1,000,000 Books

are available to read at

www.ForgottenBooks.com

Read online
Download PDF
Purchase in print

ISBN 978-1-331-16239-1
PIBN 10152461

This book is a reproduction of an important historical work. Forgotten Books uses state-of-the-art technology to digitally reconstruct the work, preserving the original format whilst repairing imperfections present in the aged copy. In rare cases, an imperfection in the original, such as a blemish or missing page, may be replicated in our edition. We do, however, repair the vast majority of imperfections successfully; any imperfections that remain are intentionally left to preserve the state of such historical works.

Forgotten Books is a registered trademark of FB &c Ltd.
Copyright © 2018 FB &c Ltd.
FB &c Ltd, Dalton House, 60 Windsor Avenue, London, SW19 2RR.
Company number 08720141. Registered in England and Wales.

For support please visit www.forgottenbooks.com

1 MONTH OF FREE READING

at

www.ForgottenBooks.com

By purchasing this book you are eligible for one month membership to ForgottenBooks.com, giving you unlimited access to our entire collection of over 1,000,000 titles via our web site and mobile apps.

To claim your free month visit:
www.forgottenbooks.com/free152461

* Offer is valid for 45 days from date of purchase. Terms and conditions apply.

English
Français
Deutsche
Italiano
Español
Português

www.forgottenbooks.com

Mythology Photography **Fiction** Fishing Christianity **Art** Cooking Essays Buddhism Freemasonry Medicine **Biology** Music **Ancient Egypt** Evolution Carpentry Physics Dance Geology **Mathematics** Fitness Shakespeare **Folklore** Yoga Marketing **Confidence** Immortality Biographies Poetry **Psychology** Witchcraft Electronics Chemistry History **Law** Accounting **Philosophy** Anthropology Alchemy Drama Quantum Mechanics Atheism Sexual Health **Ancient History Entrepreneurship** Languages Sport Paleontology Needlework Islam **Metaphysics** Investment Archaeology Parenting Statistics Criminology **Motivational**

THIRTY YEARS IN MOUKDEN. 1883-1913

BEING THE EXPERIENCES
AND RECOLLECTIONS OF
DUGALD CHRISTIE, C.M.G.

F.R.C.S., F.R.C.P.EDIN.

EDITED BY HIS WIFE

ILLUSTRATED

CONSTABLE AND COMPANY LTD.
LONDON   MCMXIV

DS
783
.7
C47

"What do we ask of life, but leave to serve? . . .
I am a road-mender, I serve the footsteps
of my fellows."   *Michael Fairless.*

MAR 29 1972

TO OUR CHILDREN

WHO HAVE SHARED SO MANY OF OUR JOYS
AND VICISSITUDES

CONTENTS

I
Is it Worth While?

Introductory 1   PAGE

II
Uphill Work

1883-1887—Beginnings of Medical Mission work in Moukden—Difficulties—Opposition—Evil rumours—Establishment of hospital—First operations . . . 4

III
Moukden: City and People

The Manchus—The people of Manchuria—Country and products—Moukden—North Tomb—Roman Catholic Mission—Protestant Missions 12

IV
Bridging the Gulf

Importance of Chinese Rules of Propriety—Politeness—Self-control—Separation of sexes—Houses—Dress—Etiquette—Officials—Unintentional offence . . . 21

V
Medical Practice among the Chinese

Principles of Chinese medicine—Ancient knowledge of surgery—Modern ignorance—Injurious methods—Useful methods — Superstitions — Devil-possession — Troublesome patients 31

VI

Climatic Conditions, Disease, and Flood

Climate—Homes of the people—Sanitary conditions—Tuberculosis—Eye disease—Epidemics—Flood in 1888—Malaria 43

VII

East and West: Mistaken Judgments

Essential similarity of Chinese to other peoples—Accused of callousness and ingratitude—Liberality and hospitality — Trustworthiness — "Squeezing" — Nervous temperament—Fatalism—Suicides—Revenge — Brute force v. "Reason"—Lack of religious devotion . . 52

VIII

Far from the Madding Crowd

Accessibility of Manchuria — Former remoteness — Old methods of travel: cart, boat—Scenery—A journey among the mountains—A Polish visitor—Mrs. Bird Bishop—The first Russians 64

IX

Progress, 1883–1894

Responsiveness of Manchuria to Christianity—Mixed population, open to impressions—Policy in mission work: the Church Chinese, not foreign—Medical Missions—Itinerating—Dispensary—Hospital—Training assistants 74

X

Side-lights on the Beginnings of a War. 1894

Chinese ignorance of foreign countries and events—Dispatch of soldiers from Manchuria to fight Japanese—Lawlessness of Manchu soldiery—Murder of a missionary—Official friendliness 83

XI

Grim Reality: The Chino-Japanese War

Bad news from the front—Quarrels among Chinese Generals—Battle of Ping-yang and death of General Tso—Anxieties in Moukden—Departure of missionaries—Japanese advance 91

CONTENTS

XII
AMONG THE WOUNDED

Red Cross work in Newchwang—Battles in vicinity—Japanese occupation—Attitude of Chinese—Peace—Return to Moukden—Government recognition of Red Cross   99

XIII
A STRANGE AFTERMATH OF WAR

Awakening of Manchuria—Desire for Western knowledge—Apathy of officials—Crowds inquiring into Christianity—Mixed motives—Rules of admission—Rapid increase of membership and self-support—Training of evangelists and pastors 109

XIV
THE STORY OF BLIND CHANG OF THE VALLEY OF PEACE

In Moukden Hospital—Witnessing at his own home—Baptism—The blind reading—The wandering evangelist—The martyr 116

XV
MISDIRECTED PATRIOTISM

Foreign aggression in China—The Reform Movement—*Coup d'état* of 1898—Rise of "Boxers"—Blindness to the danger—Peaceful condition of Manchuria—Friendliness of people and officials 123

XVI
THE BOXER MADNESS, 1900

Causes of initial success of Boxers: anti-foreign feeling, superstition, Government support—Change of attitude of Moukden Government—Imperial Edict—Departure of missionaries—Burning of Mission buildings—Reign of Terror—Martyrdoms—Recantations—Story of Pastor Liu—Hospital assistants—Boxers put down by Government 133

XVII
PAYING THE PRICE

Russian occupation—Flight of Governor-General—Anarchy in Moukden—Russian entrance—Return of Christians—Tales of suffering—Political outlook—Effects of Boxer movement on Church 151

XVIII
WAR AGAIN, 1904

Russia and Japan—Preparedness for war—Japanese advance—Battle of Liaoyang—Battle of Sha-ho—Settling down for winter—Skirmishes—Friendliness—On the Red Cross train 164

XIX
IN THE MIDST OF THE BATTLE OF MOUKDEN

The Japanese attack—Fighting drawing nearer—The Russian retreat—A blinding dust-storm—The last night—Russians left behind—Rain of bullets—Chinese attitude—Japanese spies 176

XX
THE SUFFERINGS OF THE INNOCENT

Red Cross and Refugee Aid work—Housing the crowds—Epidemics—Chinese, Russian, and Japanese wounded, in one hospital—Unexploded shells—Return of refugees—Change in attitude of Chinese to Japanese . . 184

XXI
RECONSTRUCTION
H.E. Chao Er Sun, Governor-General, 1905–1907

Reforms in Manchuria: abolition of opium, education, girls' schools, road-making, street-lighting, police, sanitation, finance—Building and opening of new hospital . 196

XXII
SPIRITUAL UPLIFT

Growth of Church—Development—Aspirations—The "Revival"—Sense of sin—Higher ideals—Uplift of women—Education—Arts College—Theological training . 207

XXIII
THE PRINCIPLES OF MEDICAL MISSION WORK

China Centenary Missionary Conference—Medical Missions an essential part of the Church's work—Logical conclusion: the establishment of medical colleges, and training of Chinese medical missionaries 216

CONTENTS

XXIV

The Beginnings of Medical Education in Manchuria

H.E. Hsü Shih Chang, Viceroy, 1907–1909.

Progress in Moukden: modern buildings, education, colleges, telephone, electric light, tramways—Need for medical education—Hindrances—The way opened—College site—Government help—Need recognized by United Missions—Appeal for funds—Response . . 225

XXV

The Black Death

H.E. Hsi Liang, Viceroy, 1909–1911

Beginning of the epidemic—Spread by rail—Plague among coolies at Moukden station—Death of Dr. Jackson—Impression on Chinese—Viceroy's sympathy—memorials 234

XXVI

Fighting the Plague. 1911

Measures taken in Moukden: inspection, isolation, placards — Difficulties — New Year calls — Snow — Villages — Tragedies—Winning the battle—International Plague Conference 246

XXVII

Moukden and the Revolution

H.E. Chao Er Sun, Viceroy, 1911–1912

Causes of revolution—Moukden Committee for Preservation of Peace—Plots—The new Republic—The Red Cross . 258

XXVIII

The Moukden Medical College

Threatened by fire—Applicants for entrance—Examination under difficulties—Teaching begun—Prospects for our graduates 270

XXIX

After the Revolution
H.E. Chang Hsi Lan, Governor, 1912

Manchuria's hopes and fears—Army Medical Service—Changed attitude to Christianity—Student movement and Dr. Mott—Day of prayer 278

XXX

Looking Forward

Stability of China—Dangers of changes—Hopes for future 288

Summary of Events 293

Index 297

ILLUSTRATIONS

A Moukden City Gate . . . . *Frontispiece*	
"Over each of the eight great gateways was a tower."	
Moukden Hospital Out-patient Department, and College, 1913 . . . . . . facing page	6
"A Slow Placid Stream, almost a Lake" . .	8
The Small River Bank in Summer	10
"Pleasure-seekers in the tea-booths gaze on the lotus."	
"Broad Streets Lead from Gate to Gate" . .	16
At the North Tomb	18
"An archway of fretted marble, behind which the main gate is barred against all."	
At the North Tomb	20
"A broad paved way with large stone animals on either side."	
Fishing on the Small River	46
Moukden Mission Church	76
"It was built in purely Chinese style."	
Manchu Soldiers	86
"With large round target on chest and back."	
Entrance to Moukden Hospital before Boxer Time	136
Refugees from Ruined Villages	186
"Where were such crowds to be housed?"	
Red Cross Work, 1905: The Sufferings of the Innocent	188
H.E. Chao Er Sun, Viceroy	196
"One of the ablest men available—a notable financier—a man of the future."	

	FACING PAGE
CORRIDOR OF THE HOSPITAL: WARDS OPENING ON EITHER SIDE	204
H.E. HSÜ SHIH CHANG, VICEROY	226
"He maintained the dignity of the Chinese Government."	
A WARD IN THE MOUKDEN HOSPITAL	230
H.E. HSI LIANG, VICEROY	236
"He had the heart of a father to those whom he ruled."	
DR. ARTHUR JACKSON	238
DR. JACKSON'S GRAVE	244
READY FOR PLAGUE WORK	250
GENERAL CHANG TSO LIN	264
"He was watching events with an alert army."	
THE MOUKDEN MEDICAL COLLEGE	272
DR. WANG	282
"The influence of a man like Dr. Wang can hardly be overestimated."	
MAP OF MANCHURIA	*At the end*
PLAN OF MOUKDEN	*At the end*

THIS is not a History, still less is it an Autobiography. It does not attempt to give a complete account of Manchuria, nor even of Moukden, nor to depict minutely its people and their customs. There are important missionary developments which are not alluded to, or only lightly touched upon. Books on Manchuria, and on its wars, and on its Missions have already been written. This only attempts to deal with personal impressions, and to give a picture of life amid the Changeless East of the olden days, and amid the rapid march of events which have brought us to the Changed East of to-day.

THIRTY YEARS IN MOUKDEN

I

IS IT WORTH WHILE?

" Oh, ye that might be clothed with all things pleasant,
Ye are foolish that put off the fair soft present."
William Black.

" A lang dreich road, ye had better let it be."
Scottish Song.

COLD November, the wind whistling over the dreary Manchurian plain of dull, brown, hard earth, with not a blade of grass, leafless brown trees, earth-coloured houses with low earth-coloured roofs, no hills, no colour, all a dead level of monotony; only the brilliant blue arch overhead and the clear dazzling sunshine mocking the dullness and chill dreariness—a complete contrast to the good old homeland with its changeful cloudy skies, and ever-varying hues of mountain, moor, and lake, fresh green grass and purple heather. And instead of friends, comrades, fellow-countrymen, with aims and ideals like our own, are thousands and millions of these inscrutable Chinese, from Newchwang on the threshold to the far interior, hostile, indifferent, or at best curious, all busy with their own daily toil, with neither thought nor desire beyond it.

On coming out to Manchuria in 1882, as a medical missionary of the United Presbyterian (now United Free)

Church of Scotland, I was faced with remonstrances and obstacles which were perhaps commoner then than now.

"Why go to China?" said one of my professors. "You have good prospects before you at home."

"Missions are a failure," seemed to be the verdict of Shanghai. "To join them is to throw away your life."

"Why go up-country?" was the question at Newchwang. "Settle here and you can easily make a good income, and do as much for the Chinese as you like at the same time."

"You are attempting the impossible," was the common opinion. "The Chinese do not want you. Their own religions suit them quite well, and they are content with what medicines they have."

"I'll give you one word of advice, young man," said one old doctor who had been years in China. "Never trust a Chinaman with anything, not even a single pill!"

One could not help asking oneself: Is it really quixotic as they say? What can a handful of foreigners do among these millions?—To make known among the sufferers that Someone cares, to share in lighting in Manchuria the inextinguishable Torch of Truth, to help to set in motion the mighty powers of the Coming Age—this is the Vision. Is it worth while to try?

Thirty years have gone by, and what is their record? Hostility and persecutions, our houses and all our worldly goods burned, wars and deadly plague, tragic death among our ranks, partings with children sent away to the homeland—they have not been smooth years, but *it has been worth while.*

We look back on almost incredible changes, and all who have shared in them feel that it has been a great thing to take part in the Awakening of a Nation, the Regeneration of a great People. Hostility to foreigners is at an end. In all public emergencies, plague, war, famine, it is the missionaries, and of necessity specially the medical missionaries, that are looked to for advice and help. We count among our friends one Viceroy after another, and all the high officials ; and those who travel in Manchuria to-day bear witness to the remarkable friendliness of the country people everywhere.

The Torch of Truth is burning brightly all over the land. Christianity is regarded with a kindly eye and respected by high and low. Christian schools and colleges are in the van in the march of education. The Church of Christ in Manchuria numbers its flock by tens of thousands.

In Moukden, not to mention other places, hundreds of thousands of sufferers have been treated, and the hospital is known far and near. From the Christian Medical College, largely supported by Government, will soon issue a stream of Chinese medical men to do their part in serving God and their country.

The Christian Ideal of Service has made its appeal, and the popular mind is increasingly responding to it, and recognizing it as the Ideal towards which China too must strive. The Government's request for a Day of Christian Prayer met with ready response in Manchuria, and drew officials and people together to our churches to express their sense of their country's need of help and guidance from the Great God over all.

II

UPHILL WORK

"Does the road wind uphill all the way?"
Christina Rossetti.

"The best is yet to be."
Robert Browning.

IN the spring of 1883 a small handful of foreigners settled down to live in the city of Moukden, the capital of Manchuria, and when it became known that one was a doctor, there was much excitement. Premises being difficult to get, a small dispensary was fitted up in our own compound, and there I began to see patients, though I had been but a few months in the country and knew little of the language. At first the medical work done was small. Crowds came, each man professing to have an ailment, and receiving appropriate medicine, but it is questionable how much of that medicine was ever used, even when the disease was genuine. The real object of many was merely to see the foreigner. This they were allowed to do without let or hindrance, the unused medicine had its use, gradually the excitement died down, the numbers diminished, and real work began.

For months, indeed years, it was an uphill fight. The patients were as much taken up with the strange foreigner as with their own ailments. The language was difficult. Having no trained assistant, I had at first to make up my own prescriptions, and administer chloroform and operate single-handed. The waiting-room was very small, consulting-room and dispensary were in one, there was no hospital accommodation at all, and those on whom I operated had to stay in their own homes or in inns.

The most serious obstacle of all was that few came to us except as a last resource, when the disease had become chronic, when native doctors had failed, when there seemed to be little hope. There was, moreover, a great deal of suspicion of the foreigner and his drugs. Some said that the missionaries were but the vanguard of an English host who were coming to invade China. Others were convinced that our medicine could change the hearts of those who used it, and compel them to follow the foreigner and believe his teaching. A mandarin came one day to have a painful tooth extracted, and so afraid was he of our drugs that he would not even wash out his mouth with the water provided. The old story was set afloat, that children's hearts and eyes were taken out and used for concocting medicine and for photographic purposes.

"How can a box see to make pictures," it was reasoned, "if it has not eyes inside?"

In one quarter of Moukden there is a large Mohammedan population, and among these were many so-called doctors. These men were alarmed lest their gains might be lessened, so they set themselves to circulate evil tales and rumours about us. As China was at war with France in the south, these were the more readily believed. Placards against us were posted up in the city and sometimes on our own gates. Efforts were made to frighten us out of the country. Our assistants and servants were threatened on the public streets, foul language and sometimes mud and stones were thrown at us, and more than once the day was fixed for the burning of our houses. Large crowds gathered to see what would happen, and there was much excited talk. This was alarming enough at the time, though nothing ever came of it.

One day, during the summer of 1884, a French Catholic

priest called on us, clad in the usual long black robe. He came in a cart, remained some time in our house, and then returned home. The dispensary was at the time full of patients, so that many knew of his visit. Next day rumours against us were floating about, and our assistants were warned not to appear on the streets. Then crowds gathered outside our gate, and there was considerable excitement. The story generally believed was as follows :

The Catholics and we were alike anxious to obtain children's hearts and eyes, and were willing to give large sums for them. When the priest called, he brought under his robe a little child. We retired into a dark room, weighed it, removed the eyes and heart, and agreed upon the price. This trade in children had been carried on for some time, and the next day three carts left the city laden with hearts and eyes. Three points of the story were true. A little Mohammedan child was lost ; a black-robed priest called on us ; and a foreigner who had been in Moukden left the city with three carts the day after the priest's visit.

Not long afterwards a mother brought her young daughter for treatment ; and while the woman was detailing to me her symptoms the girl slipped out of the room, frightened at the sight of the foreigner of whom she had heard such terrible things. When the flow of the mother's eloquence subsided she looked round, but her daughter was gone ! In great agitation she rushed back to the waiting-room, but she was not there. A general search inside and outside the compound was in vain. The mother, firmly convinced that we had stolen the girl, became violent and loudly insisted that she be given up. At last someone suggested that she might have run off to the inn where they were staying. A man was sent to find out, and there the little fugitive was, glad to have escaped safely from that awful foreigner. Even when this news was brought, it was with difficulty that the excited

MOUKDEN HOSPITAL OUT-PATIENT DEPARTMENT, AND COLLEGE, 1913
Wards are behind.

woman was persuaded to leave the compound. Of course, this was the last we saw of that patient.

These fears and suspicions gradually died out, but for some years we were occasionally reminded that the eye is a suspicious member. There was an instance even as late as 1892. A little girl was brought to us with a very unsightly growth on a blind eye. Her mother, who had been in the hospital before and had trust in us, was anxious to have the growth removed, as it seriously injured her chances of a good marriage. I performed the necessary operation, and afterwards presented the patient with a glass eye. Both mother and daughter were much pleased, for it fitted perfectly and greatly improved the girl's appearance. A day or two afterwards the woman brought the child to me and asked me to take back the eye. I have no doubt that her friends frightened her out of keeping a foreign eye.

The chief factor in dispelling such suspicions has been steady quiet medical and surgical work, done openly, and combined with Christian kindness.

It was not until we had been in Moukden nearly two years that we were able to open what we called "a hospital," in a small rickety building just behind our house. It had room for twelve patients and was crowded most of the time. It is wonderful what good results were obtained in such an unsatisfactory place. At the time of the heavy summer rains one wall of the building fell and it seemed as if others would follow, but the house was successfully propped up and compelled to shelter our sick folk for some time longer, though it was so miserably cold in winter that we had to close it for a couple of months. In the heavy rains of the following summer it collapsed and became a total wreck. Another temporary hospital was then rented with somewhat better accommodation, on the very site where now stands the Medical College, and this sufficed for over a year, by which time our permanent premises were ready for use.

Among the earliest patients in our tumble-down quarters were the two first cataract cases operated on in Manchuria. One was a merchant in the city, whose right eye had been blind for several years, and whose left eye had now failed from the same cause. There was a good deal of interest shown in this case as the man was well known, and giving sight to the blind was unheard of. Our little hospital was very dark, so the operating-table was drawn out to the open air. A number of people gathered round, including some officials, and the operation was performed in public, amid breathless expectancy. All went well, and when I held up my fingers and the people heard him count them, there was quite a sensation. While this merchant was still with us, a blind man was led in by his boy, whom he had never seen. He was a village school teacher, but for years had been sightless, idle, and poor. A few days later the table was again placed in the sunshine, and a still larger crowd gathered, for the fame of the first cure had spread. When the man realized that he could see, we could hardly hold him down on the table, until I called forward his son and he gazed on his face for the first time long and silently.

Many other operations were performed, and the fame of foreign surgery soon spread far and wide. A merchant came to us who had suffered since childhood from a painful disease. For two years he had not had a night's rest, sleeping only by snatches. He was thirty-eight years of age, but the constant pain was ageing him before his time. He had consulted me a year previously, but when I explained to him the nature of the operation which was the only means of saving his life, he refused to submit to it. He returned rather to the native doctors, of whom he consulted first to last about a hundred, besides several witches ; but their treatment only added to his suffering. He was one of those who hated the foreigner and lost no opportunity of reviling us. Now at last, as his only chance for life, he resolved to submit to our treatment.

A SLOW, PLACID STREAM, ALMOST A LAKE

It was an anxious case for us. He was well known among merchants, a class who looked with disfavour on our presence here, and among whom we had then few patients. The operation, if successful, might do much to break down their prejudices. Failure, on the other hand, might have serious consequences in raising evil reports against us. The patient was weak, emaciated, excitable, and worn out with prolonged pain and sleeplessness. The operation, however, was a complete success, and he made a good recovery. A few weeks later he sent a subscription to the hospital and put up a handsome tablet as an expression of gratitude. He always continued a warm friend to the hospital, exercising his influence in our favour among his fellow-merchants, and later on he joined the Christian Church.

It was a long time before we had a case of amputation of more than fingers or toes. This was not because diseased limbs are uncommon, for hardly a week passes without such cases coming under our notice. But many a Chinese would rather die than lose a leg or an arm; when laid in his coffin he must be complete to enter fitly on the dim Unknown. Another reason was the want of confidence in any doctor's verdict, and the lingering hope that, after all, the knife might not be necessary. This hope is less unreasonable than one would at first think, for the Chinese have wonderful recuperative powers.

When our first amputation case came, it seemed almost a hopeless one. Three months before, while the patient was carting stones, a large stone had fallen with great violence against his arm, shattering it, and knocking him down so that the wheel passed over his foot. A native doctor was sent for, who without attempting to replace the bones applied to the arm the universally-used black plaster, and told him not to move it. After a week it was noticed that the fingers were getting black, and on removing the plaster the whole forearm was found to be dead or dying. Since then matters had grown steadily worse, and now, after three months' suffering, all hope of recovery was given up, and as a last chance the dying man was carried to the dispensary, covered with bed sores and so weak that he could hardly speak. One end of the fractured bone was protruding, and a splint of millet-stalk which had supported the arm had got embedded in the tissues, so that the least movement caused severe pain and bleeding. The smell from the arm was overpowering and most trying to the patient and all near him, and his foot too was very painful. He and his friends were anxious for amputation. He was already dying, and if we could not cure him it would be an easy way to get quit of life. When the operation was performed, his heart was so feeble that for some time we feared he would not rally. He came round, however, and from that day steadily gained strength.

Very slowly the number increased of those willing to submit to amputation in order to save their lives, and even to this day many a man puts off his consent until too late. For a long time every amputated limb had to be carefully preserved and given to its owner, who kept it against his burial, that it might be put with him in his coffin, and thus be restored to him in whatever life might await him.

It was never intended that medical work should permanently be carried on in buildings meant for small Chinese dwelling-houses. From the beginning, efforts were made to buy a compound suitable for a permanent hospital and dispensary, but this was no easy matter. There was great unwillingness to sell to foreigners, and our choice was restricted to places within reach of our dwelling-house and in suitable situations. Time after time we seemed about to succeed, but the desired property slipped from our grasp. At last a friendly official, whose house was not a hundred yards to the east of ours, received an appointment to another province, and consented to sell us his compound, a site which was in every way suitable.

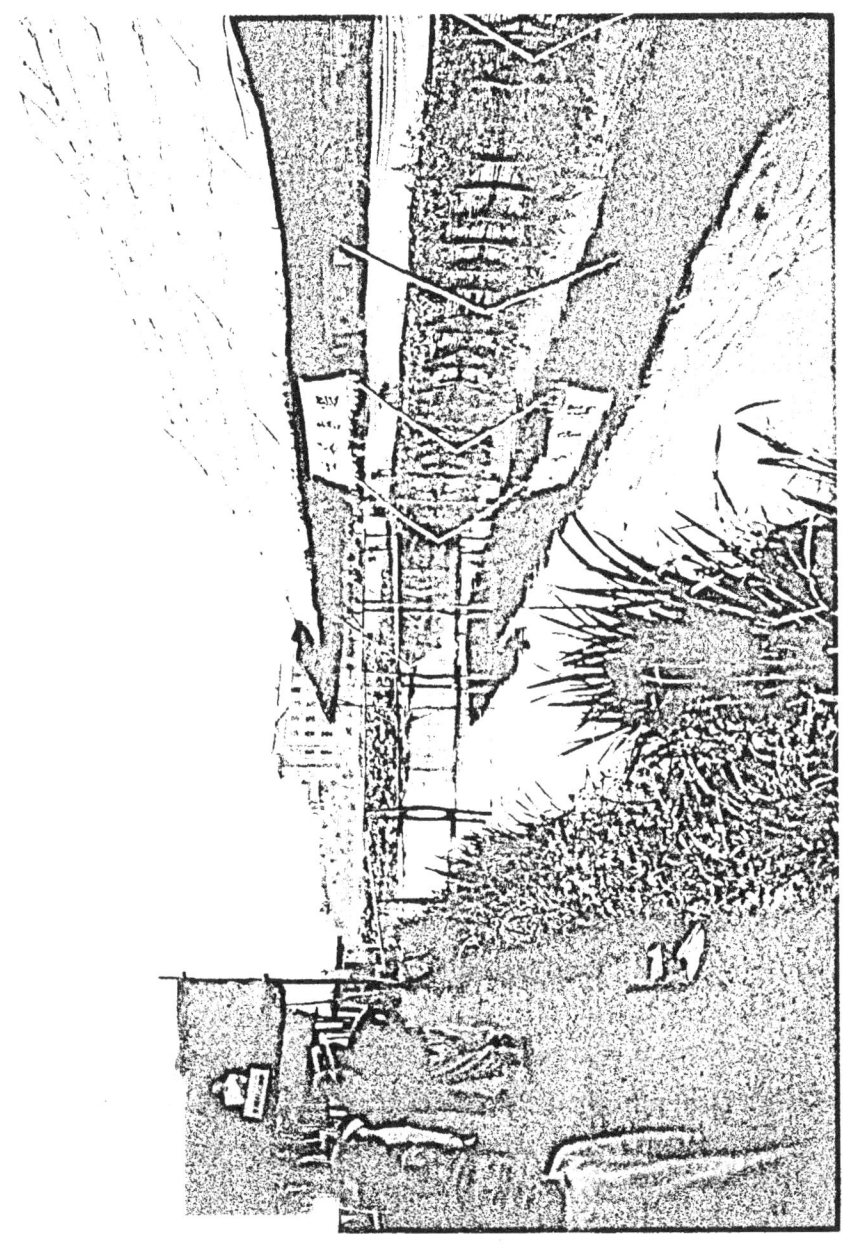

THE SMALL RIVER BANK IN SUMMER
"Pleasure-seekers in the tea-booths gaze on the lotus."

In the south-east of the city, not far from the busy streets, is a slow placid stream almost a lake, called the Small River. In summer its banks are a favourite resort of pleasure-seekers and holiday-makers, who chat and sip tea in the many tea-booths, gaze on the beautiful broad-leafed delicate pink lotus flowers floating on the water, and breathe in what is considered the best air in Moukden. On a terrace overlooking this stream we had been fortunate enough to secure two compounds for houses, and from our point of view there was no more desirable spot in Moukden than that which was now to be our hospital. The existing buildings we utilized as wards, and erected an entirely new and commodious dispensary in front. The premises were formally opened in 1887 by a friendly Manchu official of high rank, the President of the Board of War, in the presence of a large gathering of the leading mandarins of the city. On the same day an enthusiastic meeting of the Christians was held in the waiting-room, which could hold about 150. The hospital had accommodation for fifty men and fifteen women.

Thus ended the first stage of my experiences in Moukden, the initial stage of fighting down suspicion and opposition, and establishing ourselves in the confidence of the people.

III

MOUKDEN : CITY AND PEOPLE

"There is a world outside the one you know."
Rudyard Kipling.

"Who doth ambition shun,
And loves to live i' the sun,
Seeking the food he eats,
And pleased with what he gets,
Come hither, come hither, come hither;
Here shall he see
No enemy
But winter and rough weather."
Shakespeare.

ABOUT the time when all England was ringing with news of the coming Armada, a warlike tribe from the mountains in the east was threatening to overwhelm what we now call Southern Manchuria. Its wide fertile plain had been colonized by Chinese settlers, and was dotted with towns and cities. The corrupt Ming Dynasty of China was tottering to its fall, and all efforts made to beat back the advance of those vigorous mountaineers, the Manchus, were but futile. City after city fell before them, and every man who did not wish to be beheaded shaved his head and cultivated a queue. Those who thus submitted were encouraged to enrol themselves under the victorious *Nurhachu*, forming the "Chinese Bannermen." The Manchu tribesmen and their helpers the Bannermen were not content till all China lay at their feet, and so was founded that Manchu Dynasty which has just passed away, after bearing rule over China for 270 years.

Moukden was an important city before the Manchus took it and made it their capital, but the present city wall and Imperial Palace only date from that time. When Peking fell before them, it in its turn became the capital, and Nurhachu's grandson the first Manchu Emperor; but Moukden has always been regarded as the home of the Dynasty, and near it are the tombs of the old warrior Nurhachu and of his son.

Southern Manchuria was never largely populated by Manchus. Its inhabitants have always been of mixed race, aboriginal tribes of kindred stock to the Manchus originally occupying the mountain districts, but Chinese the plains. In the course of time intermarriages have obliterated differences, and Manchu, Bannerman, and Chinaman are practically indistinguishable. The Manchu language has completely died out and Chinese is universally used, the dialect spoken being Mandarin, the same as at Peking. Only in the case of old families is the distinction perpetuated, and the line proudly traced back to the time of " the Conqueror." There are still a few Manchu towns and villages, especially near the old Imperial tombs, where the people are most exclusive and only marry among themselves. Farther north the Manchu element is more distinct, but in the greater part of South Manchuria it is very little in evidence, those of the original Manchu stock having been for the most part transferred to other parts of China to garrison the cities.

To the superficial observer it seems untrue that Manchuria is really Chinese, for wherever he goes he is struck with the curious, picturesque, and typically Manchu head-dress of the women, with its sparkling silver, gilt, or enamelled ornaments. They wear the long Manchu robe, too, instead of the jacket and skirt of the Chinese woman, and they walk on their own natural feet, not on crippled and crushed deformities. How can the people be Chinese when the women are so evidently

Manchu ? The truth is that they are not Manchu but Manchurian.

"Where do you come from ? " you ask a man.

"I come from Shantung."

"How long have you been in Manchuria ? "

"Two hundred years," he answers gravely.

Every year they are still crowding in from Shantung, Chihli, and other provinces. The woman who in her old home opposed tooth and nail the loosening by the fraction of an inch her little girl's foot-bandages, follows her husband to far Manchuria and settles down among her large-footed, rosy-cheeked sisters of the north. In a few years there are other little girls growing up in the home, with natural feet and Manchu dress, and in time they will marry and put up their hair in Manchu style. They have become Manchurian. The removal of these people from their ancient ancestral homes, and the gathering together of families from various provinces, result in a marked lessening of their conservatism, prejudices, and superstitions. Local ideas and customs often vary so greatly that when brought into close contact they neutralize each other. The consequence is that the people of Manchuria are, speaking generally, more open to new impressions than their kinsmen whom they left behind in the old rut in the China behind the Great Wall.

The Three Eastern Provinces, as Manchuria is usually called by the Chinese, are not nearly so crowded as the rest of China, their total population being estimated at from fifteen to twenty millions. It is increasing rapidly by reason of constant immigration. Southern Manchuria, the province of *Fengtien*, is far the most populous and furthest developed of the three. In its rich alluvial plains are innumerable villages and many towns. It is astonishingly fertile, yielding two crops in the year in spite of the long rigorous winter. The principal produce is *millet*, without which it is difficult to see how the people of Manchuria could live. It is the staple food of man and beast, and is so productive that one grain bears eight hundredfold. The long stalk, strong but brittle, is the household fuel, and the material for roofing below tiles or lime, fences, partitions, and many other things. Every country house or cot grows its own millet, beans, and other vegetables, selling the surplus to provide the few other necessaries of life.

One feature of the landscape strikes every new-comer— the *graves*. Outside a city there are miles of wasted space with endless conical mounds, the public free cemeteries, and in whatever direction one turns there are smaller private burying-grounds. In time one learns to be grateful for the green they furnish. The vast, cultivated, level plain would be more overpoweringly monotonous but for the family graveyards dotted here and there, with their fresh green turf in the springtime, and their dark green pine trees when all else is brown.

Manchuria is not all plain, though the most populous parts are. There are also hills with cultivated slopes, abrupt heights whose wooded crags are crowned with Buddhist retreats, long winding valleys with nestling hamlets and great rivers, and away to the east are mighty mountains and the glory of snow peaks and virgin forest.

Moukden stands on the plain, with low hills in sight six or eight miles to the south and east. A river from the distant eastern mountains, the *Hun*, passes a few miles from the city, between it and the hills. Ancient Moukden was not large, the massive battlemented wall of Nurhachu, 40 ft. high and 30 ft. wide at its summit, enclosing a space of little over a mile square. At each corner and over each of the eight great gateways was a tower, besides the Drum Tower and Bell Tower in the midst of the city, so that from afar it looked a veritable city of towers. Much of this ancient glory has departed, as within recent years most of the towers have been removed, the masonry being unsafe. The grey old wall still stands, and tells how well and strongly they built of old, and in the deep arched gateways the heavy iron-studded doors still shut ponderously when night comes, and prevent the benighted traveller from entering or leaving the city.

Broad streets lead from gate to gate, with narrow intersecting cross lanes. In the centre is the brilliant orange-roofed Imperial Palace, without inhabitant for over two hundred years, but containing priceless treasures of Manchu relics and antique ware. Within the city walls are all the yamens, official buildings and residences, banks, and principal merchants, but few live there except those connected with these establishments and the many shops. Up to 1905 there were none but one-story houses and practically no attempt at architecture, and most of the buildings are still of the old type.

The principal business street was and is notable not by reason of fine buildings, but for the large, gorgeous protruding shop-signs, enormous peacocks, dragons, etc., coloured brilliantly and beautifully. At one end of this street is the old Drum Tower, where the war-drum still stands, beat of old in time of war or public danger. At the other end is the Bell Tower with its ancient bell, tolled peacefully until recent years as a curfew and to mark the watches of the night, and beat still when there is a fire in the city. A mile or more outside the old wall is a second wall of earth, about ten miles in circumference, and between these are the populous suburbs.

It is estimated that Moukden has a population of about two hundred thousand. It is the governmental, literary, educational, and commercial capital of Manchuria. Large numbers of expectant officials congregate here, because here resides the head of the Government, the Tartar-General or Governor-General, Viceroy, or Governor, as he has been variously called.

There is one marked difference between Moukden and a European, especially a British, city, and indeed between

"BROAD STREETS LEAD FROM GATE TO GATE"

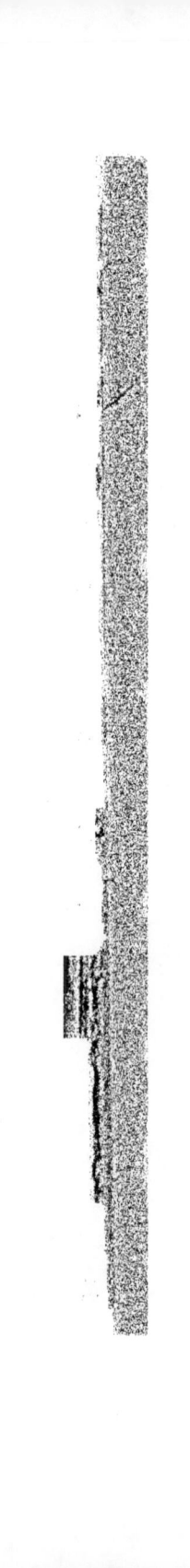

Moukden and most cities in China : the men far outnumber the women. There are bankers whose womenfolk are in far-off Shansi ; merchants in hundreds from Chihli, who go home to visit their families annually ; craftsmen and labourers innumerable, who have not yet sent for their wives from the old home in another province; besides men from all over South Manchuria, who go home once or twice a year, and would not think of bringing their wives to the city. All these live for the most part at their places of business. There are also many families following the old patriarchal customs, several generations, sometimes over a hundred souls, forming one large home. There is an ever-increasing number, however, of small homes, a man with his wife and children and perhaps an old grandfather or mother, just as in our own land.

A busy, industrious, contented people they are, prosperous and comfortable according to their own ideals, peaceable and law-abiding. Policemen were unknown before 1905. Men lived as their fathers had lived, and asked for nothing better. The shops shut at sundown, and the unlighted streets were silent and deserted till dawn.

A few miles north of the city, across an open grassy plain, is a spot which goes far to atone for the monotony and dullness of the country round Moukden—the tomb of Nurhachu's son, deep buried among trees. The outer circle is genuine wild-wood, with straggling paths seeming to lead nowhere, among wild flowers, dense thickets, and open glades. One could lose oneself for a June afternoon amid the startling beauty of white tree-blossom or trailing clematis against the vivid young green of the oaks and birches, while through the green and the white the blue gleams bluer, and the sun strikes sudden brilliant patches into the dark shadows. Deep among the trees the birds twitter and sing as nowhere else near Moukden, and overhead in the intense radiance hover and balance the keen-eyed hawks. Through the trees glistens a vivid red wall enclosing the tomb, with glimpses of yellow tiled roofs within. South of this rectangular enclosure stands solitary an archway of fretted white marble, behind which the main gate is barred against all. It is only opened when the official representative of the Emperor sacrifices at the shrine of this ancestor of the dynasty.

For many years the side gates too were closely barred, and none might see within the sacred precincts except the Manchu guard who lived there. Now to east and west the gates stand open, with an arching avenue of pines from one to the other. The pine trees inside the enclosure are arranged in such perfect symmetry that in whatever direction one looks it is down a long straight avenue. The undergrowth is cut, and the contrast is striking from the wild luxuriance and colour of nature outside, to this cool, solemn, dark-treed symmetry.

From the closed south gate there leads a broad paved way, with large stone animals on either side, to an inner enclosure, whose gate is only opened to bearers of a pass, or to those known to the wardens of the tomb. Inside is a silent paved courtyard, guarded by high towers and a broad battlemented wall, and in the innermost part of all a great round grassy mound, the grave itself, with a tree growing on the top. Behind all this, keeping away the evil influences from the north, is a long artificial hill overgrown with trees and creepers, from which can be viewed the whole enclosure with its enfolding woods, and the walls and towers of the city of Moukden away across the plain.

The first foreigners to settle in Moukden, or indeed in any part of Manchuria, were French Roman Catholic priests. This was in 1838, and by 1882 they had a fine cathedral, schools, orphanages, a priests' seminary, and a nunnery, besides dwelling-houses for bishop and priests, all in one large compound in the south suburb. The general policy of the Roman Catholic Mission seems to

AT THE NORTH TOMB

have been all along to keep their converts separate from other people. There are, dotted throughout the country, distinctively Roman Catholic villages with many Christians of the fifth and sixth generations. They are a well-behaved, clean, industrious part of the community. Their children are instructed closely and carefully, and orphans are constantly received. In the cities the priests do not seem to conduct any open aggressive propaganda, but come and go among their own people, and live quietly in their own compound, a little world in itself.

One or two Protestant missionaries visited Moukden from 1867 onwards, but no serious attempt was made to work there until 1874. At that time the anti-foreign feeling among all classes was very strong. The agitation and bitterness which had culminated in the Tientsin massacre of 1870 were felt in Manchuria also, and there was hardly a man in the city who would speak a word in favour of the detested " foreign devil." It was not easy for a missionary to gain a footing, and yet it was felt that no real hold could be taken of the province so long as only village work was done. A Chinese evangelist was sent first, who sold books, preached, had long private talks and discussions with those interested, and by his patience and tact opened the way for further effort.

There the Rev. John Ross, and Rev. John MacIntyre, of the United Presbyterian (now United Free) Church of Scotland, paid repeated visits from Newchwang, and later on Dr. Ross stayed as long as six months at a time, living in a private room in a Chinese inn. There was much opposition, much mud-throwing both literal and figurative, and more than once something very near a riot. But gradually this died down, and out of the persecution emerged a small Christian congregation. A preaching chapel was opened on one of the busiest streets, where daily public preaching for outsiders and evening worship for the Christians were held. At last it became possible to get property for a missionary dwelling-house. First one compound was acquired on the Small River bank in the east suburb, then another, until now there is quite a little colony there, with hospitals, houses, schools, and Medical College. A church is not far off, and three miles away, in the west suburb, are another church, an arts college, and missionaries' dwellings.

AT THE NORTH TOMB
"A broad paved way with large stone animals on either side."

IV

BRIDGING THE GULF

"If you do not learn the rules of propriety, your character cannot be established."

"The Superior Man subdues himself, and submits to these rules of propriety; he neither looks, hears, speaks, nor makes any movement contrary to them."—*Confucius*.

UNFORTUNATELY for the foreigner, the "rules of propriety," according to Chinese usage, are often diametrically opposed to the customs of the West. The European gentleman, even if he has a University education and polished manners, seems a mere boor to the uninitiated Chinaman, and offends at every turn against the strict etiquette of this ancient civilization, an etiquette which in its main points is observed by the lowest coolie. The character therefore of the European or American is "not established." The very appellation "foreigner" means an *outsider*, a man from a country outside this Middle Kingdom where the Golden Mean prevails.

Wherever he goes, the foreigner helps to confirm this opinion of him. He is travelling in the interior, it may be on horseback, and he rides through the quiet country hamlets as he would at home, at a rapid pace. As he passes a group of men he calls out:

"Which is the way to X——?"

He probably gets no reply, and rides on thinking what unmannerly louts these Chinese yokels are.

A rough uneducated countryman is the next traveller. He pulls in his horse to a slow amble as he enters the village,—this is one of the "rules of propriety." On reaching the group of villagers he dismounts,—rule number two.

"May I borrow your light?" he asks. This is an apology for troubling them,—rule number three. Then he too inquires the way to X——, and receives ready help; if need be a man will even accompany him to point out the way. Thereafter these same yokels not unnaturally remark to each other what unmannerly louts foreigners are, ignorant of the most elementary rules of propriety.

All over China the experience has been general that in settling down in a new city or district, the foreigner, be he merchant or missionary, meets with opposition, suspicion, and misunderstanding. Of course it is possible to ignore this, and go one's own way regardless of what people are saying and thinking. But the secret dislike and misjudging of foreigners, so common still in many parts of China, spring from this very ignoring of the feelings and opinions of the people. It would seem a wiser policy to study the causes of the dislike, to seek to remove them, and to avoid every possible occasion of offence.

For instance, great indignation has more than once been roused, almost amounting to a riot, by the careless use of paper with Chinese characters on it. The sacred characters were being degraded; when such paper is no longer wanted it should be burned. Again, a leading characteristic of the Superior Man as depicted in the Confucian Classics, and as admired by all classes of Chinese, is *self-control*,—he "subdues himself." The ordinary man never dreams of putting this into practice, but he expects it from anyone who claims to be a scholar or a leader. Many a foreigner takes up the position of being greatly superior to the Chinese around, while all the time these Chinese are contemptuously laughing in their sleeves at this stranger who so easily loses his temper.

To strike or kick under any provocation whatever brands a man as an uncultured barbarian. Western impatience too calls forth contempt. The Superior Man takes everything philosophically, and bears calmly all delays and disappointments.

In the early days, the freedom of intercourse between foreigners of different sexes, especially in the Treaty Ports, was a great offence to the Chinese, and was the beginning of the low opinion of foreigners so commonly held. In Manchuria women were much less restricted than in other parts of the country, but there was still an invisible line which held society in two parts as by a bar of iron. To a foreign mind the things which might and might not be done were wholly unreasonable. But then to a Chinese mind the foreign rules of propriety had still less reason, indeed they were both wrong and ridiculous. It is then no easy task that a foreigner sets himself when he decides to avoid offending Chinese ideas. In its entirety it is impossible, but it is well worth while to do all one can to gain the respect and friendship of any people among whom one is going to live.

When we settled down in Moukden our first need was houses. In Manchuria, as in the greater part of North China, there were no two-story buildings except a few temples.

"Gods may dwell in towers, but not men," is the saying.

To build a foreign house in those days would have been to court trouble; a two-story house would have meant a riot. So the *compounds* were Chinese to outward seeming, with massive gateways, and servants' quarters at the entrance. The house in its garden behind the inner wall might have foreign windows and doors, foreign flooring and stoves, but nothing of that could be seen by the passer-by, or even by the visitor to the outer yard.

There came the question of clothing, for a foreigner's

dress was the first thing which attracted attention. A man appearing in public, clad in a short jacket and tight-fitting trousers, was at that time an offence to the Chinese sense of common decency; a respectably dressed man always wore a long robe. A woman in a closely fitting dress was still worse in their eyes, the Chinese female garb being loose and flowing. So for a good many years loose robes, long coats, dressing-gowns, tea-gowns were affected by most of the foreigners in their intercourse with Chinese. The native dress was not commonly worn by them—there are practical difficulties in the way of adopting it entirely, and half-measures seemed of little use—but such foreign garments were chosen as would harmonize with popular ideas of propriety.

These questions of housing and clothing were easily settled. The study of the Chinese laws of etiquette was a more complicated matter. It was not difficult to master enough of the general rules and customs to get on fairly well with the lower classes of the people, and carry on work successfully in dispensary and hospital. But I was early brought up against the question of intercourse with officials, where detailed etiquette is of the first importance. One may so easily make a mistake which amounts to insulting an official before his underlings, and which will probably cause him to curse the unmannerliness of the foreigner, and effectively prevent any further intercourse with him.

When an official visitor is announced, gate and door must be opened wide ready to receive him, and the host should meet him between the two. The position of honour is north before south, east before west, so the host must keep to the west of the pathway and house door, which always faces south. He must not walk exactly beside his guest, but always half a step behind. When inside the room it is important to offer the proper seat, but a foreign house being differently arranged from a Chinese one, it is not always easy to know which this is.

It should be as far from the door as possible, and the host must sit nearer the door, and to the west of his guest if he can. Tea is always served whatever the time of day, but the correct moment must be chosen for offering it. On formal occasions or first visits, the host takes the cup with both hands and places it with a bow before his guest, who rises and receives it in both his hands, saying something polite. The host then invites his guest to drink, and this they do simultaneously, taking the same number of sips, and replacing their cups at the same moment. It will easily be seen how readily the foreigner may offend, for there are a hundred minor points which give opportunity to show different gradations of respect and cordiality.

When a foreigner pays a return call on an official, the occasions for blundering, and thus rendering himself ridiculous or offending his host, are perhaps even more numerous. He must not go on foot, however near the house may be. He must remain in his cart while his own servant takes in his card, and he must not alight till invited. On entering, and at each successive gate or door, he must stand aside and urge his host to enter first, and must not be too easily persuaded to proceed. He will be given the seat of honour, but must be unwilling to take it, and only do so after some protesting. He must not actually sit down until the same moment as his host, and if a second visitor arrives he must rise at once and offer him his seat. On a first visit he must not stay too long, nor yet may he be over-hurried in his departure. There are many other everyday rules which are only slowly mastered, but which gradually become second nature when associating with officials.

For anyone who is going to live permanently in a city, hoping to make his presence and influence felt, it is obviously desirable to come into contact with all classes of the people. The lower grades are much the most easy of access, and it is possible to live and work for years in their midst and know very little indeed of the officials, the *literati*, the gentry, or the influential merchants. Many causes contribute to producing this gulf between them and the foreigner, besides that prominent one already indicated—his neglect of the "rules of propriety." One is the language, for it takes years to become quite at home in it, and few ever speak it without a marked foreign accent.

At the outset, a doctor has the great advantage that he may have an opportunity of relieving bodily suffering, and thus gain an entrance. The maintenance of a friendly footing afterwards, and the extension of acquaintance among these classes, will depend largely on the extent to which he himself cultivates these same "rules of propriety." Our relation with the officials was a most vital matter thirty years ago, as the common people were greatly influenced by the attitude taken up by them regarding us and our work. We were fortunate in having a call from an official of some rank within a month after our arrival in Moukden. He was suffering from disease of the lower jaw, several of his teeth had fallen out, he could hardly speak, and extreme pain was wearing him out. The diseased bone was easily removed, giving immediate relief, the cure was perfect, and he remained our staunch friend till his death a few years later. From him I received hints and suggestions as to etiquette which were invaluable. He was the means of introducing many official patients from the Governor of Moukden downwards, and others came without introduction. The Governor was specially grateful for a bit of practical help. He had lost two front teeth, and this disfiguration made it awkward for him to appear before the Emperor, and therefore might hinder official promotion. Knowing something of dentistry, I was able to provide him with false teeth, which meant a good deal to his career.

One of my most intimate official friends was a *Tao-tai*

named Gao, who had been for some years at the Chinese Legation in Paris, and been through the siege there in 1870. He had also visited England and America, and was a most enlightened man, thoroughly in sympathy with Western ideas and with Christianity. I was early installed as his family physician, and had constant intercourse with his whole household for many years. Through him also we came in touch with other mandarins, and as years went on I had an extensive circle of official acquaintances. This was a great help to our work, giving us an assured position, and going far to prevent the riots and other troubles which were so liable to occur.

It was not long before we began to have soldiers also among our patients. Soon after our first hospital was opened, a small band of robbers was creating much trouble among some villages and scattered homesteads in the far east. A company of sixteen soldiers was sent to put them down, but weeks passed before they could even be found. At last some villagers gave information as to where the gang was lodged. When night came the soldiers surrounded the house, but the robbers escaped all but one, who took his stand behind the door. This was small, admitting only one at a time. A fine young fellow volunteered to lead the attack, and the door was soon forced, but the robber was well armed and made a desperate resistance. The soldier wounded him severely on the head with his sword, while the brigand lodged the contents of his pistol in the intruder's thigh. Other soldiers pressed in and overcame the ruffian, who was bound, taken to Moukden, and executed.

A fortnight later a military officer called on me, presenting the card of the Moukden *Tao-tai* (circuit judge) and asking if I would do His Excellency the favour of treating the wounded soldier. When the man was admitted, his health had suffered considerably from the knocking about he had sustained in travelling, the injured leg was much swollen, and suppuration had set in. After two days' rest, suitable food, and proper dressing of the wound, the inflammation had somewhat subsided, and the situation of the bullet was detected. The *Tao-tai* sent an officer to witness the extraction, an operation which native doctors could never attempt. The bullet was removed without difficulty, and the officer took it away to present to his General, *T'so Pao Kuei*. The patient left us after a month, able to walk as well as ever.

This case was of great use in making our work known and disarming suspicion, especially among soldiers and military mandarins. General Tso, the Commander of the Chinese forces in Manchuria, became our good friend and remained so ever afterwards, being many a time of great help to us. His soldiers were constantly sent to the dispensary and hospital for treatment, and when wounded were sometimes carried hundreds of miles to be put under our care. There was at that time, and for a good many years later, absolutely no attempt to provide medical or surgical help for the army. It depended on the kindheartedness of the General whether anything at all was done for the sick and wounded, but with the best heart in the world it was impossible to provide efficient aid. General Tso did all in his power in this direction. Though a strict disciplinarian and a terror to law-breakers, he was beloved and trusted by his men and respected by all classes. He established and maintained a Foundling Hospital, kept a soup-kitchen open for the poor for a couple of months every winter, and, while remaining a strict Mohammedan, subscribed liberally to our hospital.

Though we did our best from the first to promote friendly feeling, we sometimes unintentionally brought trouble on ourselves. In the second year of our residence in Moukden, a party of five men, including some visitors from Newchwang, started on horseback, escorted by a

Chinese gentleman, to visit some points of interest. Outside the west of the city, near a Lama temple, was a large open space where cavalry were in the habit of exercising. Here once a year was held a review of Manchu and Mongol horsemen, which our guide said was well worth seeing. These were not disciplined troops, but principally wild Mongols from the desert, with some Manchus. They wore no uniform, each being dressed as he pleased, with sheepskin coat and turban, or fierce-looking hairy cap. All were fearless riders, and many carried long spears. Their mounts were rough little ponies, full of spirit, and as unaccustomed as their riders to city crowds.

Unfortunately, as we approached, one of our horses, excited with the shouting and galloping, became unmanageable and rushed forward with its unwilling rider among the other horses. Immediately he was surrounded and cut off from the rest of the party by a noisy crowd of angry Mongols, who kept riding closely round him, whooping and shouting, and frightening still more his excited pony. The rider, finding himself jostled nearly out of his seat, struck the nearest horse with his riding-whip. In return the soldier made a fierce blow at the foreigner's head with a heavy stick. Seeing this, one of the other visitors spurred his pony straight at the Mongol brave, and knocked him and his beast into a large pool of mud and water. Meantime on the outskirts of the crowd we had succeeded in finding some officers, and were apologizing and explaining to them about the restive horse. With their help we gathered our little party together as quickly as possible and rode away, just in time to avoid serious consequences.

In spite of all our efforts to avoid anything which might be disliked by the people, and in spite of the friendship of many officials, civil and military, there was for long an undercurrent of ill-will in many quarters, and a readiness to take offence. Had we made no efforts at conciliation, and had we had enemies instead of friends in high places, it is difficult to say how that undercurrent might have affected us and how many years might have passed before our work in Moukden would have been firmly established.

V

MEDICAL PRACTICE AMONG THE CHINESE

> "And happed to hear the land's practitioners,
> Steeped in conceit sublimed by ignorance,
> Prattle fantastically on disease,
> Its cause and cure."
> "Epistle of Karshish"—*R. Browning.*

THE beginnings of medicine in China are in the dim distance of 4500 years ago, and its chief medical classic dates from the third or fourth century B.C. This is a book on medicine and physical science, treating of the human body, the two principles " yin " and " yang," the five elements, the circulation of the five elemental vapours in the body, diseases, acu-puncture, and so on. Other books were added to this later, but the theories as to the cause and cure of disease have been stereotyped for many centuries.

As long as the five elements of which the body is composed—metal, wood, water, fire, and earth—are in equilibrium, health is enjoyed; when they are out of proportion disease ensues, and the object of treatment is to bring them back to their normal relations. Medicines are classified according to the five colours and the five tastes, corresponding to the five elements and the five organs of the body. All treatment must accord with the various cycles of five, of which the following are a few:

Elements—

    metal   wood   water   fire   earth

Colours—
white	green	black	red	yellow

Tastes—
acrid	sour	salt	bitter	sweet

Organs of the body—
lungs	liver	kidneys	heart	spleen / stomach

Productions of the organs—
breath	ligaments	bones	blood	muscles

Senses—
nose	eyes	ears	tongue	mouth

Directions—
west	east	north	south	middle

For instance, if the heart is feeble there must be too little fire; fire is produced by wood, which corresponds with the liver; therefore to strengthen the heart the liver must be toned up, the medicine should be sour and of a greenish hue, and anything bitter must be strictly avoided. If, on the other hand, the lungs are affected, then earth is needed to produce the lacking metal element, the spleen and stomach must be stimulated, the medicine should be yellow and sweet, and everything acrid must be avoided. There are many other points too intricate to describe in detail.

Disease is diagnosed by the pulses, of which there are also five varieties. The left indicates the condition of the heart, liver, and kidneys; the right that of the lungs and stomach, and also of the "gate of life." When a patient enters the consulting-room for the first time, he does not expect to be asked questions. Silently he stretches out one hand after the other, and the doctor, by placing three fingers on each pulse in turn, is supposed to recognize the nature and seat of the disease. In the early days a friendly native doctor used to bring patients to see how

I would examine and treat them. One day a man appeared who, on account of an abnormality, had no pulse in the usual situation. I asked my Chinese friend to examine this case by his method, but finding no pulse at all he was completely nonplussed, and was greatly interested and astonished when I explained.

The ancients in China had some knowledge of surgery. There is evidence that they knew of the circulation of the blood, that they dissected the human frame as far back as 600 B.C., and that they were using anæsthetics and performing abdominal operations in the third century A.D. Unfortunately this knowledge seems to have become extinct. Their ideas now as to the position and functions of the various internal organs are most vague and inaccurate, and modern Chinese doctors own that they know nothing at all of surgery. They cannot tie an artery, amputate a finger or perform the simplest operation.

The only mode of treatment in vogue which might be called surgical is *acu-puncture*, practised for all kinds of ailments. The needles are of nine forms, and are frequently used red-hot, and occasionally left in the body for days. Having no practical knowledge of anatomy, the practitioners often pass needles into large blood-vessels and important organs, and immediate death has sometimes resulted. A little child was carried to the dispensary presenting a pitiable spectacle. The doctor had told the parents that there was an excess of fire in its body, to let out which he must use cold needles, so he had pierced the abdomen deeply in several places. The poor little sufferer died shortly afterwards. For cholera the needling is in the arms. For some children's diseases, especially convulsions, the needles are inserted under the nails. For eye diseases they are often driven into the back between the shoulders to a depth of several inches. Patients have come to us with large surfaces on their backs sloughing by reason of excessive treatment of this kind with instruments none too clean.

Another very injurious method of treatment is the application of a black resinous plaster, universally used for all kinds of aches and pains, bruises and swellings, wounds and sores. A small pimple or abscess appears, at once the plaster is applied and free discharge prevented. The result is often serious disease. Indeed, in almost every case of bone or joint disease which comes to us, the condition is aggravated, if not caused, by this deadly plaster; and yet the Chinese have unbounded faith in it. A boy of nine was brought in a basket, and when the plaster completely covering one leg was removed, the smell could almost be *heard*, as the Chinese say. A large part of the *tibia* was quite bare and projecting. His mother said that no medicine had been applied except this plaster, which had first been used about fifteen months before, when there was only a small sore place, caused by a fall. He was now much emaciated, with weak rapid pulse and bad cough, and death seemed not far off. We took him into the hospital, treated the leg rationally, and after a few days removed the diseased bone entirely. In a month he was walking about, rosy, strong, and merry, and with great enthusiasm learning to read and sing hymns. Such cases are very common in every hospital.

When there is an open sore in any part of the body, the native doctors often put in medicine having caustic properties, causing much mischief. For instance, a young man suffered from disease of the cervical glands, a common complaint here. An abscess having formed and burst, caustic medicine was put in. He came to us in great pain, and I found that the caustic had burrowed its way under the muscles, setting up severe inflammation of the deeper structures. By cutting down and removing the irritating substance, relief was given.

Any man who wishes may practise medicine, and as even the most famous and learned doctors know nothing of the structure of joints, patients often suffer much at their hands. A little boy twisted his leg one day when playing.

He complained of pain, but continued to limp about. As there was no doctor in the village, one old woman after another was consulted, but in spite of their rubbing and kneading the pain continued, so he was taken to a well-known doctor in Moukden. With great violence this man pulled and twisted the limb till the boy was screaming with agony. Until this operation he could walk, but now he could not even stand, and the limb was bent and shorter than the other. Three weeks later he came to us. The hip was much swollen, and so painful that examination was impossible without chloroform. The joint was found to be dislocated, doubtless as the result of the heroic treatment to which it had been subjected. It was easily reduced, and the little fellow was soon all right.

After the removal of a piece of bone one day from a severe gunshot wound, to my surprise a quantity of pure mercury poured out.

"That is the melted bullet!" said the patient.

Chinese doctors make no attempt to extract bullets, but often put mercury into the wound, which they say will melt the lead, and the patient is easily made to believe that it has done so.

With so much that is injurious, the Chinese have also some harmless and helpful methods and some useful drugs. They use *massage* constantly, not certainly in a scientific way, but intelligently and with much benefit. They also realize, indeed overestimate, the value of *counter-irritation*, and there is a somewhat peculiar method in common use. The skin is pinched up and twisted repeatedly and sharply between the fingers or knuckles, or with two bits of wood or copper coins, until it becomes livid. Cupping is also a common method. People are constantly seen with round livid patches on the forehead.

"What is wrong?" one asks at first in alarm. But the inevitable surprised answer is :

"I had a headache, that is all."

Blisters of many kinds are also freely used, and the actual cautery. The value of *perspiration* in illness is universally appreciated, and without calling in a doctor medicines are given to induce it.

Among their useful *medicines* are such as rhubarb, gentian, nux vomica, calomel, Epsom-salt, and so on. Little, however, is understood of the action of drugs on the system.

Vaccination is of comparatively modern date. Until recently a method commonly employed was to blow the lymph up the nostril, but this was very uncertain in its action, and now the foreign practice is usually followed.

The most valuable asset for the healing of disease which the Chinese possess is their wonderful *recuperative power*. Wounds heal by first intention under conditions which would be deadly to a European. A woman has her breast removed for cancer, and is put in a low smoky room 16 ft. by 10 ft., along with her attendant, three other patients, and a baby, one of the patients having a foul-smelling abscess; yet she makes a speedy and perfect recovery. In our hospitals we constantly have cases of remarkable recovery from wounds and diseases of bones and joints, which in the West would certainly prove fatal without amputation.

The power of resistance to nervous shock is also noticeable. A man is mending a gun in a blacksmith's shop, not knowing that it is loaded. It explodes, blowing off his hand. He calmly throws a handkerchief over the stump, and holding the wrist tightly with the other hand, walks three miles across the city to the hospital.

There are many strange and superstitious ideas about disease and its causes, which had their origin long before Buddhism or Taoism, and will doubtless linger in the country districts long after these religions have passed away. Unlucky days are blamed for many diseases, and lucky days are chosen for taking medicine. A hair is often twined round a limb above a sore, "to keep the poison from going up to the heart." A man, explaining the origin of his sickness, bowed his head and said, evidently with the deepest repentance :

"I have offended the Tiger-god. I was up among the hills and ate tiger's flesh, and this is the punishment."

A fine-looking old man brought his daughter to the dispensary in the last stages of pulmonary consumption, so weak that she could hardly stagger from her sedan-chair to the consulting-room. When the nature of the disease was explained, the father politely but firmly replied :

"You are mistaken. There is no disease of the lungs. I too am a physician of no mean reputation, but I am not a surgeon. It is because I have heard of your skill with the knife that I have brought my daughter to you, that you may remove the evil thing that is preying on her life." Then he explained that, many months before, a tortoise had begun to grow in her abdomen, and had increased rapidly till it was now the size of a hand. It lived on the patient's blood, which it drank three times a day.

"See!" he said, "you can feel its head moving from side to side under your hand, just below the heart. Can you not take it out ? "

Poor old father! the "tortoise" was but the fluttering aorta, whose beat was easily felt in the patient's thin, emaciated body.

Mothers are often credited by foreigners with heartlessness for throwing out the bodies of their little ones to be devoured by the wild dogs, but there is a reason. The untimely death of a young child is caused by the evil dog-spirit, which can only be appeased by the yielding of the little body to actual dogs. If this is not done, the same ghostly malevolence will cause the death of child after child in that family, so in love to the living the mother sacrifices the dead.

The belief in evil spirits is universal, and all forms of disease are attributed more or less to their agency. Besides the doctors who follow the ancient books, there are therefore sorcerers, witch-doctors, and devil-charmers, who are consulted even by men of rank and intelligence. Their prescriptions are of a varied nature. A paper with mystic characters may be burned, its ashes mixed with water, and the concoction drunk by the patient; or the characters may be worn as a charm. Sometimes a cup of water is covered with a cloth and shaken steadily until bubbles begin to appear; then it must be drunk quickly by the patient, while mysterious words are solemnly pronounced.

Madness, epilepsy, and extreme hysteria are usually regarded as being caused by devil-possession. Without any inquiry into the origin of the condition, most cruel methods are resorted to in order to drive out the evil spirit, such as forcing the patient to stand barefoot on red-hot iron, and there is always severe and merciless beating. Fortunately for the poor sufferers, life cannot long sustain such extreme torture, and death brings release. A girl of seventeen was brought to me, evidently a case of extreme hysteria. The witch-doctors, after trying several cruel methods without success, had finally thrust a red-hot poker down her throat to expel the demon. The girl died shortly afterwards. The electric battery has come to be recognized by the Chinese as the foreign cure for devil-possession, and many an "evil spirit" has been thus banished.

Medical science in China being in such a chaotic condition, and the methods of treatment so fantastic and inconsistent, it is not to be expected that patients should have great confidence in their doctors. The idea of a "family physician" is unknown. When the medicine of one doctor fails to cure within a few days, his prescription is set aside as unsuitable or disapproved by the gods, and another man is called in without the first being even informed. It is quite common to use the medicines of several doctors at once, in the hope that if one does not cure, another may. For this reason, visiting patients in their homes is most unsatisfactory.

There was a well-to-do merchant whose life was saved in the hospital in the early days, and who became an intelligent Christian. Some years later he had a severe attack of pleurisy, and wanted to come to the hospital, but the weather was extremely cold, little above zero, so it was thought wiser to leave him in his own comfortable home. Minute instructions were given, and one of my assistants visited him several times daily. The progress of his malady was most incomprehensible. One day he would improve so rapidly that we thought him out of danger; next day he would be worse than ever. Had I known then what was found out afterwards, I would have risked his removal to the hospital as his only chance. All the time that we were doing our utmost for him, his wife, who secretly hated Christianity and held to her old religion, was consulting native doctors. The alternations of medicines accounted for the strange, rapid improvements and sudden relapses. I had sent a man to sit up with him and administer the medicines, and we were hoping that the worst was over. But my man was sent home, the wife insisting that she would do all that was wanted. Next morning he was worse. In the evening I found her administering the contents of our medicine bottles, but they only contained water. It was now too late to save him.

Patients are quite unaccustomed to obey a doctor's instructions to the letter. Melons and cakes are eaten against orders; people grow tired of lying down when told, and are found walking about. A woman came to us with hip-joint disease, and after operation her leg was put in splints. She at once began to complain of the discomfort and cried herself ill, so that the splints had to be removed. She promised to lie quite flat and straight, but in a few hours was found sitting up with her leg bent. Some days later she was seized with dysentery, which would not yield to treatment. A small piece of the rind of a coarse kind of melon was found among her bed-clothes. A friend had smuggled it in, and she had eaten it entire, except this scrap. She was once more improving, when she began to cry to go home. She was tired of our strictness in diet, and saw no connection between food and her disease.

"I am going home to eat as much fruit as I like," she said. "If I don't die, I'll come back to have my leg cured. If I am fated to die, I die, and there's an end of it." She went home and died in four days.

On the other hand, a readiness to trust us blindly often causes difficulty, as when a man swallows the prescription along with the pill, or crunches a clinical thermometer to powder before he can be stopped. A man was brought to us who had suddenly lost the power of speech seven months before. He had been under one native doctor after another all that time, with no improvement. It was evidently a case of hysterical aphasia, so I did my best to secure his confidence, and then gave him some powders which were to last him four days. He, however, took the whole packet at once, which caused severe vomiting, but immediately his speech returned. In a day or two he went home, proclaiming the magic cure. Some days later a dozen sick people arrived from his village, insisting on being cured instantaneously of all their old chronic ailments. We had a similar experience with a cataract case, who led from his village and neighbourhood a long string of blind people, mostly incurable, some with no eyes left, all pleading on their knees to have their sight restored as his had been.

There is a general willingness to accept anyone as a doctor who professes to be able to cure. As soon as the suspicions of all things foreign began to pass away, people were only too ready to buy foreign drugs from

MEDICAL PRACTICE AMONG CHINESE

any quack who happened to sell them. A man acts as coolie in the hospital for some months, sees how wounds are dressed, and learns the names of the commonest medicines. He leaves us, invests a few dollars in castor-oil, santonine, boracic, and some lint, goes off to a village, and sets up as having learned medicine in the foreign hospital. A lad is brought to us in a dying condition, his leg is amputated, his life saved, and by and by he also sets up in the same way. This is not necessarily rascality nor hypocrisy, for they do not understand how little they know, nor how much there is to know.

In Tieling there was a man who had never been near a hospital, nor were his drugs really foreign, but he found he could get a readier sale if he called them so. To convince people of his connection with the foreigner, he quietly went to the Tieling Church a few times and learned one of the hymns. Then day by day he set up his little tent on the street, sang the hymn which he did not understand, and displayed his medicines, and guaranteed them as the genuine foreign article.

METEOROLOGICAL TABLE FOR ONE YEAR.

MOUKDEN.	Thermometer.							Barometer.				Rainfall.			
	Maximum.		Mean.	Minimum.		Mean.	Mean for month.	320 feet above sea-level.			No. of days		Maxi-mum in 24 hrs.	Total.
	Highest.	Lowest.		Highest.	Lowest.			Max.	Min.	Mean.	Rain.	Snow.		
January..	40·4	−0·6	16·29	25·3	−28·2	−9·28	3·51	30·31	29·63	30·09		5		·75
February	37	6·2	25·53	13·9	−25	−5·02	10·25	30·45	29·74	30·15		3		·45
March ...	68	20·	43·34	39·1	−8·7	20·73	32·01	30·45	29·34	29·93	1	2		·4
April	77·2	42·2	63·45	52·4	29	38·05	50·75	29·88	29·42	29·69	5		·32	·93
May	86·9	58·1	73·26	59·	32·7	49	61·13	30	29·51	29·69	7		·65	2·3
June	96·1	70·8	83·5	69·7	51·9	60·8	72·15	29·75	29·34	29·56	8		2·2	5·27
July	95·9	74·2	89·05	76·2	64·5	70·25	79·65	29·73	29·41	29·55	6		3·26	4·62
August ..	95·2	72·6	85·28	76·2	48·6	63·77	74·52	29·82	29·27	29·59	7		3·35	4·63
September	86·7	63·3	75·5	59·9	38·5	50·1	62·8	30·13	29·53	29·83	5		1·72	3·42
October..	76·1	35·3	54·3	49·3	23·1	34·7	44·5	30·27	29·73	29·94	4	2	·8	2·58
November	54·2	29·	39·7	42·6	−6·9	13·8	26·8	30·27	29·78	30·01	1	1		1·
December	47·2	10·8	25·4	23·9	−17·4	4·	14·7	30·29	29·62	30·11		5		·72
For year .	96·1	−0·6	56·2	76·2	−28·2	32·6	44·4	30·45	29·27	29·84	44	18	3·35	27·07

VI

CLIMATIC CONDITIONS, DISEASE, AND FLOOD

"A nation's wealth is in the health of its people."

IT is probably not generally realized that Rome and Chicago are about the same distance from the Equator. They and Moukden alike are about 42° N. The climate of Manchuria is distinctly continental, with extremes of heat and cold. It is not affected by ocean influences, and its wide level plain has no shelter from the cold blasts which in winter sweep over Siberia and Mongolia. The absence of forests and larger vegetation also influences the temperature and humidity.

The summer is hot, but rarely in Moukden is it above 95° Fahr., and for a part of the season the dryness is absolute, so that the sensations do not indicate the real temperature. During the wet season the heat is moist and oppressive; the summer rains are torrential, several inches often falling in a few hours. Spring and autumn are short, winter lasting about five months, for four of which every stream and pond is firmly icebound. In Moukden the minimum in an ordinary winter is 20° Fahr. below zero, though 33° have been registered, with occasional days when it does not rise above zero at all. The excessive dryness, however, the prevailing bright sunshine, and the clear calm bracing atmosphere, prevent this extreme from being realized. There is usually a good deal of snow, but not enough to allow sledging within many miles of this city. In spring the changes of temperature are great and sudden, high dry south winds prevail, and there are also quiet wet days which remind one of the homeland.

Manchuria has on the whole a desirable climate, healthy for Europeans, if they are careful in their eating and moderate in their drinking, if they are well housed and protected against the cold, and if they take proper precautions in the heat; for each extreme renders them more susceptible to the other. Its most trying feature is its extreme dryness, which, especially in winter, stimulates the nervous system, encouraging men to overwork without knowing it, and tending to produce insomnia, hysteria, and other diseases of nervous origin.

When we examine the conditions of life among the inhabitants of Manchuria, we are at first surprised that the race should be physically so well developed, strong, and healthy as we find it to be.

The houses of the common people defy all our laws of sanitation. The floors are either of earth or brick, and are on much the same level as the ground outside, or even lower. In the city they may be several feet below the street. The dwellings are planned with a view to economy of fuel. Half of the room is occupied by a brick platform, the *kang*, covered with matting, whereon people sit cross-legged, and eat and work in the daytime, and spread their bedding at night. At one end of the room a small kitchen is partly partitioned off; here is the millet-stalk furnace, under a large pot, and the flues of the chimney pass back and forward inside the *kang*, raising its surface to a comfortable heat which lasts for hours. If liberally fired twice or thrice a day when cooking the food, the warmth will linger in the bricks all the rest of the time; but the smoke of the millet-stalk fuel fills the apartment, making the eyes water and the throat smart.

No attempt is made at keeping the whole place clean, nor at sweeping behind cupboards or in corners; it is considered sufficient if the *kang* is clean, and a great many houses are unspeakably dirty. The windows have paper instead of glass, allowing very insufficient light to penetrate. Few rooms have proper ceilings, and the dust and cobwebs of years hang about the roof-beams. The number of people living, eating, and sleeping in one room is excessive, and all these expectorate freely on the floor.

The surroundings of the houses are also dirty and insanitary. Stagnant water is allowed to accumulate and every kind of garbage and filth, dogs and pigs being the only scavengers. Until 1905 there was no attempt at sanitation, and there is still no drainage of any kind except some open ditches, which are roaring torrents or foul-smelling holes, according to the weather. In the city there are large stagnant ponds, the natural drainage of the rainwater from the streets, and in these the people clean their vegetables and wash their clothes.

Personal cleanliness is expensive. Many have to buy their water from water-carts or pay to have it carried from the nearest well, as women cannot draw water unless the well is at their door. For six months of the year the houses are too cold, and all the year they are too crowded for baths to be easy or even possible. There are public baths in the city for men who choose to pay, but none for women. The wadded winter clothing is made in autumn and worn without change until spring, though the better off and the more particular wear inner garments which are washed regularly.

Mothers have no idea of the proper rearing of children. They are usually nursed to the age of three or four, and the use of cow's or goat's milk is unknown. When the mother cannot feed her child, she gives it rice, flour, or millet slops. During the long winter the little children of the poorer classes are kept indoors owing to insufficiency of warm clothing, and huddle together on the *kang* with neither fresh air nor exercise.

Under such circumstances we are accustomed to think

that no people could thrive. We would expect rickets among the children, but it is non-existent; we would expect diphtheria, typhus, and typhoid to be endemic, but they only appear in occasional infrequent epidemics. We would expect to find a stunted development, whereas the people are notably big and strong. There are certain conditions which counteract the influences adverse to health.

The houses are never overheated, and constant ventilation is afforded through the chinks in the ill-fitting doors and paper windows, and by the opening of the doors direct from outside to the living-rooms. In summer, windows and doors stand wide open all day, and for seven months of the year the children practically live out of doors except at night, adults also to a much lesser degree. The people live " the simple life," rise early, work hard, use no stimulants, do not hurry, and do not worry.

The general result is a strong body, the digestion of a horse, healthy tissues, and a wonderful power of resisting disease. Were the characteristics supported by a proper attention to infants during their first few days of life, precautions against tuberculosis, scientific treatment of disease, and general attention to hygiene and sanitation, there would be nowhere a stronger or more healthy people than the inhabitants of Manchuria.

But these matters are woefully neglected. Thousands of infants die of convulsions within a week of birth, owing to ignorance and dirt; many more are blind for life; others have their health permanently undermined.

Tuberculosis is the scourge of Manchuria. The idea of the communicability of the disease has not yet entered the Chinese mind, and owing to the general practice of expectoration, the atmosphere of many a crowded room must be loaded with bacilli. Phthisis is very common, especially among students and among young women of all classes. Girls are often married at fifteen or sixteen, and then their duty is to stay indoors doing the work of

FISHING ON THE SMALL RIVER

the household, cooking, and sewing, and many a young wife dies of "decline" within a few years. In our surgical wards, too, we have a large proportion of tubercular cases.

Eye diseases of every kind are very prevalent, especially trachoma with all its complications. The principal irritating causes are the smoke of the *kangs*, particularly where, as in some country places, they are fired with wood; and the frequent dust storms. The sand and impalpable dust which then load the atmosphere are driven by the strong wind, filling the eyes, ears, and nostrils of any who are out of doors, and penetrating into every corner of even the best built house. Smallpox among children is responsible too for a great deal of eye disease and blindness. Eye ailments are almost invariably neglected in their early stages, and diseased eyes are constantly wiped with dirty cloths, so that many come to us in extreme conditions such as are never seen at home.

Dyspepsia of all kinds is common, as millet, the staple food, is hard to digest, and is commonly gulped down in great quantities, often imperfectly cooked, without any attempt at mastication. Raw and under-cooked vegetables are also often eaten. During the hot season there is a great deal of dysentery, diarrhœa, and other diseases of the alimentary system. The uninstructed do not associate diet with disease. Many a death is caused by the practice of eating the greater part of the rind of the melons and cucumbers which are so abundant and cheap in summer.

Infectious diseases, such as chicken-pox, measles, scarlet fever, and smallpox, are always more or less among us, for no precautions are taken against their spread, The last is regarded as an ordinary children's ailment. and is usually of a mild type. Yet a great many die of it, and many more are badly disfigured by pock-marks, or have other sad traces of the ravages of the disease.

Several terrible epidemics of *cholera* have swept through the country during the past thirty years. The worst was during my first summer in Moukden. Native treatment was worse than useless, consisting largely in piercing with needles. The disease was of a most malignant type, and the mortality was terrible, 20,000 coffins being carried out through the city gates during August and September. We were kept busy from morning till night trying to save lives. We had no hospital, nor even a shed to shelter patients, but day by day crowds of people came to us or were carried on shutters and stretchers, and I did what I could for them in the open air. Another serious cholera epidemic followed the Chino-Japanese war, and there have been several less severe visitations.

In the summer of 1888 a calamity overtook us quite as serious as an epidemic, and more far-reaching in its results. It was an exceptionally hot and dry season in Moukden. All June and July the ground was parched and dry, and there were processions to plead for rain. In the mountains in the far east where our rivers rise there was, on the other hand, an unusual amount of rain, so that the River Hun, a couple of miles east and south of the city, was flowing full and strong. Then our rains came, incessant heavy downpour for a fortnight. Dark rumours began to be circulated of floods among the hills, and men shook their heads as the water steadily rose in the river. On 13 August the rain ceased, but late that night the water in the Small River in front of our hospital and houses began slowly to rise, amid much excitement. Early in the morning I heard shouts outside : " The water is rising ! The water is rising ! "

I went out, to find our terrace or " Bund " crowded, and the road between it and the river completely under water. Suddenly in the quiet flow, rippling in the bright sunshine, there was a swirl and a tumultuous rush of waves. When it subsided, the water had risen a foot. Another onrush of waves—another rapid rise—again—again—till it was lapping the edge of our terrace. It had risen 15 feet in about three hours.

What was the meaning of it all?

During the night a large volume of water from the hills had come down the *Hun* valley, carrying destruction with it. Village after village was swept away, and in some none were left to tell the tale. From one village the only survivor was a woman who was carried down ten miles supported by a piece of wood under her arms. There was a small hamlet some fifteen miles above Moukden, where the water rose so rapidly and with such terrible force that there was no time to escape to higher ground. House after house collapsed, and the inmates gathered in the darkness on the fallen walls, with little hope of life. All that night and the next day they clung to the ruins, the water reaching the waist and armpits, and no food being obtainable. When at last in the evening the flood began to subside, eleven of them were missing.

Meantime the torrent had swept onward until, at a point about two miles east of Moukden, where stood a large wood yard and a village, the banks of the Hun gave way. A great mass of water left the course of the river, and wave after wave poured down in the direction of the Small River, submerging miles of low-lying closely populated country.

The quiet slow water before our gates was now a deep foaming torrent, beyond which stretched as far as the eye could reach an angry sea, with clumps of trees showing here and there, and men and women clinging to the branches. Past us were swept logs from the wood yard, bundles of millet-stalk, trees, tables, carts. Then came horses, mules, cows, dogs, some already drowned, others struggling for life; then human beings clinging to floating pieces of wreckage, or huddled together on hastily constructed rafts. The water was still rising. Our terrace was transformed into an island, and quite cut off from the hospital. At our gate the water was several feet deep, all our compounds were submerged, and water was under and in the houses. The eastern wall of our compound was swept away, part of our gatehouse collapsed, and we saw a sedan-chair and other of our possessions float into the swift current. At last, about 4 p.m., we found to our relief that the water had ceased to rise. It was now 20 feet above its usual level.

The violence of the current was such that it was impossible to render much assistance to those who were drowning, but we did what we could and some lives were saved. A ring attached to a rope was whirled through the air to the help of more than one struggler, and in one instance a rough raft with half a dozen people was by this means guided safely in at the hospital gate. Towards evening, as the water was slowly falling, a man was seen struggling at some distance away. Without a moment's hesitation one of our Christian elders, a sturdy old man from the coast of Shantung and a good swimmer, threw off his coat, jumped in, and struck out into the stream, followed immediately by his son. They dived and swam, but could make but slow progress, and the drowning man had disappeared long before they reached the spot. After a fruitless search they returned, evidently unconscious that they had done anything worthy of praise.

It is hardly possible to estimate the loss of life caused by this flood. Besides the submerged villages, a large part of the suburbs of Moukden was under water, and several hundred were drowned. The loss of property was still greater, many families being reduced from easy comfort to extreme poverty. All over Manchuria the rivers were flooded, so that the distress was widespread.

The immediate effects of the flood, however, were not the most disastrous ; only when the severe cold of winter set in was the misery of the great mass of the people realized. The harvest was destroyed in extensive regions of rich grain country, and famine followed with its attendant fever. This condition of things was made known in the British newspapers, a Mansion House Fund was opened, supplies of grain were soon forwarded, and the missionaries worked hard for months at famine-relief. The hospitals too had their hands full, treating fevers and other ailments resulting from insufficient and unsuitable food. The most trying time was the following summer, before the harvest was ready. General Tso, willing as always to help the needy, offered the temporary use of a large barracks for famine cases. Several hundred were taken in who would have died on the streets, and many thousands were provided with food, medicine, and other help. Though the harvest was exceptionally good, much distress continued throughout the next winter, and it was years before the country recovered its prosperity. This famine-relief work had one good effect, the banishing from many districts of the suspicions and prejudices against foreigners.

Another and still more prolonged result of the flood was the development of *malaria*. Before this it was uncommon, twenty-eight cases being recorded in our dispensary from 1883 to 1888, several of which were from other parts of the country. During the floods the subsoil was saturated, and large ponds and marshes were left which became stagnant, offering a suitable breeding-place for mosquitoes. In the next spring an increase in malarial cases was first noticed, and the numbers rose rapidly in summer and during the following years, until we treated as many as 4000 in a year. Then some dry summers caused the drying up of many ponds, and stretches of marshland were drained and cultivated. Our numbers fell steadily, and now we have few cases of malaria from the neighbourhood of Moukden.

VII

EAST AND WEST : MISTAKEN JUDGMENTS

" There is neither East nor West, Border, nor Breed, nor Birth,
When two strong men stand face to face, tho' they come from the ends of the earth."
Rudyard Kipling.

" Man to man, the warld o'er,
Shall brithers be, for a' that."
Robert Burns.

THERE is a general widespread impression that the Chinese are in all things the opposite of other men, that they never feel or think or act as other peoples would. Externally there is some truth in this : their customs, ways of speech, methods of action are often the direct antithesis of ours, and they look upon many things from quite a different point of view. In fact, the longer one lives in China the more he realizes this difference, and feels the impossibility in everyday life of getting behind the outer screen, as we do with intimate friends of our own or similar nationality. But when we come to the elemental passions at the foundation of our common human nature, then we can grip their hands as brothers, for we find them strong, virile, and reliable in those deeper feelings which are the mainspring of action. Their family affection, their staunch friendship, their unselfishness to those they love, their homely joys, their love of children, their kindliness to friends and neighbours, their warm-hearted gratitude, their fortitude in trouble, their patience in enduring, will compare with those of any nation.

Their action may often take a different form from ours,

which we forthwith condemn; but when we examine into causes and influences at work, we find that our hasty surface judgments were wholly mistaken.

A man is taken suddenly ill when walking alone along a busy city street. He staggers and falls near the door of an evidently prosperous shop. What happens? Passers-by glance at him curiously and go on; a few stand and look at him, but no one touches him or meddles in any way; the shopkeeper keeps studiously out of sight. He is unconscious and a stranger, so no one can inform his friends, but after a time the shopkeeper gives notice to the *yamen* which has charge of city affairs, and he is removed. All this time no one has so much as brought a cup of water, or tried to make him more comfortable.

" Callousness ! " exclaims the foreigner. " Hard-hearted, selfish indifference ! "

But what is the standpoint, what are the customs of centuries, the laws of the land, which lie behind this action or rather inaction? The law is that those who house, or feed, or attend to a man who dies, thereby accept responsibility for him. If no friends claim him, they must bear the expense of burial. If friends appear, these may accuse the meddlers of causing the man's death.

The daughter of my early friend, the Tao-tai Gao, had married a wealthy and prominent official. One day she found a poor wretch on the street, lying half dead, starving, and very ill. She hired men to carry him to the hospital, but on the way he died, and she paid for his funeral. The man's relatives heard of it and gathered round her like vultures. Great lady as she was, she had to pay them hundreds of taels to hush the matter up. Is it any wonder that dying men are left to die on the street?

One day when I had not been long in Moukden and was not conversant with this point in law, I saw a crowd on our river bank and went down. In the water was a drowning man, now unconscious, a case of suicide. To my indignation, no one was attempting to save him, and when I called on the hospital men to help to get him out of the water, they obeyed most unwillingly. When at last the man was, to the astonishment of the crowd, restored to life, I learned that, had the man died, only the fact of my being a foreigner would have prevented serious consequences to those who had touched him.

This law is doubtless the crystallization of an old custom which might once be useful enough in preventing murder. People own that it is not a good law, but customs which date from the time of Abraham are not easily changed.

Another charge frequently brought against the Chinese is that of *ingratitude.* Many a foreigner does things which he considers kind and benevolent, he acts the part of Lady Bountiful, or the *deus ex machina,* and the very people whom he has benefited requite him with ingratitude and even dislike. The truth usually is in such cases that donor and recipients do not understand one another. They think that he is paid for all he does, or has some ulterior motive, so why should they be grateful? Or his benefits may be bestowed in such a way as to offend them, and while too polite to tell him so, they cannot go the length of gratitude.

When Chinese realize that they are being kindly treated and receiving what they have no claim to, their gratitude is both deep and practical. In the hospital we have had thirty years' experience of this; indeed, we meet with far less ingratitude than do infirmaries and hospitals at home. All our patients pay for their food, except the destitute, for whom there are free beds. Besides this, many subscribe liberally. One day a man brought me a shilling, explaining that he was that amount in debt to us when he left the hospital, so before going back to his distant home he had hired himself out for a month as a farm labourer until he had saved this.

"You cured me for nothing," he said, "I must surely pay for my food!"

Often have patients returned with the present of a fowl, or a basket of eggs, or even a bag of hazel nuts from their own trees. A Mongol boy dislocated his elbow, and was brought to us after a year. The joint was stiff and immovable, but an operation restored its usefulness, and father and son went joyfully home. Months later a fine black Mongol cow was driven into the compound with the compliments and thanks of the whole family. At the Boxer time there was a rumour that I had not escaped, but was in hiding in the North Tomb woods, outside the city. There was a horse-dealer who had been treated in the hospital, a regular cheat and rascal who to this day would rejoice in getting the better of me in a bargain. He bought a basketful of various kinds of food and went secretly to those woods, where he searched in vain for me for a whole day. It was at the risk of his life, for anyone known to help a foreigner would have been killed.

Liberality is a marked feature of the Chinese, in spite of the popular idea of their closeness in money matters. They are not good at systematic giving, nor indeed at anything systematic, but they respond warmly to any call for a donation. Their presents to each other at marriages, funerals, the birth of a first son, and other occasions seem to us quite out of keeping with their means. When a missionary goes home on furlough after years among them, he is overwhelmed with gifts from those who can never expect to be repaid in any way. We have had happy experience of this liberality in our hospital and college, which have been built and maintained largely by voluntary contributions from the Chinese.

Akin to this is their great *hospitality*, of the open spontaneous kind. Marriages, funerals, and births are the occasions of feasts to which crowds are asked, tents being erected on purpose. They do not confine their hospitality to such stated occasions, but are ready with it at all times and to all comers. The invitation we so often hear when we stop to speak to a man outside his door : " Will you not come in and rest, and drink a little water ? " is not a mere formality. They mean it.

One summer afternoon we were caught by a thunderstorm when out walking in the country. Near by was a tiny little hut, built of mud bricks, with a thatched roof. For this we made with all possible speed, as the drops were heavy and our clothes thin. Seeing us running, its inmate opened the door and, before we could ask breathlessly for shelter, begged us to come in. He apologized for the poorness of his humble dwelling, and at once began to prepare hot water to offer us, excusing himself for possessing no tea.

"Had I known that such honourable guests were coming, I would have prepared some," he said, and no doubt he would. He made the children at home, showing them all his little possessions, and had he been a lord he could not have entertained us more courteously. He was not a Christian, nor had he ever been near the hospital, nor even spoken to a foreigner before. We were simply fellow-beings in need of shelter, and he gave it gladly.

We often hear of the deceitfulness and dishonesty of the Chinese,—" ways that are dark, and tricks that are strange." Yet those who come into close contact with Chinese merchants consider them as reliable as any in the world. During over thirty years' experience I have always found the word of a respectable merchant or tradesman as good as his bond. I have known of contracts between foreigners and Chinese where the Chinaman from some unforeseen cause lost money instead of making a profit, yet he took it as a matter of course that he should honourably fulfil his contract. It is a common experience that lack of trust or lack of understanding those with whom one is dealing causes deceit and dishonesty, whereas trust breeds trustworthiness.

EAST AND WEST: MISTAKEN JUDGMENTS

Foreigners may be met with who have lived a lifetime in China and have not a good word to say of the Chinese. A man may lightly dismiss a servant on suspicion, or in anger, or for some breach of foreign custom, in a way which the Chinese regard as unjust. It is difficult for him to find a second servant of real trustworthiness. If a misunderstanding again occur, he becomes noted as a man to whom no good servant should go, and all his life he will suffer from a succession of undesirables, who take service to make what they can out of him, by theft or other means.

One cause of the common imputation of dishonesty is the universal Chinese custom of *commissions*, or, in Anglo-Chinese parlance, "squeezing." In buying or selling, an uncertain percentage may remain in the hands of each person who has to do with the transaction. This is the system of the country, from highest to lowest, and is regarded as a man's lawful right. No doubt it is a bad system, open to endless abuses, but it is universally recognized and is not considered dishonest nor unjust if kept within limits. It is not to be compared with the calculated rascality in swindling met with in some so-called Christian countries, though unfortunately the Chinese are beginning to learn such things also.

One day I was visiting a Chinese official, an intimate friend, whose family were away. His head cook came in on business, and the master said to him :

"You must be badly out of pocket now with so few to provide for. Here is something to make up." And he handed him some money. I was interested in the episode, and asked about this custom, which is so objectionable to us.

"He gets about 5 per cent on all his purchases," said the official. "The other servants see that he does not take too much. The Governor-General's people will take double that, there are so many to get a share, and the Emperor pays most of all."

The same principle runs through all official life. The nominal salary is a mere trifle.

"I don't get enough to pay the food of my horses," said one official. There are endless perquisites of office which form the real salary. The evil of the system is that it is left to each official to determine what are his rights, and while there are many conscientious, fair-minded men who take no more than their due, there are not a few who, regardless of the people, grasp at all they can.

The Chinaman is usually credited with being *stolid*, whereas he is in truth, under certain conditions, one of the most nervously excitable of men. He will endure a great deal if he thinks it inevitable, and not complain, and his feelings do not readily show themselves in his face; but deal with him contrary to "reason," or in a way which he considers touches his honour, and he quickly becomes so excited that he loses all control of himself. A common cause of illness is a "fit of anger." I have seen a man's temperature rise four degrees in a few minutes, solely because of rage at some news from his home. There was a patient in the hospital who one evening suddenly lost the power of speech and developed alarming symptoms with very high temperature. I found that his servant had just left him, and he had been very angry; so we got the man to return to his duties, and gradually the patient was restored to his normal state.

This nervous susceptibility is often worked upon by the innate *fatalism* of the East. When a man believes a thing will happen, that goes far to make it happen. An elderly man suffering from severe dysentery was brought to us by his son, and after four days' treatment had greatly improved. On talking with him I was surprised to find that he was firmly convinced that he was dying. At the beginning of his illness he had consulted a fortune-teller, who said that he would certainly die at 4 p.m. on a certain day. This the family tried to prevent by sending him to us.

"You may do what you like to cure me," said the old man, " but I have to die all the same. It is the Decree of Heaven." In spite of our remonstrances and the entreaties of his wife and son, he got men to carry him home on a stretcher, and on the afternoon of the appointed day he died.

With a people of this temperament one would expect *suicide* to be common, and so it is, but not from the same reasons as principally cause it in Europe. In China a man kills himself not because he is tired of life, nor from the cowardly desire to escape shame or distress; but either in ungovernable anger or because he knows that *his death will put the other party in the wrong.* You lend a man money and he cannot pay; you make it unpleasant for him, and "take away his face," i.e. his honour *vis-à-vis* the world; he dies to revenge himself on you, and you are blamed for the death. Or you have a lawsuit and win your case, but your opponent commits suicide, and it would have been better for you to lose.

There was in Moukden a wealthy family who had land in the country adjoining that of some comparatively poor people. A dispute arose as to boundaries and they went to law. Having money to back him, the rich man won the case. Next day a son of the poor man committed suicide at his door, and he had heavily to compensate the parents. When that was settled, another son did the same, calling on all to witness that he did this because of the injustice his parents had suffered at the hands of this man. This time a much heavier indemnity was demanded, and, after months of haggling, was paid. Then a third son killed himself, and the payment of the still further increased blood-money reduced the once wealthy man to be poorer than his rival. Again the lawsuit was heard, and this time the country family won the case. The sense of family honour is strong, though manifesting itself very differently with us.

When a young wife is unhappy, suicide by jumping

down a well is not uncommon. Immediately her own parents or relatives demand money from the father-in-law, because she must have been ill-treated or she would not have killed herself. It may have been done in a fit of anger, and the quarrel may have been entirely her own fault, but this would be difficult to prove, and in most cases the husband's family consent to pay hush-money. This custom acts as a wholesome deterrent to the ill-treatment of young wives by mothers-in-law.

Revenge or retaliation in some form is looked upon as a duty. If a person injures you, you " lose face " if you do not take some measures against him. Among the rough and illiterate the methods of revenge are sometimes terribly brutal. A man came to us with part of his tongue cut off by an enemy, another with his eyes gouged out and both hands chopped off, a third with all four eyelids cut off. (We were able by plastic operations to supply some protection to the poor staring eyes.) In general, however, the use of brute force is condemned, and the tongue is considered a more dignified weapon. When we hear with astonishment a cultured, well-dressed person indulging in the most extreme vituperation, and ask how this is possible, he answers calmly :

" He reviled me, so of course I must curse him, or I would lose face." The Christian precept, Bless them that curse you, does not commend itself to the natural man in China.

The Western world has regarded China as far behind in all civilization, largely because of her slowness to develop those lethal weapons a modern army and navy. In spite of her teeming millions, she could be coerced by a gunboat ; therefore she was despised. It is a question, however, whether her ideal of civilization is not of a higher type than that which acts on the principle that " might is right." In China it has long been recognized that mind is superior to matter, intelligence to physical strength, the appeal to reason better than decision by force of arms. Arbitration is her ideal. A certain force of soldiers was always necessary, but it was an armed provincial constabulary rather than an army, and the difference in rank between a civil and a military official shows how fighting was looked upon.

Reason is regarded by all as supreme, and is appealed to on every occasion. No stronger condemnation can be passed upon a man, a family, a community, a nation, than that they are devoid of " reason, reasonableness, right principle," as the word may variously be translated. When, at the point of the sword, a nation makes a demand which is manifestly without *right*, and when China has to give in, no one considers that the superiority of the foreigners has been established, but rather the reverse. For it is a poor cause that has to resort to force; its supporters evidently realize that they have not *reason* behind them.

This is carried out in communal and individual life. To appeal to a man's sense of reason has far more effect than threatening him with arrest. The settlement of quarrels by means of middlemen or arbitrators is universal. Until the Russo-Japanese war brought Western ways among us, there was not a policeman in Moukden nor any other city, and none were needed. Night-watchmen there were, and " yamen runners " who would come to arrest a man if sent for, but the peace of the city was in the hands of its citizens.

The patriarchal family system, from 20 to 150 souls living as members of one household, has often been blamed for causing family quarrels. But could we imagine such a system enduring in the West at all? The dispeace would be so constant and bitter as to be almost unbearable. As a matter of fact, most of these populous homes live in a wonderful measure of amity and affection, all the members being ruled by the old grandfather or mother, whose word is law, and who acts as arbitrator in every dispute.

After a foreigner has become accustomed to his first impressions and has concluded that the Chinese are diametrically the opposite of ourselves, he will, if he lives among them and learns to know them intimately, gradually change his mind, and find out how like we are after all. A country farm with boys and girls growing up in health and merriment around parents and grandparents, attending the village school or helping on the farm, while the grown folks work hard in the fields and in the home, and the old people totter in the summer sunshine, and doze in the warmest corner in winter—it is really much the same as the life on a croft or small farm at home, except that the religious background of life does not exist.

This is in reality the one vital difference. As a general rule, religion counts for nothing in Manchuria. A man has nothing great to live for, no high ideals, nothing to glorify his monotonous daily round and common task, no desire for moral and spiritual growth and development in this life, no hope for any life to come. He may subscribe to the building of a temple, or burn incense before an idol, but that is not usually a religious act at all. He does it as a form of insurance, to bribe the evil influences which might otherwise harm his home, or to secure some temporal boon which he earnestly desires, or at the most to turn aside the punishment which his own evil doings, known and unknown, would naturally bring.

Those who profess to be religious in the only way he has heard of, Buddhist or Taoist priests, or devotees who have vowed to do all kinds of uncomfortable things in the name of religion—he sees indulging at the same time in every form of vice. Being an eminently reasonable man, he recognizes this practical divorce of religion from morality, and concludes that religion is of very little use. At the same time, for an upright life, even if he does not practise it, he has a very great respect, inherited from generations of ancestors who have been taught the high morality of Confucius.

For the great bulk of the people, outside those who follow a few Buddhist sects, religion, properly speaking, does not exist, though there is a vast deal of superstition. This material life is all they know or care about. Even their respect for uprightness and morality is based on the experience that in the long run they pay best. What will make money, furnish creature comforts, and above all give security for the coming years, that is to be followed after. A man is loyal to his ancestors, and faithfully worships at their shrines; and when his time comes he will be gathered to his fathers, and his children whom he has instructed will in their turn worship at his shrine. What good will it do to him? we ask. And the many millions of Manchuria all give one answer: "Who knows?"

VIII

FAR FROM THE MADDING CROWD

> " No sooner was I fairly found
> Pledged to the plain, after a pace or two,
> Than pausing to throw backward a last view
> To the safe road, 'twas gone ! grey plain all round !
> Nothing but plain to the horizon's bound ! "
> "Childe Roland to the Dark Tower Came."
> *Robert Browning.*

THERE are few parts of the world where the modern change in ease of access has been more marked than in Manchuria. One can now leave London at nine o'clock on a Monday morning, and after a comfortable sleeping-car journey drive through the Moukden streets in the afternoon of Friday, eleven days later. The contrast with thirty years ago, and indeed with thirteen years ago, is greater than the contrast between that time and the days of sailing ships.

Manchuria used to be one of the remote parts of China, little known and seldom visited. After the six weeks' voyage from London to Shanghai, a coasting steamer to Newchwang must be waited for, perhaps as long as ten days. Arrived there after a three or four days' voyage, another stay of a few days was necessary, to hire carts and prepare for the journey up-country. Bedding was needed for the inns by the way, a servant to prepare food, pots and pans to cook it in, knives and forks to eat it with, plates and cups for those who did not care to use the scanty and coarse inn supply, and a store of sufficient foreign food to eke out the native fare of the inns, on which few foreigners can maintain health.

Inland travel was no easy matter, and it remains the same to this day aside from the railway lines. Made roads are non-existent. Rough tracks lead across the country from village to village, usually below the level of the surrounding land, and deep ruts are worn by strings of heavy carts conveying the produce of the district to the nearest mart. In times of rain these roads become streams or a succession of ponds and quagmires, and the weary mules have to struggle on at a snail's pace, sometimes only succeeding in making five miles a day. Occasionally a mule is drowned in the road.

The passenger travels in a springless cart drawn by three horses or mules, which are guided chiefly by the voice of the driver. The jolting is most trying, conducive to headache or sickness, especially to the inexperienced. Many a traveller concludes it to be preferable to walk, until fatigue drives him back to the questionable comfort of his cart. When approaching darkness makes a halt necessary, he has to content himself with a Chinese inn. To the experienced this is no hardship, but the newcomer feels a brick bed very hard, in spite of the mattress he has with him; the smoky rushlight gives a miserable light; and the prying eyes peering through the holes, so easily made in the paper partition or windows of what is called a private room, cause an uncomfortable lack of privacy. Then the carter always insists on starting in the small hours of the morning, when in winter it is bitterly cold. The journey of 120 miles to Moukden by cart used to occupy from four to eight days, according to weather and the condition of the roads.

In summer, instead of carts a boat might be hired, a rough river-craft used for beans and other cargo. The passenger took the place of the beans in the bottom of the boat, a matting tent giving privacy and protection. Here, with a fair degree of comfort, the journey might be made in anything from three to ten days, more probably the latter. If the wind was favourable the boat sailed along pleasantly among green fields or between high banks with overhanging willows, but at every bend the long poles were needed to keep her off the banks or shallows. Going up-stream, more often the men poled for hours at a time, the monotonous tramp of their bare feet resounding on the narrow deck which runs on either side of the boat. At other times, when the wind was adverse or the contrary current strong, the crew took to "tracking." A rope was fastened to the top of the mast, so as to clear bushes and trees on the banks, and the two or three available men toiled with it along the tow-path, while one remained on board to steer. For those who knew the language and could chat with the boatmen and the villagers, these journeys by river were a pleasant variety, even when the boat stuck on a sandbank and it took some hours to get her off. For a stranger, however, the journey by road or by water was not inviting, and it is not to be wondered at that Inland Manchuria in those early days saw very few visitors.

In winter the feeling of isolation was intensified by the difficulty of getting into or out of the country. Towards the end of November the Port of Newchwang, the one gate to Manchuria, "closed," and remained ice-bound for at least four months. Letters came by swift couriers overland from Shanghai, taking more than a month, but to travel that way was out of the question. Exit by the north was still more impossible, as the Siberian Railway had not even been thought of. To the east was the Hermit Kingdom of Korea, where no foreigner could enter. Dalny had not yet been created, and the only way of crossing the sea in winter was to trust oneself to the storms in a Chinese sailing junk, after an overland journey of a week or ten days to Port Arthur or one of the bays near it.

Those foreigners who lived up-country remained there

for the most part all the year round. There was no summer resort within reach, and the only change possible without great expense was to pay a visit to some other station, or to go on a tour into the farther interior.

Itinerating tours were and are often taken in winter, when the roads are frozen hard and the cart can rattle over them or along the ridges of the bare brown fields at a trot, and cover as much as forty miles in a day. Then the people are at leisure from their farm labour, and have time to listen or to bring their sick folk. A journey in spring is a delight to the soul, with the fresh green life bursting forth all around after the dreary winter, and the wild flowers rejoicing in their new life. But the body has to pay dear for such soul-luxuries, as the cart bumps and toils in the mud and deep ruts. In summer the colour dies out, the freshness and greenness become wilted and dull, the heat makes travelling a burden and a danger to a foreigner; then too come the heavy rains, the streams are swollen and hard to ford, the roads become rivers or quagmires.

An early autumn journey is through quite a different land. The cart or riding-horse jogs along the country roads and lanes with tall twelve-foot-high millet on either side. The traveller cannot see more than a few yards away, except the road behind and in front and the cloudless distance overhead. Only now and then as he reaches some rising ground he draws his breath at the rich beauty before him, miles and miles of millet, the heavy red-brown heads of grain waving cumbrously on their thick stalks in the blue sunshine, while here and there a farm or a hamlet nestling amid its trees, or a field of other grain or vivid green vegetables, breaks the ride monotony.

My first country journey was in the spring of 1884, when I had been a year and a half in Manchuria. With a light heart I put aside all my language-study books, packed into a cart my bedding and a few other belongings, a good stock of medicines and some instruments, and took three days' journey south to Haicheng, to join my companion, a senior missionary, the Rev. John MacIntyre. He also had a cart with bedding and other things, and a stock of Gospels and Christian books and tracts. We ourselves rode on horseback, much the pleasantest mode of travel. From Haicheng we struck away into the hill country to the south-east, and I began to realize what a beautiful land Manchuria is. Spring had come with a rush, violets were carpeting the woods, bluebells were ringing joyously, and the trees eagerly " uttering green leaves." Undulating hills gave place to high mountains with grand passes, reminding us of our own Scottish highlands. The summits and clefts of these heights were still white, and clear streams from the melting snows ran in the valleys. A striking feature on these rivers is the many weirs and water-mills with turbine wheels, in use here for hundreds of years.

In every town and village where we stopped we made known that we would see patients, and crowds of astonished people surrounded us. Many ailments were cured and minor operations performed, the existence of a hospital in Moukden was made known, many books were sold, thousands listened to our preaching, and all went away saying that " this Jesus religion must be quite a good thing." We went as far as the River Yalu, the border of Korea, then turning north returned by a different route.

One day towards dusk, in a sparsely inhabited district, we found ourselves several miles from the only inn, and between us and it was a river, swollen with the melting snows. It was quite evident that the carts could not cross.

" We can swim if need be," said Mr. MacIntyre, " and so can the horses; let's ride across." So we plunged into the clear rapidly-flowing stream. Fortunately swimming was not necessary, the animals kept their footing and struggled through to the other side. We found our way to the inn, reaching it about dark, a poor hovel, only one common room, with two old men as innkeepers. We were tired and glad of a resting-place, humble though it was. There was neither candle nor lamp, but the end of a tarred rope was lit, hanging from a beam, and by this dim light I looked at my watch.

" What is that toy ? " asked one of the old men.

" It tells the time," I answered.

" What time ? What do you mean by *time* ? "

" It shows where the sun is."

Turning to his brother, he asked in a puzzled way :

" But the sun's down long ago: how can he tell where it is ? "

" *Ai-ya !* " said the brother, with awe. " He can still see it in that glass ! What can these foreigners not do ? "

We were ravenously hungry, but there was no food of any kind in the inn except dry cobs of last year's Indian corn. These we had boiled, and thus took the edge off our hunger. At last, about midnight, our carts arrived, and we were thankful to have a second and more digestible supper, and our beds. Early next morning we were astir, preparing to go on. As our horses were being saddled the old man again began to question us :

" How far away is your country ? "

" Many thousand miles."

" And did you ride all the way on that horse ? "

Some days later an untimely snowstorm overtook us. Snow in Manchuria is usually dry as powder ; but the first early fall and the late snow of spring are like the home article, finding their way damply into every nook and cranny, penetrating even into the recesses of bedding and bundles in the carts, so we were weather-bound in a wayside inn. Many people gathered to look at us, to watch us eat, to listen to us speaking to each other in a foreign language, to examine our strange clothes and belongings, to tell of their ailments, to question us as to what made us come here. Among them was a man with an enormous unsightly tumour over one eye. He had heard of our Moukden work, and came to us begging to have this taken away. Forthwith a table was brought, antiseptics prepared, and there in the middle of the gaping crowd, amid much excitement, the tumour was removed and the wound sewed up. It was dressed that evening and next morning, then left to Nature's care. I afterwards heard that it healed most satisfactorily.

The arrival of a foreigner in Moukden in those days was quite an event. One winter evening early in 1885 our servant came in to say that there was a foreigner at the gate, but he evidently hesitated to bring him in. I went out, and there was an elderly man in decidedly dirty and ragged Chinese clothes, the colour of whose shaggy beard proclaimed at once that he was no Chinaman. As he knew no English, nor could I make out his language, we were reduced to conversing in Chinese. He was a Pole who had been shipwrecked more than twenty years before in the south of Manchuria. According to his statement, he was the only survivor from the wreck, and the British Consul in Newchwang had helped him, and had sent him away to the far borders of Manchuria to find out about the "Fish-skin Tartars." He travelled north day after day, until he found himself near the region he sought; but his money was exhausted, so he hired himself as farm labourer to a Chinaman and settled down there.

It was a wild lawless country, quite beyond the control of any Government, and was at that time under a brigand chief who had power of life and death. A common punishment for those who thwarted him was burying alive. Here the Pole worked hard and behaved well, so that he won the confidence of the people, and got a piece of ground of his own to farm. He married a Chinese woman and lived happily with his family for a good many years.

Then a tragedy befell them. A terrible flood swept away wife, children, homestead, crops; and now, alone and desolate, his thoughts turned to his mother, sisters, and country. He was trying to work his way slowly to Newchwang, where he hoped to get a ship and return to his native land. For all these years he had heard no news of European events, and he listened eagerly to the story of the Franco-Prussian war and the rise of the German Empire. But what of Poland? When I told him that the last effort for independence had failed, and that there was no Poland, and showed him the map of Europe, he wept like a child.

The Chinese Christians were greatly interested in the man, especially when he told them he too was a Christian, and they collected among themselves a considerable sum to help him on his journey. We rigged him out with old foreign clothes, entertained him for a few days, and then sent him down to Newchwang with a letter to the British Consul. Afterwards we heard that he went straight to the Roman Catholic Mission in Newchwang, saying that he was a Catholic, which was no doubt true, and the priests gave him money. He also went to the Consul and others with my letter and got money from them. Then one day he disappeared, but not by steamer, and no one heard of him again. Doubtless he was a political exile who dare not return to the Poland he yearned for.

Sometimes we had visitors of a very different type, as when Sir Henry (then Mr.) James, and Sir Francis (then Lieutenant) Younghusband, and Mr. Fulford (now Consul-General) spent a few days with us on their way to explore the regions of the "Long White Mountains."

Some years later we had a visit from the distinguished traveller Mrs. Isabella Bird Bishop. She was in Korea when the revolt broke out which ushered in the Chino-Japanese war, and with other ladies was ordered out. Her plans being thus overturned, she came to Newchwang and took boat for Moukden. A few hundred yards from our door her cart was upset in trying to avoid a black pool of unknown depth; she was thrown out against a stone, receiving bad bruises, and her arm was seriously injured. For over five weeks she remained in Moukden, taking a deep interest in our work and in all that happened, visiting the hospital constantly, inquiring into the history of each patient, and taking photographs. We were greatly impressed by her energy and keenness in the face of ill-health and suffering. Her right arm being disabled she immediately set herself to learn to write with her left hand, and in this way part of the MS. of her book on Korea was written. She was with us during a trying time of deep anxiety and some danger at the beginning of the war, when she endeared herself to us all, and ever afterward she remained a staunch friend to us and our work. A part of the Medical College here is erected in her memory and with her money.

As a general rule, as long as there was no railway, months passed without our seeing any European outside our own little circle. It was in the winter after the Chino-Japanese war that we first began to feel that the great world outside was stretching its covetous fingers into the plains and valleys of Manchuria. One day we had most unexpected visitors, a Russian colonel and lieutenant, attended by four Cossacks, the first we had ever seen. They had travelled through Korea, had passed northward into Manchuria, and had now come south as far as Moukden. We invited them to spend an evening with us, and had a most pleasant time with them. That night as I stood at our gate, and saw them mount their horses and ride off at a gallop by the light of the brilliant winter stars, and heard the hoofs clatter in the distance on the hard roads, it seemed like a warning that old times were passing away, and that Manchuria was to be left to her isolation no longer.

IX

PROGRESS, 1883–1894

" Take up the White Man's Burden—. . .

" By open speech and simple
    An hundred times made plain,
To seek another's profit
    And work another's gain.

" And when your goal is nearest,
    The end for others sought,
Watch sloth and heathen folly
    Bring all your hopes to nought."
Rudyard Kipling.

MY first Sunday in Moukden, the service was held in a small room, with under a score of Chinese present, all men. It was a warm-hearted, united little company, very hopeful too, in spite of obloquy and persecution, looking forward to the time when Manchuria would be conquered for their King. But I do not think that the most hopeful would have believed it possible that thirty years later there would be twenty-six thousand Protestant Christian members of the churches, besides many more adherents, and that in Moukden alone about a thousand would gather every Sunday to worship God in three different churches or halls.

Speaking generally, Manchuria has been more responsive than any part of China, in proportion to the number of foreign missionaries at work. This is due partly to the mixed nature of the population. Men who have been transplanted from various parts of China do not naturally hold on firmly to their old local superstitions and beliefs. Where so many experiences in life are new, a new religion does not seem so impossible. The inward impulse to find some settled faith to hold by has caused thousands of these Manchurian Chinese to enter Buddhist sects, groping after truth. These sects have been manifest feeders of the Church, furnishing some of her most earnest votaries and deepest thinkers, and at the same time also her keenest and most determined antagonists.

The progress of Christianity in Manchuria is still more largely due to the policy adopted from the beginning in mission work, the most prominent principle of this policy being that the Christian Church must be Chinese, not foreign. The members have been encouraged to undertake the spreading of the light themselves. From the first, responsibility was laid on Chinese evangelists and Christians, and it is they who have brought in these thousands. The Church is also Chinese in its organization and administration. Where foreign rules and customs have been introduced, it has only been until the people themselves chose to alter them. Denominationalism has been conspicuously absent, at least ninety-nine of every hundred members to-day being unaware that there have all along been several independent missionary societies at work, viz. the United Free Church of Scotland, the Irish Presbyterian Church, the British and Foreign Bible Society, and since 1895 the Danish Lutheran Church. To the Chinese mind there is but one—the Christian Church of Manchuria.

Then when the church in Moukden grew large enough to need a special building, this was not erected among or even near the houses of the missionaries, but in a more central and convenient situation near the inner city gate. It was built in purely Chinese style, with a pagoda tower of which the Christians were very proud, and it could accommodate seven or eight hundred. Adjoining it were built later on first one and then a second "manse," in which live the two Chinese pastors of the congregation, so that there is no trace of foreign domination.

Another principal factor in breaking down the prejudice against Christianity and in making its teachings widely known, has been Medical Missions. This method has been largely used in Manchuria, more so than in most provinces. Moukden came first as a medical centre, and was followed at intervals of a few years by Liaoyang, Kwanchengtze, Kirin, and others, until now there are hospitals in eighteen different centres dotted over the country.

In Medical Mission work the general methods are much the same everywhere: we itinerate, we see out-patients, we open a hospital, and we teach.

1. ITINERATING is at first of very great use in a double sense: it enables the people to know us, and us to know the people. It spreads the news of the existence of a foreign doctor, medical work, and the Christian religion, and gives us the opportunity of making friends. Later on it becomes unnecessary, and is felt to be waste of time and money in comparison with hospital work. Here are some extracts from the journal of a journey made in 1886, the route being north to Tieling, south-east to Yungling, and west to Moukden, about two hundred miles in all.

"*Mon.*, Nov. 23.—Cold stormy day, snow falling heavily. Saw out-patients early, and called on two official patients. Started on journey 2.30 p.m. in a snowstorm. Am advertised to see patients on Wednesday at *Ilu*, a village 25 miles distant, and hope to meet Webster there. A courier has been sent before to intimate our coming all along the route, and bills have been posted up explaining the object of our visit. Roads hard, very rutty, progress slow. Only made 3 miles, putting up for the night at a village. Inn small, smoky, filthy.

MOUKDEN MISSION CHURCH

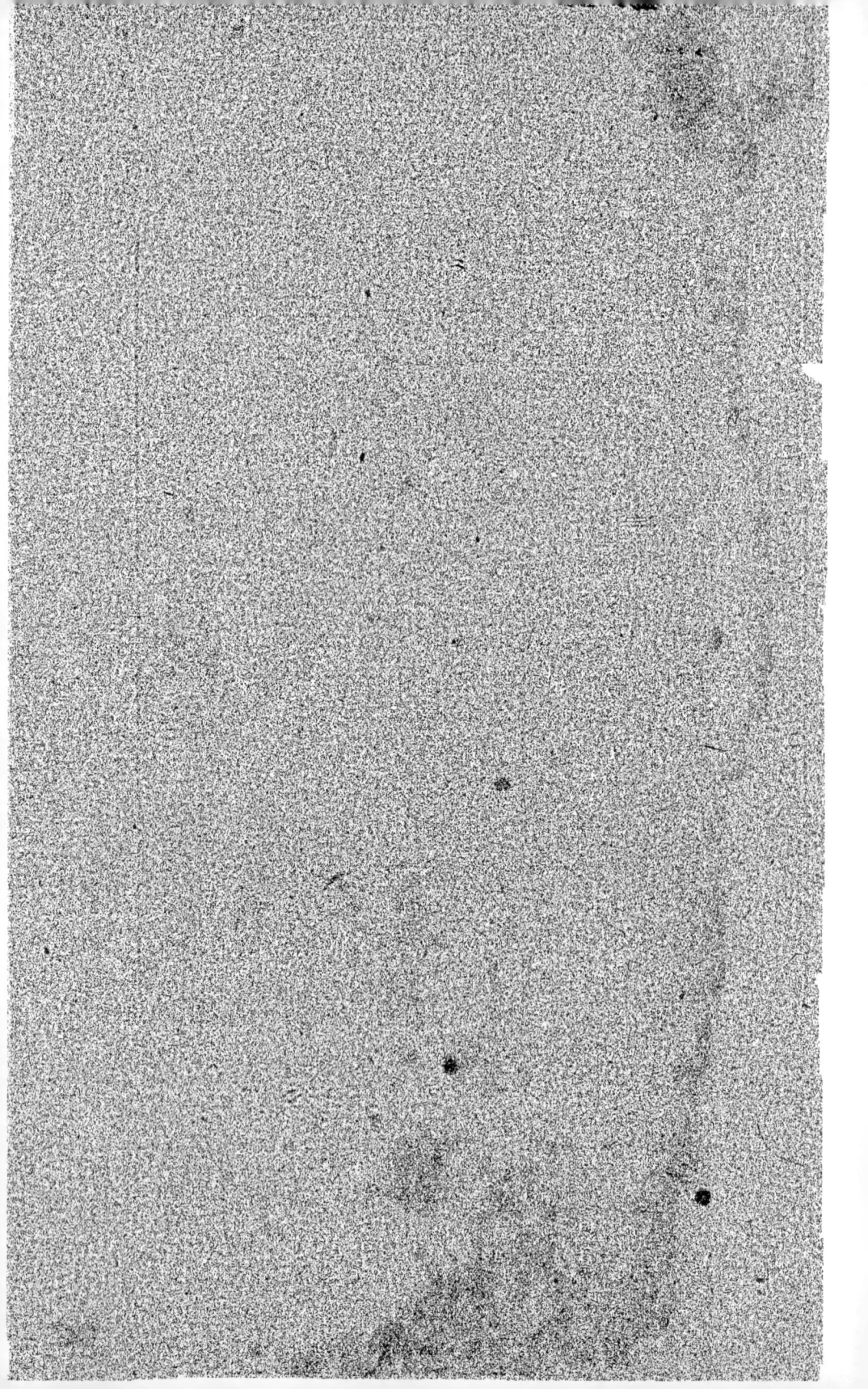

"*Tues.*, 24*th*.—On road at daybreak, keen north wind. Reached large village about 9.30 a.m. Innkeeper friendly and loud in praise of Englishmen. Professed to be anxious to understand our religion, but sincerity doubtful. I was recognized by several as the 'Moukden free-healing doctor,' and greeted heartily. 5 p.m. Got to *Ilu*, Webster awaiting me. Seems a place of some importance.

"*Wed.*, 25*th*.—After breakfast saw 34 patients, and at the same time there was preaching, and tracts were given away. In afternoon walked 20 li to next village, where we stayed the night.

"*Thurs.*, 26*th*.—Saw patients and was asked to visit several in their homes, which means a decided increase of confidence. Left at 1 p.m. and reached *Tieling* at 5. Fine city, beautifully situated. Has two distilleries and twenty pawnshops, the latter being used like banks and regarded by the Chinese as a sure mark of prosperity. Mr. Ross and Mr. Webster were stoned out of this city not long ago.

"*Frid.*, 27*th*.—Patients began to gather early, and I went on examining cases and, with Webster's help, dispensing medicines as long as daylight allowed, and for some time with the feeble glimmer of a native candle. Preaching in chapel from morn till night. Pleasing to see the good order and friendliness in the large crowd. An old patient who was cured in Moukden a year ago presented himself, and his account of his cure, which he was proud to repeat again and again, did much in inspiring confidence.

"*Sat.*, 28*th*.—Dispensed until noon—saw in all 120. Left at 1 p.m. for the south-east and entered beautiful hill scenery. Rich country, well cultivated, densely populated. Spent night at village with 400 people. Slept in small outer room whose temperature was several degrees below zero. In the evening we rolled ourselves in our fur rugs and coats on the *kang*, and began to explain our message to some who gathered to look at the foreigner. All promised to read our books. At midnight we were awakened by the loud squealing of pigs, barking of dogs, shouting and general uproar. A pack of wolves had come down from the hills, and one, finding its way into the compound, had a desperate fight with the dogs. . . .

"*Tues.*, 1*st Dec.*—At a town of 1000 inhabitants. People very hostile and suspicious. Servant was asked by several what was the secret purpose at the bottom of our visit. Feared none would trust us or our drugs. At last a young man came forward suffering from a simple abscess. An incision gave great and immediate relief, and did wonders in our favour. Saw 42 cases.

"*Wed.*, 2*nd Dec.*—Passed through fine mountainous scenery, where are tigers, etc. Yesterday two cows were devoured, and last winter a young man was carried away by a tiger from quite near a house we passed, and never heard of again.

"*Thurs.*, 3*rd Dec.*—At one village people very suspicious. The sight of my stethoscope made a man run for his life.

"*Frid.*, 4*th Dec.*—Reached Yungling, a large Manchu town. Expected opposition, but found the opposite. A mandarin who was treated in Moukden called on us and this influenced the whole town."

2. THE DISPENSARY is our widest opportunity. Here the people come in crowds. For the first twelve years we saw men twice a week and women twice, the other two days being reserved for operating. By the summer of 1894, the beginning of the Chino-Japanese war, we had sometimes two hundred patients in a forenoon. After that war there was a separate women's hospital under lady doctors, and we began to see patients four days a week. In the summer of 1913 we have had over four

hundred men in a forenoon, besides the three hundred at the women's dispensary.

These patients begin to gather at an early hour, especially in summer, and preaching goes on all morning in the waiting-room. Some who have time at their disposal remain to hear more after being examined and prescribed for. Much of what is said there is but seed by the wayside, but now and again there is a little "good ground" too. A man who has begun to listen because he had nothing better to do while waiting, may go on to inquire, because "the words are good." And on the hearts of many who go their way apparently untouched, an impression is made, so that when, perhaps years afterwards, Christianity once more comes near them, they receive it with gladness. Some buy books and tracts, and these find their way to distant homes where a missionary has never been seen.

3. Both itinerating and dispensary lead up to the HOSPITAL where our best work is done, both medically and spiritually. There we can see that our drugs are properly used, and watch their effect; we can operate, and dress the wound as often as we wish; we can find out our patient's real standpoint, talk over his difficulties, answer his objections; and, what tells perhaps more than anything else, we can show him day by day Christianity in action. Attendance at religious services is purely optional, but the majority of the patients come gladly, the hymn-singing being a great attraction. We have always employed a hospital evangelist, for some two years, to preach to the out-patients, conduct the services, instruct all who care to listen, and follow up "inquirers" who have left the hospital. But this work has never been left to the evangelists alone. Doctors, assistants, dispensers, all do their part, and many is the man to-day an intelligent member of the Christian Church, who heard of Christ first in the wards of the hospital.

The opening of the New Hospital in 1887 gave us much more scope than we previously had, and the roomy outpatient department caused our numbers rapidly to increase. In the early days patients used frequently to be baptized from the hospital, so that we could reckon in numbers the additions to the Church which were the direct fruit of our work. During four years fifty-four patients were baptized. Later on a new arrangement was made. The Church had greatly extended, persecution had in large measure died out, and it was feared that some might enter it from gratitude without realizing what was implied. So it was agreed that, unless under exceptional circumstances, no man should be baptized until after three months' probation, changed some years later to nine months. Thus our patients are not reckoned as hospital converts, but each man in his own home enters the Church like anyone else; and we can have no idea of how many are brought in through the Medical Mission. We are chary of being over-confident of any man whom time has not proved, for sometimes those of whom we are most hopeful fall back sadly. There is one instance of a whole village becoming practically Christian through the influence of an ex-patient, who himself afterwards returned to opium-smoking and other evils.

4. TRAINING ASSISTANTS.—In opening medical work, the first difficulty that arises is that no intelligent assistance can be had. The doctor sees the patient, writes the prescription, makes up the medicine, performs the operation, and does all the dressings. The beginnings of medical education in China have been therefore in scattered hospitals, where the force of necessity has compelled the practical training of men more or less suitable.

To begin with, I engaged a man called *Hung* as my Chinese teacher. He had entered the Church a few years before, but, though a good Chinese scholar, was in the utmost poverty, earning a miserable pittance by drawing pictures. After a few months I began to teach him the English, or rather the Latin, names of drugs, and how to make them up. He soon became very useful, and was afterwards head dispenser.

Wei, who became my chief assistant, was a young man of a very different stamp. His family were well-to-do farmers, he had received a good education, and had been employed for some years in a large drug shop in Moukden. From boyhood his mind had a religious bent, and at one time he wished to become a Buddhist recluse, so when Christianity was brought before him he accepted it readily. It was the custom that at certain seasons two of the shop assistants should go to the temple of the god of medicine to worship and present offerings. Shortly before our arrival in Moukden it had come to *Wei's* turn to go, and he refused, with the result that he was summarily dismissed. It was impossible for him to get a similar situation, his family were very angry and would not help him, so he was glad to accept the post of assistant, though the salary was but small. He proved a most faithful and capable helper, making it possible for me to do twice the work otherwise possible. These two men I taught together, taking them gradually through a systematic course.

It is obvious that it cannot be very satisfactory for one medical man to see out-patients, run a large hospital, superintend the evangelistic work, see patients in their homes, pay visits to officials, and at the same time give students regular tuition. This, however, is what had to be done for many years. One of the drawbacks of the system was the impossibility of binding these students to stay long enough for a satisfactory training. Again and again a man who seemed just what we wanted left us as soon as he had learned a little, and set up for himself a foreign medicine shop, professing to understand the healing art. When the new hospital was opened we took in four students. Within a year two left, and the others, after having much time and trouble expended on them, had to be dismissed later on.

Hung too failed us, after ten years' useful work. The Roman Catholic Bishop in Moukden offered him a large salary, twice what he was getting, if he would go to them and be their doctor. He need not become a Catholic, he was told, but he would have a free house among them. He went, and before long found it advisable to turn Catholic. A few years later he died of cholera. It is interesting to note that his son, who in his baby days used to visit his father in the hospital, and boast that he was going to be a doctor, is now a student in our Medical College.

At the beginning of 1892 we again made known that we would receive and train Christian young men as medical evangelists, and eight were enrolled for a five years' course of study. It was impossible to devote to their training as much time as was desirable, but they had regular lectures and clinical instruction all the year, they dispensed all the medicines, and each had charge of a ward where he did all the dressing as well as a good deal of what is done by nurses in our home hospitals. Some of these men proved the most satisfactory and useful we have had. So things stood when the Japanese war broke in upon our work.

X

SIDE-LIGHTS ON THE BEGINNINGS OF A WAR
1894

> " They now to fight are gone,
> Armour on armour shone,
> Drum now to drum did groan,
> To hear was wonder ;
> That with the cries they make
> The very earth did shake,
> Trumpet to trumpet spake,
> Thunder to thunder."
> "Agincourt"—*Michael Drayton.*

THE only foreign figure commonly seen in Moukden long ago was that of the Korean. His curious tall hat was a conspicuous object, especially when a Korean embassy passed on its way to present tribute to the Suzerain, the Emperor of China. Everyone knew and despised the Koreans, and most people in the towns had also some idea that there was another country beyond Korea called Japan, inhabited by a race of dwarfs, who, of course, must also be under the suzerainty of the " Son of Heaven." Even this inaccurate knowledge had not filtered through to the remote country districts, and in any case countries were hardly worth reckoning which were outside the " Middle Kingdom." All outside countries were supposed to be much the same, though divided up into many petty States, such as France, Great Britain, and Russia.

When therefore in 1884 there was war with France in the south, it was only known in Moukden that China was "fighting the foreigners," and for some months our position here was precarious. Similarly in 1891, the anti-foreign riots on the Yang-tze caused a wave of excitement, and placards were again put up calling for the burning of foreign property on a certain day. But the excitement fizzled out in rain, the day was wet, and not a man appeared.

Popular knowledge of public events and movements closely affecting China was scanty, vague, and inaccurate, such matters being regarded with indifference as concerning the officials only. The Korean border was not two hundred miles away from Moukden, but no one in Manchuria cared what happened there. We foreigners read in our weekly Shanghai paper of plots and risings, but few dreamed that these seemingly insignificant disputes in an insignificant country were to be the prelude to the strife of nations which was to rend Manchuria again and again.

In the early summer of 1894 a cloud no bigger than a man's hand rose on the eastern horizon, and soon the whole heavens were black. The immediate occasion of the war is of little importance. The Japanese had for years been preparing to assert themselves, and to get the upper hand in Korea. We know now that had this occasion not served, another would soon have been found.

Our first local warning of the coming trouble was near the end of July, when telegraphic orders came from Peking that our friend General Tso Pao Kuei and his entire forces were to start for Korea at once overland. His were the only real soldiers in Manchuria, well-trained, always maintained ready for action, and accustomed to fierce fighting with brigands. The first companies left within forty-eight hours, and the General himself with his staff a day later. He came first to bid me good-bye, not with a light heart. He had trained his men to the best of his knowledge and equipped them as well as he could, and they would follow him to the death; but he knew how poor was his best compared to the modern organization of the Japanese army, and he was fully aware of what was hidden from us, the lack of cohesion among the Chinese forces and Generals.

"This is different from fighting brigands," he said. "I am not likely to return." And he was right.

During the following weeks many thousand troops of a very different stamp were summoned from all parts of Manchuria, till the road from Moukden to the Yalu River was one line of straggling soldiers on the march. Many were raw recruits, straight from their farms, or sturdy beggars swept in from the streets, who halted for a week or two here to be drilled before starting for the front. In a large barracks just behind the hospital we saw company after company "licked into shape." Rifles were put into the hands of youths who had never seen a gun, and there was neither time nor teacher to instruct them. There were not nearly sufficient weapons of one make, so some companies had old rusty muzzle-loading muskets, or ancient Chinese matchlocks, or even bows and arrows, and many were armed after the ancient fashion with a short sword and a long wooden lance with a red tuft at the end. The chief thing these lancers practised was to make a simultaneous lunge forward, thrusting out their bristling lances and yelling "*Dza!*" which means *stab*. On asking why they made so much noise, we learned that it was to frighten the enemy.

It was pathetic to see these poor deluded fellows preparing to be mown down by modern fire. When their short training was over, they marched cheerfully to their doom, clad in the gay unserviceable soldiers' garb, bright red jacket with large round target on chest and back, every tenth man carrying a pole with a streaming red flag. The general view of the coming war was that the Japanese had presumed to rebel, and of course China must crush them—an easy task.

A great number of the soldiers came from the extreme

north for the first time in their lives. Many were Manchu reservists who had always drawn pay but never done work. All the Manchus, reservists or inactive regiments, were bigotedly and blindly anti-foreign, recognizing no difference between the foreigners they were to fight, against whom their passions were roused by tales true and false, and any others they might chance to encounter. They even looked on the Chinese with scorn, and regarded them as their natural prey. At first the passing of a company with their strange fire-arms or gay flags drew all the women and children out to see; for General Tso's men were allowed no looting nor licence, the shooting of a few offenders stopped that at the outset. But within a few weeks the villages on the line of march were deserted, the women and children and all animals which had not been seized having gone into hiding, and little work was being done on the fields. The large inns were forcibly kept open by the soldiers.

"They have devoured all my grain," moaned one poor innkeeper, "they have burned all my fuel, they have smashed all my dishes, they have ruined my house; and now when I show them my empty hands, and say I have nothing to give them, they beat me!"

"The Chinese soldiers are not so bad," people would say under their breath, "it is those awful Manchus!" One natural retribution quickly fell on them: before long we heard that the soldiers *en route* were suffering from lack of food.

There was one special regiment of Manchus who were turbulent and fierce beyond their fellows. On their way definitely "to kill foreigners," they were ready for anything. In Moukden some of them began to make trouble. Most of the shopkeepers shut their shops and put up their shutters, and the soldiers began to threaten the Tartar-General and his guard. It looked for a time as if there would be fighting, but their officers managed to pacify them, and to withdraw them from the city to a camp

MANCHU SOLDIERS
"With large round target on chest and back."

outside. A friendly official told me afterwards that a Manchu official of high rank had said to him at that time : " Why do we delay till we get to Korea ? Are there not some of these foreigners in this city ? Let us kill them at once."

Meantime a large company of the same regiment had reached Liaoyang, a city forty-five miles to the south. It was a hot afternoon, Friday, 10 August. Bands of these men were roaming about the streets, terrorizing the shopkeepers and helping themselves to whatever they fancied. Some of them saw a preaching-chapel, and with venomous glee they set themselves to wreck it completely, after beating those who were there. A man ran to tell the missionary in charge, Rev. James Wylie, who lived in a Chinese house not far off. Mr. Wylie at once started on foot for the yamen a little distance away, to ask the mandarin, who was very friendly, to take steps to stop the rioting. Unfortunately he encountered a band of the marauders who had just raised the cry to look for the foreigners' houses and kill them all. With a yell of bloodthirsty triumph they fell upon him, and before long he was left for dead on the street, battered and gashed with many blows and wounds.

This had, however, diverted the murderers from their purpose of finding the other foreigners. The magistrate having heard that there was a serious disturbance came out in his official chair with a guard to quell it. Caring nothing for mere Chinese authority, the soldiers turned on him, smashed his chair, beat his men, and he escaped for his life on foot in the gathering dusk. Darkness prevented further outrages ; the Manchus returned to their camp outside the city, and the gates were closed. Mr. Wylie was fearfully injured and quite unconscious. Sorrowing Chinese carried him before dark to the doctor's house on the outskirts of the city, where he lay for six days and then died.

In Moukden we heard vaguely from officials the news

of the disturbance the day after it occurred ; then letters came with details, and a mounted messenger summoned me down for consultation. It was the end of the rainy season, the roads were flooded and cart-travelling quite impossible, so that the natural course was to go on horseback. But I was suffering severely at the time from an injury to my foot, and was compelled to hire a sedan chair.

It was well that this was so, for I had to pass through the midst of the very men who had threatened the Tartar-General a few days before, and they had heard of the success of their comrades in killing a foreigner in Liaoyang. I drew the curtains of my chair completely, and they thought it was occupied by a high official. The chair-bearers, in mortal terror, were only too glad to encourage this idea, and so we passed them. But immediately afterwards we came to a river which must be crossed by ferry, and I had to leave the chair. The boat had just pushed off from the bank when a soldier caught sight of me and raised the cry: "A foreigner! Kill! Kill!" The boatmen, greatly alarmed, poled with all their might. Several guns were raised to shoot, but an officer evidently remonstrated. This gave us time to reach the other side, where we were quickly out of sight behind the banks. Unfortunately I arrived too late to see Mr. Wylie alive.

During the following weeks foreigners all over the province kept as quiet and unconspicuous as possible. No one attempted to go a journey, and in Moukden we confined ourselves to the district round our houses where we were well known. A few days after Mr. Wylie's death an Imperial Proclamation for the protection of foreigners was posted on all the city gates and scattered throughout the country.

About the same time a prominent Manchu official of the Imperial Clan, who had been cured of a dangerous disease a few months before, presented to the hospital a "tablet" as an expression of his gratitude. It came at a most opportune time. The large black board, with its glittering gold characters proclaiming the wonderful powers of the Healing Hand, was placed on a draped and gorgeously decorated platform with a brilliant yellow canopy, and promenaded through the streets for a whole forenoon, preceded by what stood for a band, discoursing discordant music; so that it was known through the length and breadth of the city. In general we did not encourage this form of gratitude, nor relish the necessity for giving a substantial gratuity to the musicians, but on this occasion we welcomed it, and felt the money well spent. The same afternoon the official, as well as his wife and a large number of friends and attendants, called, a company of mounted soldiers escorting them. The lady suggested that I might act as mediator between Japan and China!

Next day Lady Tso, the wife of the General, called with their five children. She had heard that we were leaving Moukden and came to say good-bye. She was in very good spirits, having that morning received a telegram that her husband was quite safe. The publicity of these marks of official friendliness was of great value to us, especially in the eyes of the army.

The common people were now quite friendly, as there was hardly a lane in Moukden without an old patient. The medical work went on as usual, though country people were few in number. In their stead we had soldiers by the dozen. Those in camp behind us were our very good friends, and sometimes twenty at a time would come for treatment. It was arranged that all soldiers should be seen at once when they came, without awaiting their turn, and this pleased them greatly. The people were looking forward to the winter with much apprehension, because of the many soldiers on the march in some districts, and the great increase of brigands in others owing to the withdrawal of General Tso's troops. Everyone assumed as a matter of course that the Chinese would be victorious, but General Tso had sent for his men's winter clothing, and that meant delay. Defeat was unthinkable at the hands of an insignificant people like Japan.

XI

GRIM REALITY : THE CHINO-JAPANESE WAR

"The giant shades of fate, silently flitting,
Pile the dim outline of the coming doom."
"Pauline"—*Robert Browning.*

INTO the midst of the bright harvest weather of September came a whisper of a crushing Chinese defeat in North Korea, where General Tso had gone. At first no one cared to believe it, but soon it took definite and even exaggerated shape. The Chinese army was defeated and scattered, perhaps annihilated, General Tso was killed, the Japanese were advancing on Manchuria. The consternation of the Moukden officials was complete, for the impossible had happened, and what would come next ?

And yet it was easily explained. The Commander-in-Chief of the Chinese forces at the front had for weeks been sending false news to Peking of victories over the Japanese, and had received rewards and honours, while in reality he was neither fighting nor making any preparations for the inevitable battle. Many of the Chinese officers were lingering on the Manchurian side of the Yalu, while part of their regiments went to the front. Most of the Generals hated and mistrusted the Commander and each other; those from the metropolitan province looked down on those from Manchuria ; Manchus would have no dealings with Chinese; everyone seemed fighting for his own hand.

General Tso drew out a plan of campaign specially for

the defence of Ping-yang, a city which was considered the key to the situation. In spite of jealousies the plan was agreed to, but at the critical moment the Commander-in-Chief and other Generals withdrew their men from Ping-yang. Part of the army engaged the Japanese outside the city, but without any co-operation with General Tso, who was left to defend the citadel alone, with inadequate forces. During the battle thousands of Chinese and Manchu soldiers were within reach, but were restrained from striking a blow. When it was evident that a Japanese victory was likely, all these Generals and their men retired as speedily as possible, some to a town on the Korean bank of the Yalu, others across the river into Manchuria, where they seemed to think no Japanese could follow.

In Ping-yang General Tso made a spirited defence, though outnumbered many times, and his men were confident that if he had lived they would have held the city. The battle lasted the most part of three days, the Japanese occupying the surrounding hills and woods, and bombarding the fortifications. In the afternoon of the 15th, General Tso was directing the fire of one of his heaviest guns when the gunner was killed at his side. The General, who had already received several wounds, stepped forward and fired the charge himself, but at the same moment fell shot in the leg. Binding the wound hastily with a piece of cloth, he got up and urged his men to greater efforts, but as he was shouting to them another bullet struck him, and he fell mortally wounded. Some of his men were placing him on horseback to attempt to escape, when a shell fell among them, killing all except one, a cavalry captain, who told me the story. He was stunned, and when he came to himself the day was lost, the Japanese were in the city. One more effort was made to carry away the dead General's body, but a party of the enemy advanced, and the men had to abandon it and flee. The Japanese recognized in General Tso a foeman worthy of their steel, buried him with military honours, and erected a monument over his grave.

On the death of their General the Chinese resistance ceased. Under heavy fire, the cavalry escaped as best they could through the Japanese infantry lines, cowering down on their horses and galloping full speed. The captain who had been with the General at the last took part in this wild charge. A bullet passed through his right knee and killed his horse, but after lying still for a little he succeeded in mounting a riderless steed and escaped. Another young fellow, aide-de-camp to the General, told me that the bullet which passed through his lung entered the head of a companion in front, killing him on the spot. The wounded man galloped on till his horse was shot under him. Then he just managed to crawl in among some long grass, when he lost consciousness. When he awoke it was dark, and he pressed on until early in the morning he reached a Chinese camp on the retreat. About a fortnight later he came to the Moukden hospital, where he made a rapid recovery. He and other Chinese soldiers frequently spoke of the silence of the Japanese army in battle, contrasted with their own men, who all shouted at once.

"They fight as if they were at drill," said one.

There was great mourning and fear in Moukden when it was known that our good General was dead, the one man who could protect Manchuria. High and low united in respect and love for him, and for us it was the loss of a personal friend. His memory is still cherished affectionately, and no other General has ever arisen to fill his place in the popular mind.

A good many men wounded in Ping-yang were received into our hospital, the Governor-General having repeated the orders of General Tso that all wounded were to be brought straight to us. The great majority of the injured, however, lay helpless in the Chinese frontier towns, where nothing could be done for their relief.

Just about this time an unfortunate episode caused us much anxiety. During the summer the agent of a German firm had been in Manchuria selling guns to the Governors of the Three Provinces. He returned to Moukden from the north just when the news of the General's death and the great defeat was causing much excitement. This, the violent death of Mr. Wylie a few weeks before, and probably also business worries, seem to have preyed upon his mind and upset his reason. I was called out of the Chinese church one Sunday to go to him in an inn, where he had tried to commit suicide by cutting his arm with a razor. His Chinese servant had bound it up and sent for me, and was watching over him. He had not slept for four or five nights and was in terrible excitement and fear, suffering from delusional insanity. I at once brought him over to our house, and we arranged a room for him in the hospital.

Under sedatives his excitement gradually passed away, but the delusions continued and he was very difficult to manage. He believed that he was a spy, who had in some way done great harm to the Chinese, and that very soon he was to be taken to the execution ground and killed, and with him all who helped him. The slightest noise of footsteps made him tremble. "They have come to take me!" he would say. There was imminent risk that he might attack someone or kill himself, and in the excited condition of the public mind, this was a general even more than a personal danger. For some days he had to be watched constantly, the various members of our little missionary circle taking it in turn to try to converse with him, take him short walks, and divert his mind. To our great relief he gradually calmed down sufficiently to be sent off by boat to Newchwang, and afterwards he returned to Germany.

As days passed by and no reliable news of a Chinese victory came to reassure the public mind, the excitement and fear in Moukden were great. In vain were false reports of victory circulated to allay the alarm. The trouble grew and stirred, and the wildest rumours were circulated. It was said that two hundred British soldiers were concealed in our hospital compound, or, according to some, in the tower of the church. Some officers called on my assistant to find out if this was true, and he showed them all over the premises to see for themselves. The better-class inhabitants began to leave in large numbers, some by the long overland route through the Great Wall into China proper, others by boat to Newchwang, there to find steamers or junks.

The question was now raised whether it was wise for foreigners to remain in Moukden. We were most unwilling to leave unless it should be absolutely necessary, and were we all to go at once it would likely cause a panic, for the people watched us closely, knowing that we had more reliable news than they. On the other hand, travelling by road to Newchwang was impossible, boats are docked for the winter early in November, and after that retreat would be cut off. Finally it was decided that ladies, children, and most of the men should at once begin to leave in detachments, taking with them valuables and necessaries for the winter. All Moukden was preparing to take refuge in the northern and eastern hills, and if once the exodus began, carts to the river would be unobtainable. Our colleagues in Liaoyang had already left, that city continuing in a very disturbed condition, and missionaries from the north also were all on their way down.

Our medical work now diminished rapidly; the women's hospital was empty, the men's not half full. The Governor-General again issued a proclamation commending us, and the rumours died down for a time, but it was only the lull before the storm. On the evening of 25 October I called on an official friend named Gao, the son of my old friend the Tao-tai, already mentioned. From him I heard privately that a telegram had just arrived, that the Japanese had crossed the Yalu by night, that the Chinese had been defeated in a battle on Manchurian soil, and were driven from the chief fortified city of that region, and that the Japanese were marching on *Feng-huang-cheng*, the ancient Phœnix city. He advised strongly that the two of us who still remained should go to Newchwang without delay, as the Chinese army was quite unable to stay the advance of the Japanese, and there would soon be in Moukden a rabble of retreating soldiers whom no one could control.

On the morning of the 28th the news of defeat became known, and the city was in excitement bordering on panic, so we delayed no longer. Reliable men were left in charge both in the church and in the hospital, and our assistants felt safer without our presence. There was also a watchman for each house, but we felt it likely that they would be looted if not burned before we could return. With some difficulty we got carts to take us to the river, where few boats were now to be seen. Had we waited much longer we should have been shut in for the winter.

It was not only in Moukden that people were fleeing in hundreds from the impending trouble. When we reached Newchwang we found that junks and steamers were all crowded with refugees. Soon the junks ceased, and steamers became few. One day the last steamer on the river, when about to leave, was besieged by a struggling crowd of native boats. The passenger accommodation was already full, but the determined travellers swarmed up ropes and boathooks and crowded the decks, the roofs of the deckhouses, even the masts and rigging, to the number of about three thousand, until bluejackets from the foreign gunboats forced them back to their boats.

The Japanese were steadily advancing and occupying one town after another—Port Arthur, Kaichow, Haicheng. Some towns and villages were destroyed, scores of innocent people being killed, and hundreds left homeless at

GRIM REALITY: CHINO-JAPANESE WAR

the beginning of the rigorous winter. In other cases, Haicheng for instance, the battle was fought at some distance, and the Chinese army fled to re-form again to the north or west, leaving the city unprotected. The civil magistrate of Haicheng quietly withdrew next day after opening the two city gates on the Japanese side, and they entered without firing a shot. But this official was, according to law, degraded for not preventing the Japanese entrance. My friend Gao, who had warned us to leave Moukden, was appointed magistrate of Kaichow. He knew the Japanese would take the city and that he would have no soldiers to defend it, so he feigned illness, and asked for two months' leave of absence before taking up his appointment. He too was afterwards degraded, as if he had deliberately given up his city to the enemy, and he never received another appointment.

All through the war couriers continued to make their way between the principal cities, so that we kept in touch with Moukden. Each fresh tidings of defeat caused panic there. Half the population fled, household property was sold for a song, the military were occupying the city in thousands, and large stretches of country were overrun with marauding soldiers. Rewards were offered for the capture of any who helped the enemy, and innocent men were constantly seized and executed. Villages were deserted, those who could not flee north digging pits in the hillsides, where were concealed the women and children and all movable property. Many who tried to flee were waylaid by robbers, deserters from the army, their carts seized, the men killed, the women and children carried off. The dumb suffering of the country people as that winter dragged on will never be known.

To us in Newchwang the fighting drew ever nearer, until one beautiful peaceful winter Sunday a new sound came into our ears, never again to be forgotten. The sky was intense blue, the sunshine radiant, mere living seemed good and evil non-existent, when from the unseen distance across the plain there came, low but distinct, a dull insistent booming, the sound of cannon fired to kill. It seemed as if clouds ought to veil the sun, the blue should change to grey, but all day it continued—the pitiless blue, the mocking sunshine, the relentless hollow roar which announced that moment by moment our fellow-men were being mangled and torn. Since then we have become accustomed to it. There were other battles much nearer to Newchwang, we were wakened before dawn by cannon roar, our windows shook as the shells screamed over our heads, and in the war ten years later we lived in Moukden for months with that sound in our ears. But nothing ever brought that sense of awe, that vivid realization of the incongruity, the unhumanness of war, as did that dull distant booming which broke upon the Sabbath calm.

XII

AMONG THE WOUNDED

" When the days were torment, and the nights were clouded terror,
   When the Powers of Darkness had dominion on our soul,
When we fled consuming through the Seven Hells of fever,
   These put out their hands to us, and healed and made us whole."
                                            Rudyard Kipling.

IN the Chinese army of 1894–5 no provision was made for the wounded. Where a man fell, there he lay, to die of slow starvation or the more merciful cold. With a temperature many degrees below zero, one night was enough. If the wounded man was fortunate enough to find some place of refuge, or if his comrades carried him under shelter, it was often only a more lingering death, for no one could treat his wounds.

As the scene of war drew nearer to Newchwang, efforts were made to establish a Red Cross hospital there. Ambulance work was impossible, but with the approval of the Chinese magistrate an inn was rented, put in order, and opened on 3 December. At first the wounded came by twos and threes, but the news spread rapidly through the army, the early cases cured did much to establish confidence, and the proportion of wounded who came under our care increased with each fight, so that a second inn had to be rented. When a battle was fought in January at *Kaichow*, twenty-five miles away, the wounded continued to arrive for three days, 169 being admitted.

There were fortunately eight medical men in Newchwang at this time. Dr. Daly, the medical officer of the port, took general charge of the Red Cross work, and its success was largely due to his able and energetic administration. He was assisted by the doctors of the two gunboats, American and British, and five medical missionaries, and non-medical help was also freely given. One of my medical students had come down in November, another got through the lines later, and they were invaluable all through. A Red Cross Society had been formed in Shangai, which liberally met all expenses.

Our "hospitals" were far from satisfactory, being dark and dilapidated, with low roofs, and crevices in their mud walls through which wind and snow found a ready entrance. Their sanitary condition could not have been worse, and operations were performed in small dark rooms which no amount of cleaning could make clean. Our medical supplies ran very low, communication with the outer world being practically cut off. We had to use native cotton-wool, and the ladies helped by making bandages and surgical dressings.

On 24 February a battle was known to be going on ten or twelve miles to the east. Our hospitals were full from previous fighting, but we emptied them of all convalescents in preparation for new arrivals. This time the Chinese General sent the wounded direct to us, so that the rush was far beyond our anticipation. It would have been still greater, but that the temperature that night was 10° Fahr. below zero, and many died of cold. The scene in the hospitals next day was beyond description. The compounds were crowded with farmers' carts and animals hired by the officers, while many serious cases arrived in improvised litters, baskets, and chairs. Some were already beyond our aid. Dead were lifted from the carts as well as living. One man died at the door, others within an hour of admission. By evening our two hospitals, and even every outhouse, were crowded out. Early next morning a third inn was rented, then a fourth, but while these were being put in order the overcrowding was terrible. The *kangs* were packed with double rows of wounded, as close as they could lie, and we had to pick our way along the mud floors, stepping over the poor fellows lying on heaps of straw.

Every available foreigner was pressed into the service, valuable assistance being rendered by the officers and men of the British gunboat "Firebrand." Our operating-rooms were busy from morning to night, and in the wards the work of dressing was carried on by Customs officials, pilots, business men, seamen, and missionaries.

While to us the hospitals seemed miserable dens, to the men themselves they were havens of rest. They had seen comrade after comrade die on the frozen ground, or lie groaning in some wretched hovel without medicine, comforts, help, or even sufficient food. Here they had a warm *kang*, kind attention, soothing medicine, good food if they could eat it, and surgical aid. It did not matter how crowded the room was, nor how foul the smells, nor how unskilled the nurses, to them the Red Cross hospital was heaven.

Things were gradually getting into order in our inn-hospitals, and the patients being made more comfortable day by day, when on 5 March the news spread that the Japanese were coming. Old Newchwang, thirty miles to the north, had fallen the day before, after an exceptionally fierce and bloody fight, and it seemed as if the Port of Newchwang would be surrounded, so the Chinese army was being withdrawn and concentrated at *Tienchuang-tai*, ten miles away to our north-west.

The people, in great fear and excitement, made what little preparations they fancied might serve to conciliate the Japanese. Here was a rough signboard with "enG-LisH HOusE" printed on it, there in large Chinese characters the words "foreign religion," and many a red cross was painted on boards or sewn on flags. In the main street we noticed a very conspicuous Red Cross flag over what was manifestly an opium-den. The owner emphatically protested his right to fly it, as he had been in the service of a foreign doctor years before. It was pathetic to see a little mud hut with poor tattered paper windows, and some half-naked children huddling at the door, to watch their father put up a stick with a bit of dirty cotton at the end, on which were sewn some scraps of red in the rough form of a cross.

" What is it for ? " we ask him.

" To protect us when the foreigners come."

" But what does it mean ? What is the red cross for ? "

" Who knows ? They say foreigners won't touch you if you have that."

In the Red Cross hospital itself there was little confidence in the protection of the flag. Panic seized our patients. They were convinced that the Japanese would kill them all. In spite of our assurances and entreaties, very many fled during the night of the 5th and the following morning. Fortunately the majority of these had only slight wounds, or were convalescent, but a few serious cases hired bearers to carry them on stretchers. Some of them must have died by the way. One man was taken nearly ten miles, but hearing that the Japanese were quite near, the bearers fled, leaving him helpless by the roadside. After six days of agony and privation he succeeded in getting back to us.

Early in the morning of the 6th I went to our hospitals, now half empty, to help to pacify the terrified patients who remained, and prevent more from going. We vacated the two more recently occupied inns, concentrating in the original two, and put up very large and conspicuous Red Cross flags. Newchwang was by this time almost clear of soldiers, the magistrate and his guard having fled in the night across the river on the breaking ice. No resistance was to be offered to the entrance of the Japanese, who could now from the housetops be seen approaching the open unguarded gates.

Leaving the hospital during the forenoon, I made for

my own home on the outskirts of the town. While crossing a piece of open ground, I suddenly heard the sharp report of rifle-fire quite near, and three Japanese scouts came quickly round the corner of a house. Instantly they levelled their guns at me. I stood still and shouted to them, holding up my hands to show I was unarmed. Slowly they lowered their rifles, then nodded and laughed and ran on, firing down a street at a few Chinese soldiers who had been tardy in making their escape. As they ran they looked all round apprehensively, till they disappeared in the direction of the gate outside which we had seen the approaching army.

An hour later the Japanese quietly occupied Newchwang. It was the first thaw of spring. Until a few days before it had been bitterly cold, but now in warm sunshine we watched the men struggling through deep slush, with their heavy winter overcoats thrown open. From every house curious eyes were peering, and before long some, bolder than their fellows, offered the conquerors drinks of hot water or tea, according to the degree of their poverty. Newchwang breathed a sigh of relief : all was over, the town was taken, and nothing dreadful had happened.

On the afternoon of the same day there was a sudden crash of cannon very near us, the scream of shells over our heads, the bursting of shrapnel in the air. A Chinese fort a couple of miles off had opened fire on the Japanese on the plain. Their aim was most uncertain; indeed they were almost as likely to strike the town itself as the enemy, and for a few hours while the artillery duel lasted there was much anxiety. But night fell, and after spiking their guns the plucky little garrison withdrew.

The Chinese headquarters were now at *Tienchuang-tai*, ten miles off, on the other side of the River Liao. Here were gathered the broken remnants of the army, guarding a large store of munitions of war. We were awakened at dawn two days later by heavy cannonading, the Japanese attack on this position. Severe fighting continued all that day and part of the next, and then the Chinese fled. The Japanese fired the town, as it did not suit them to hold it, and all evening and for days afterwards the sky was black with the smoke of the burning.

A few days later some of us visited the place. It had been a flourishing town with ten thousand inhabitants; now there were but desolate ruins. Some houses were still smouldering, and the large fleet of hundreds of boats docked for the winter had shared in the conflagration. The streets were strewn with the slain, and fierce skeletons of dogs were prowling about and devouring the bodies. We found a few, very few, wounded hiding among the ruins. When the starving wretches saw that we were not Japanese, they crawled out from their holes, or hailed us, and we made arrangements for their conveyance to the Red Cross hospital. This was the last battle of the war.

The Chino-Japanese war was one of the first where comparisons could be drawn between the wounds caused respectively by the old heavy leaden bullet and by the newer hard-jacketed bullet of small calibre and high velocity. The new type of rifle had recently been introduced into the Japanese army and was used at Ping-yang, but a good many regiments were still armed with the older weapon, which was responsible for most of the cases treated in Newchwang. I had therefore an opportunity of comparing the two, and published the results of my observations at the time in the medical journals.

During the few months of the existence of this Red Cross hospital over a thousand wounded were admitted. In spite of the unfavourable conditions, the mortality was remarkably low. Most of the deaths were cases where pieces of dirty wadded clothing had been carried into the wounds. In many of these, life might have been saved by prompt amputation; but few were willing to submit until symptoms of septic absorption developed, when it was frequently too late. Not a few, when the alternative was laid before them, calmly but firmly decided to die. Many of the wounded were also severely frost-bitten. One had a bullet wound which healed quickly, but he lost both feet, as they were frozen before he was found lying unconscious.

The good results of the Red Cross work were not confined to the healing of wounds and saving of lives. A lasting impression was made on the minds of all who came in touch with it. Of direct Christian teaching there was necessarily little, but it was remarkable to see the number of convalescent patients who voluntarily attended the Sunday services in the Chinese church. Some months later several of these men were baptized, and one we still know as a prominent Christian in a church in a neighbouring province. Hundreds took away at least some knowledge of the religion of Christ, hundreds more a friendly and grateful respect for the foreigner whom they formerly hated and despised.

The Chinese officials publicly recognized the Red Cross, and showed readiness to help. In February the chief magistrate of Newchwang telegraphed at my request to the Governor-General in Moukden and to my assistant, Mr. Wei, as I wished more of my students to come, and this was impossible without protection. Carts, money for the journey, and a military escort were provided by the Governor-General. Unfortunately, when half-way, the fall of Newchwang compelled the party to return.

In the early months of the war the coming of the Japanese was universally regarded with terror. Many hundreds faced the known dangers of flight rather than the unknown horrors of falling into the hands of the enemy. In spring their successful conquest of many miles of populous country was accepted by these same people with equanimity. This change of attitude was the result of the unexpected mercifulness and equity of the Japanese rule. At first there were many excesses; people were summarily turned out of their homes, property was seized without payment, furniture was used for fuel, and for women it was never safe. But as time went on the soldiers were kept more strictly in hand, and when civil governors were appointed over towns, people found themselves under a just and orderly government.

Newchwang was specially fortunate in its administrator. Complaints were promptly attended to, justice impartially administered. A few cases where Japanese were punished for oppressing Chinese made a great impression. Sanitary conditions were improved, road-making vigorously carried on, lamps erected on the main streets. In several other large towns the administration was of the same benevolent, just, and enlightened nature.

The acquiescence of the people was helped by their bitter resentment against their own Government, especially *Li Hung Chang*, who was universally believed to have " sold the country." Stories were common, with what foundation it is impossible to say, of shells filled with sand instead of explosives, of hundreds of boxes full of cartridges which were practically blank, and of guns which would not fire. Certain it is that there were stores of cartridges which did not fit the rifles, and loads of rifles with no ammunition.

Had all the Japanese been like the civil administrators the people might have been sorry to see them go. But there were others. Following the army as coolies, baggage carriers, etc., were a miscellaneous crowd of the very lowest class, who were regarded by the Chinese with contempt mingled with fear. Their uncouth garments and naked limbs called forth constant expressions of disgust. Drunkenness and other vices were common among them, and they were not under strict discipline like the soldiers.

While the towns were well governed, the rural districts were practically without law. Robbers overran the country, many armed with magazine rifles. During the

AMONG THE WOUNDED

spring and summer months the River Liao swarmed with pirates, and travelling by road or river was most dangerous. The whole land groaned for a settled government. Greatly exaggerated reports, however, were taken to Tientsin by the retreating soldiers. Newchwang was said to be burned, the country laid waste, the inhabitants massacred. The telegraph wires were cut, no mails had got through for weeks, there was no communication by sea as cold weather returned and the river remained frozen, so the truth could not be ascertained.

Towards the end of March a British cruiser was sent as near to Newchwang as possible, to find out the fate of the foreigners. A steam-launch came as far up the river as the ice would allow, and landed a small party who walked six miles to the town carrying heavy bags of mails, our first news from the outer world for over a month. This welcome relief party was fêted joyfully, and escorted to their launch with as heavy mail-bags as they brought.

Peace was signed on 8 May. Manchuria was to be rent asunder, and the southern part to belong to Japan. Immediately thereafter came startling news : certain European Powers had interfered, Japan was to give up the conquered territory, receiving Formosa instead, South Manchuria was still to be Chinese, and Korea independent.

It was some time before the country was sufficiently settled for anyone to return to the interior. Not until the end of July did we receive our passports, board our boats, disregarding pirates, and gladly sail away up the river. We had been prepared to have our houses looted, but when we entered them after nine months' absence they were absolutely untouched, even to a pair of scissors left carelessly on a mantelpiece. It was good to be back, with peace reigning once more.

We found that our Red Cross work was well known to the Government. Mr. Wei was presented with a button of the fifth rank in return for his services to the wounded, and in recognition of all our hospital had done. Some time later the doctors who had taken a leading part in the Red Cross work received from the Emperor the decoration of the third grade of the Order of the Double Dragon.

The Red Cross Society in Shanghai found itself now at the close of the war with a balance, out of which they made grants in aid to hospitals which had done Red Cross work. Fifteen hundred taels (about £240) was given to the Moukden hospital, with which an adjoining compound was purchased, a most necessary addition.

XIII

A STRANGE AFTERMATH OF WAR

"Let us admit it fairly, as a business people should,
We have had no end of a lesson; it will do us no end of good."
Rudyard Kipling.

"For mankind springs salvation by each hindrance interposed."
Sordello.

IN many parts of China the war awakened no interest, and the great bulk of the people did not even know that China had been defeated. In Manchuria, and to a lesser degree in all North China, it was naturally far otherwise. Out of their contemptuous and deluded calm the people had been rudely shaken. Now, after months of mental earthquake, blind suffering, and terror, they were able to look about them again, to take stock of what had happened, to think of what it all meant.

The foreigner had conquered them! And it was not even the Western foreigner, who with all his barbarian ways had wonderful skill in mechanics, guns, surgery, and such-like; but it was this neighbouring people who had always been their inferiors. Who were these Japs? Mere savages, who had borrowed Chinese civilization, the Chinese written character, Chinese literature. And yet they had conquered China. What was the explanation? It was because *they had learned Western methods.* Their soldiers were dressed in Western clothes, drilled Western drill, understood Western guns, followed Western ways. Of course, Chinese ways were really the best, but evidently, if one wanted to get on nowadays, these new ways must be learned.

Such questions were asked and such answers given in every village and hamlet the length and breadth of Manchuria. The country was shaken to its foundations. Never again could it sleep the sleep of the centuries. The people began to grope after light, but there was no one to lead them. Their nominal leaders, the officials, were unchanged, here and there a man whose eyes were open and who saw, but for the most part poorly informed conservative gentlemen, going on in the old ruts, averse to any novelty. The new Governor-General was an illiterate old Manchu soldier, who had commanded the forces guarding the mountains south and east of Liaoyang. The Japanese had not driven him back, and he believed that his prowess had served the country. For three years he remained in office, just at the time when the awakening aspirations of the best among the people would have welcomed an enlightened and progressive ruler. No improvement of any kind was made, in education or in any other direction.

Left to themselves, most of the people were powerless to advance; they talked, grumbled, and did nothing. Some joined secret anti-dynastic societies and discussed in private the woes of their country and the iniquities of officialdom. A Buddhist sect, the *Tsai-li-ti*, which was strictly vegetarian and bigotedly anti-foreign, also became popular. On the other hand, many read any modern or foreign translated books they could lay their hands on; and wherever there was a Christian Church school, preaching-hall, or little gathering, numbers came to learn what " the foreign religion " was like, for they connected in some hazy way the foreign religion with the foreign victory.

During the four years from 1896 to the spring of 1900, it was flood-tide for the Christian Church in Manchuria, a tide which gained strength year by year. The Church

A STRANGE AFTERMATH OF WAR 111

and the missionaries were embarrassed by the crowds seeking instruction. Village after village sent requests for evangelists and teachers: here were a hundred inquirers, there two hundred. During 1896 over a hundred patients in our hospital gave in their names as desirous of entering the Church, and one after another returned to say that he had gathered a score of inquirers who were awaiting instruction. Books were sold by the thousand. In 1897 £200 worth of Scriptures and single books of the Bible were sold in Manchuria, and £300 worth of other Christian literature, in spite of the general illiteracy and poverty of a large proportion of the population. This means much more than the same sum in England, as an ordinary man's wage was 3s. or 3s. 6d. a week.

Among the younger and more progressive officials Christian books were commonly read, and the general standpoint of the Christian Church began to be dimly understood. One day, when a case was being tried in Moukden, it came out that the man had been a Christian, but was so no longer. He evidently thought that having given up the foreign religion would be a point in his favour. Further evidence showed that he had been excommunicated from the Church.

"Ah!" said the magistrate, "if you had been a good man you would not have been put out of the Church! Set that down against him."

The thousands who wished to enter their names as "inquirers" on the Church lists may be divided broadly into four classes. There were many absolutely ignorant, with no idea of what Christianity really was.

"Why do you want to enter the Church?" they were asked.

"They say it is a good thing," was a common answer, often representing the man's entire knowledge. Many such grew quickly tired of the instruction, and dropped off from sheer indolence of mind, saying that they "did not understand." But a good many others developed a genuine interest, became first candidates for baptism, and then members of the Church.

Then there were those who knew a little about the Church, and regarded it as something like a Friendly Society. The members gathered to listen to good words on Sunday, and were bound to be kind to each other. They helped the poor and aged, and stood by each other in trouble, so that altogether it was a good society to belong to, seeing trouble comes so often. Many of these too learned the deeper meaning of things and ultimately entered the Church.

There were also a large number of men who put down their names from more or less unworthy motives. Lawsuits were usually decided largely according to the influence or money of the litigants. Now that the Church was strong and of good repute it had much influence, and could if it wished bring pressure to bear in settling disputes, either privately or in the courts. Specially would this be so if a foreigner could be persuaded to take up the matter and send his card to the official. The Roman Catholic Bishop and priests claimed the right to take part in any trial where one of their converts was concerned, and many of our people failed to understand why Protestants should not have equal privileges. The Buddhist sects too were always ready to help their members. There were many instances of men leaving in disgust after a few months' instruction, being finally convinced that, in spite of their conformance to the troublesome rules about attending services and renouncing gambling and opium, the foreigner did not mean to help them in their affairs. Some of the Christian elders did not at first agree with this policy of inaction.

"If our brethren are in trouble, defrauded or accused wrongfully," they would argue, "and if we have the power to help them, should we not do it?" And they very often did.

Gradually, however, it became more and more evident

to the Chinese as well as to ourselves, that the only way to keep the Church pure was to refuse to meddle in any way in such matters, whether right or wrong. The Presbyterial gatherings of the elders of the churches in Manchuria discussed these subjects, and finally the use of the name of the Church in litigation was unanimously condemned by them. There are throughout Manchuria to-day not a few zealous Christians who were first attracted to Christianity because of its supposed advantage in their worldly affairs. They came seeking a stone, and they found the Bread of Life.

Besides those who came in ignorance or by mistake, there were a goodly number who had read Christian books, or talked with Christian friends, or watched the daily life of Christian neighbours, or spent some time in a hospital, and who had deliberately made up their minds that they would learn more of this Way, and walk in it.

As the numbers increased of those seeking to join the Church, it became necessary to make the rules of entrance more stringent. No inquirer was enrolled as a catechumen or applicant for baptism until the evangelist in charge, or the " session " of the congregation, was satisfied that he was of good moral character, neither opium-smoker, gambler, nor in any way bringing shame on his profession ; that he understood what he was doing ; and that he had no worldly motive in becoming a Christian. After being accepted as a candidate, a man must attend services and classes, and continue to prove himself sincere and consistent for nine months, then he might be baptized. In spite of all precautions, a good many were admitted who were a source of weakness to the Church. The rapid increase in numbers was not an unmixed good.

With this urgent demand everywhere for instruction, the insufficiency of trained Chinese workers became lamentably evident. Could their number at that time have been trebled, there would still have been more than enough for all to do. In looking back on those years we cannot but feel how very inadequately the great opportunity was met. Many must have lost interest or dropped away because of the incapacity of the local Christians and evangelists to meet their needs.

In spite of all drawbacks, the mixed motives of inquirers, the difficulty of detecting insincerity, the insufficiency of evangelists both in number and in education—the advance of the Christian Church in every way was by leaps and bounds. In 1896 the membership was 5788, with 6300 on the lists of applicants, not including the many "inquirers" whose names had not yet been accepted. A year later there were 10,255 members and 9442 candidates. At the end of 1899 the numbers were 19,646, and over 7000. The growth in independence, self-support, and management of Church matters by the Chinese themselves was equally rapid. Chapels were built without foreign help, preachers were supported by their people, Christian schools were started and financed. The amount contributed by the Christians for such objects in 1896 was £261; in 1899 it was £2000. One congregation after another was formed, and elected elders who attended the meetings of Presbytery, where rules for Church government were decided, and the business of the Church transacted.

At the same time there was a new development of the sense of personal individual responsibility for influencing others, and a marked increase in the number and intelligence of women members. It had never been directly through foreign missionaries that any large number of Chinese in Manchuria became Christians, nor even principally through the preaching of outstanding Chinese leaders. The chief factor in attracting men was and is the quiet personal influence of humble unlettered folk, and the patient line upon line instruction given by obscure evangelists.

It was obvious that the most urgent needs of the time were a well-trained Christian pastorate and a supply of capable evangelists. Missionaries did not take up the position of pastors of congregations. They considered it the right of the Church to have men of their own race as pastors and spiritual leaders, the foreigner keeping himself in the background as adviser and friend. Up till now there was but one native pastor in Manchuria, supported by and ministering to the Moukden congregation. Comparatively few Christians were of the cultured class, so that preachers of real education were uncommon; some who came to be trained could not write, and some were even poor readers. There had been for long a regular system of training for these men, courses of lectures, books prescribed for study, annual examinations. Most of them were genuinely in earnest in their work, and it was sometimes found that the least cultured were the most successful in winning and guiding men. Something more, however, was needed for the Pastorate. Systematic Theological Training was now arranged by the two missions, Scottish and Irish unitedly, a number of the best evangelists forming the first class. At the same time there was increased provision for lecturing, at several different centres, to evangelists and any members who attended voluntarily; and at the annual examinations about 120 presented themselves.

At the close of the war, the Danish Lutheran Church sent a number of missionaries to work in the Liaotung Peninsula, from Port Arthur and Dalny northwards. There too the general awakening was felt, though to a lesser extent.

The hospital work in Moukden had its share in the increasing prosperity, and numbers grew rapidly. A separate women's hospital and dispensary were established in 1897 under two lady doctors, and the staffs of both institutions had their hands full.

XIV

THE STORY OF BLIND CHANG OF THE VALLEY OF PEACE

"Doth God exact day-labour, light denied ? "
Sonnet, *Milton*

" Doing the King's work all the dim day long."
R. Browning.

IN a small hamlet in the remote Valley of Peace, there lived many years ago a man of the name of *Chang*, well known in the neighbourhood as a gambler and bad character, and also as a member of an earnest Buddhist sect, distinguished by their keen search for Truth. Blindness having come upon him, he heard with interest of a foreign doctor in Moukden who could restore sight. Chang was an exceptional man, of great strength of character, and in spite of the fears, warnings, and mockery of the neighbours, he sold his belongings, tied up his money in a cloth, and started on his quest. But the road was long and dangerous, and when still several days from his goal robbers fell upon him and took from him his treasured hoard. Still he struggled on, but illness attacked him, and he reached our Moukden gate at last, a pitiable wreck.

Our small tumble-down hospital was already overcrowded, and there was not a corner for him, so he was given medicine and told to go to an inn until there was room. With pathetic vehemence he pled his cause, the 120 weary miles he had walked, how ill he was, how his money was all gone. At last the hospital preacher

THE STORY OF BLIND CHANG

offered to give him his bed, and so Blind Chang was received.

His eyes were incurable, only a little glimmer of light being restored, but this seemed of small import to him, for during the month he was with us a flood of light illumined his inner vision. From the first day he listened with absorbed interest to what was told him of Him in whose name the hospital was opened.

"This is just what I have been seeking for years," he exclaimed, as he drank in with avidity all that was said. It seemed as if his mind had been ready waiting for it, and before many days he began to preach eloquently to the other patients. It is not often that the story of the Saviour meets with such joyful acceptance, nor His claims with such immediate whole-hearted loyalty. It was not unlike the man of old: "See, here is water, what doth hinder me to be baptized?" But the cautious rules of the Church enacted that he must be tested first. He must return to his home and make known his new faith, and he would be visited there later on. Much disappointed, he betook himself once more to the northern road, and was lost sight of.

Six months later, Rev. James Webster took his journey to the north, and from a town on the main road set out to look for the Valley of Peace. It was difficult to find, and the road was bad.

"We came to a place," writes Mr. Webster, "where it seemed impossible for the cart to cross. The carter talked of giving it up, so I dismounted and proceeded on foot, well assured that the cart would follow me somehow. When at last I reached the village, I was led with much ceremony into the house of Mr. Li, the village schoolmaster. We drank a cup of tea, he telling me the while tidings which made me forget all hunger and weariness, to the effect that when Blind Chang came home from Moukden he began to tell the people about this religion of Jesus, going from village to village, and into as many houses as received him, and in the evenings preaching sometimes to hundreds under the shade of the willow trees; how at first everybody laughed at him, or thought him crazed, and pitied him;—('It's all very well for him to reform,' they said, 'for he cannot gamble without eyes.')—how, when he still went on preaching and giving practical proofs of having undergone a change, people got divided about him. Some were for him, some against him; some blessed him, some cursed him; in short, the whole countryside was in an uproar. Week after week passed, Chang daily praying his prayer for help from on high and singing his one hymn learned in Moukden, and then sallying forth, groping his darkened way with his staff, to tell of Jesus the Son of God. 'And the upshot of all this is,' said Mr. Li, 'that there is a large number of people earnestly inquiring about the doctrine, and several are thoroughly convinced, and heartily believe, and desire to become members of the religion of Jesus.'

"But where was the blind man all the while? He had gone to visit one of the inquirers, and I had missed him on the way. Mr. Li left his school and accompanied me. At last we met, and I accosted Chang. He stood stock still for a moment, and then his face became perfectly radiant with joy, and great tears dropped from his eyes as he said in a voice quivering with emotion:

"'O Pastor! you promised, and I always said you would come!'

"We directed our steps to the inquirer's house, talking as we went of all that had taken place. The few remaining hours of light were occupied in speaking to the household of old and young who had gathered, answering questions, and instructing inquirers. When it was time to retire, the inquirer, the blind man, and the evangelist who accompanied me began to talk. All manner of questions were started and discussed, and difficulties explained. Midnight, the small hours of the morning passed, and at last I fell asleep in the midst of a discussion of Confucianism as compared with Christianity. Whether the three ever slept I do not know, but the first thing I was conscious of was shrill voices in earnest converse, as on the previous night. We had a crowded house all day. I met each applicant for baptism privately, and I have seldom had more satisfaction than with these men. Nine were baptized, headed by their blind guide."

At this time Chang was able to see light, but unfortunately he trusted himself to a native doctor, who promised to cure him by piercing the eye with needles, with the not unnatural result of complete blindness. Some time later arrangements were made for him to join the School for the Blind at Peking, under Mr. Murray. Here he spent three months learning to read and write, and then returned to his valley with his books in embossed type. Crowds gathered round him to see the marvel of a blind man reading with the tips of his fingers, and what he read he explained and enforced with fluent eloquence. He had a marvellous memory, and as the years went on he laid aside his cumbrous volumes and recited the Scriptures by heart. He knew the entire New Testament, chapter and verse by number, and a good deal of the Old. When a text was announced—say 2 Corinthians ix. 6—he would at once begin to repeat the words from that exact verse. He meditated on the Scriptures constantly, bringing forth wonderful new interpretations of his own, and was neither pleased nor convinced when the missionaries did not agree with these.

Chang's personal devotion to Christ, his loyalty and zeal in making Him known to others, his untiring energy in instructing converts in the elements of the faith, were unequalled. He was a difficult man to work with or control, but his very weaknesses seemed to contribute to the spread of the Light. His was a restless spirit, hating to be tied down. The missionary who had engaged him as an evangelist might leave him in charge of a certain district, to preach and instruct there, but on returnnig a few months later would find him gone. Some inward impulse had led him, he had cast aside his stated duties, and set forth to some distant town or village, there anew to gather crowds of hearers and inquirers. Thus he wandered, staying a few weeks here, a month or two there, and then returning to the work he had undertaken. Wherever he went he left behind him a knot of interested inquirers. He did not seem capable of giving prolonged systematic instruction, but the seed he sowed seemed to live in the hearts of his hearers.

"If Chang Shen had not lost his sight," said one of the Christians of that wide district, "there would have been no Church here."

One of his wanderings was to a remote valley, a hundred miles from the Valley of Peace, among the mountains in the far east which had formed the Imperial Hunting Grounds. These were opened to settlers, one of whom was a relation of Chang's. To seek him out the blind man took this long journey. Here again he gathered a group of converts, and the history of the Valley of Peace was repeated. In answer to his summons two missionaries travelled for days across a sparsely populated region where the name of Christ was quite unknown, and found in the distant "Valley of Victory" a little group of believers asking for baptism. Some time later Blind Chang went again to this valley and was asked to remain there. He received no salary, and was under no one's orders, but moved about from house to house receiving his food wherever he happened to be, and the women provided his clothes.

For two years no foreigner could visit nor communicate with the valley, owing to the Chino-Japanese war, brigandage, and other causes. At the end of that time there were in the district four distinct meeting-places where worship was held regularly, and a Christian school. One of the earliest of these Valley of Victory believers

THE STORY OF BLIND CHANG

is now an ordained Pastor over a congregation in a neighbouring valley, which supports him entirely, and there are several other self-supporting congregations in the district.

A special feature of Chang's work was his instruction of women and children. While the men were working in the fields, the women were cooking and sewing and grinding corn in the homes, and he sat and talked to them and the children as a sighted man could not have been allowed to do. Then when going about the country the boys were always ready to act as his guides, and as they went he talked. A good many members of the Christian Church to-day look back on these talks on the mountain-paths as the very foundation of their life. Chang must have been the means of personally leading to the faith many hundred individuals, but his work was now nearly done.

It was the summer of the fateful 1900, fourteen years from that evening when a blind, sick, and penniless man moved our compassion at the Moukden hospital gate. Chang was again in the Valley of Victory when the Boxer storm broke. It is a mountainous region where the concealment of individuals is not difficult, and he being a marked man was hidden away in the recesses of the hills, the faithful people sending him food. The band of Boxers, exasperated at losing their most conspicuous prey, threatened not only to kill the Christians, but to lay waste the whole valley with fire and sword. At last someone told Chang, and at once he came forth from his hiding-place and let himself be taken prisoner. He was brought to a neighbouring town whose headmen were allied with the Boxers, and in a temple was ordered to worship the idols or die.

" I can only worship the one living and true God."

" But we will kill you."

" That is of no importance, I shall rise again."

" Will you not repent of your wickedness in following the foreigner ? "

" I have repented of all my sins."

" Then you will believe in Buddha ? "

" No, I believe in my Lord Jesus Christ," and he began to preach to them.

Afraid to kill him themselves, his captors sent some distance for some Boxers, and for three days Chang lay in prison. Then he was bound and taken through the town in an open cart, the Christians following behind, and marvelling at his fortitude as he joyfully sang the old hymn learned in the Moukden hospital, " Jesus loves me, this I know." Outside the town, in front of the temple, he was made to kneel down. " Heavenly Father, receive my spirit," he prayed. But still the sword tarried. A second and a third time he prayed, saying the same words. Then " they gnashed on him with their teeth, and cried out with a loud voice, and ran upon him with one accord," attacking him from behind with their swords, and cutting him to pieces.

When the deed was done, the superstitious fears of the murderers began to work. He was a *blind* man, and therefore specially under the protection of spirits and demons. And what did he mean by " rising again " ? To prevent such a possibility they burned his body, and scattered the ashes on the mountain streams. Still their fears were not laid. He was a *good* man, so much so that he might become a god. His ghost was said to be haunting the place, and the Boxers departed precipitately, leaving the Christians of that district unharmed.

Some years later the Government erected a monument to Chang's memory in the county town of that district, but none marks the resting-place of his ashes, for they are scattered afar, fit emblem of the Gospel he loved to preach. Indeed, he and the other martyrs have already " risen again," in the many churches and little Christian gatherings which have sprung up all over Manchuria since that terrible Boxer summer.

XV

MISDIRECTED PATRIOTISM

"Who is here so vile that will not love his country?"
Julius Cæsar.

"My large kingdom for a grave!
A little, little grave, an obscure grave."
K*ing Richard II.*

WHEN the war with Japan was over, Manchuria and all China expected to settle down again just as before, while many of her more vigorous sons sought to nurture a gradual and quiet reform from within, which might in time work upwards to the Government, and outwards to the whole nation. But this was not to be. The war had set many conflicting forces in motion, its consequences have been multiplying ever since, and none can foretell the end.

Simultaneous with the striking growth of the Christian Church in Manchuria, and with the new interest in science and in all things foreign, were development in other directions. Manchuria did not greatly concern herself at that time with what went on in Peking or elsewhere, but she soon had it brought home to her in her own borders that things could never be the same again. Russian diplomacy prevented Japan from retaining possession of Southern Manchuria, and *Li Hung Chang*, said by his enemies to be in Russia's pay, could hardly refuse to negotiate a Treaty which expressed China's gratitude in a practical way. All Russia asked at first was to be allowed to run the Siberian railway across the north of Manchuria. That was the beginning.

In Moukden little was heard of it for some time. Russian engineers surveyed and made maps and went away again, and it was reported that they were making a railway over the desert mountains in the far north. Gradually people grew accustomed to Russian visits, but when the news spread that Port Arthur and Ta-lien-wan (Dalny) had been " leased " to Russia, and that the railway was to run right through the heart of Manchuria, there was much fierce indignation, and cursing of *Li Hung Chang*. The seizure of *Kiao-chou* in Shantung by the Germans shortly before, hardly noticed at the time, and the occupation of *Wei-hai-wei* by Britain which followed, assumed importance in men's eyes, enlightened as they were by Russia's action in their midst. Parts of the country were being stolen on all hands, and a bitterness against foreigners grew and fermented in the minds of many in Manchuria, as well as all over Northern China.

There were thus two streams of feeling and impulse developing at the same time. Both had their origin in the first conscious stirrings of that patriotism which had lain dormant in the Chinese mind, but was roused by the humiliation of the defeat by Japan. Both were intensified by the actions of the European Powers.

On the one hand were those who realized China's weakness, and who sought to learn everything possible from Western nations, in order ultimately to be able to resist with success all unjust aggression, and to stand unashamed before the world, a strong, independent China.

On the other hand were those in whom resentment of foreign treatment of China grew to a passion, who blindly hated all foreigners, good or bad, and all their works, and who were willing to go to any length to rid their country of what they regarded as an incubus which caused all her troubles.

Between these were the old, the timid, the conservative, the unadventurous, and the great inarticulate mass of the common people, working for their daily bread, asking for nothing but to be allowed to earn it in peace and security, and recking little of what foreign Powers or their own Government might do.

For a time it seemed as if the forces that made for Reform were to have the ascendancy. The war was hardly over when the Emperor commanded the construction of railways from Shanghai to Nanking, and from Tientsin to near Peking, and instructed his ministers to further the study of Western science throughout the country. Later on a railway to Hankow was sanctioned, and in 1898 the establishment of a University at Peking on foreign lines, with foreign professors. The Emperor was privately studying the Bible and other books, Christian and scientific, and insisted on close personal intercourse with a number of progressive Reformers, such as had hardly been granted previously to the highest Ministers of State. The anti-foreign agitation following on the seizure of the three seaports, Kiao-chou, Port Arthur, and Wei-hai-wei, he answered by a vigorous Imperial Edict for the protection of missionaries, in which the officials were instructed to see that his Christian subjects did not suffer for their faith. Many among the younger officials, *literati*, merchants, and gentry followed the example of the Emperor. There was a great demand for all kinds of Christian literature, and books on History, Political Economy, and Science. Newspapers sprang up with an enormous circulation, where previously few had cared to know what was happening outside their own neighbourhood.

Then came the momentous and fatal month of September, 1898.

For three crowded weeks there poured forth a series of most remarkable Edicts. Education was to be modernized, science and other subjects introduced into the stereotyped examinations for degrees, temples turned into schools, a University and Middle Schools established at once, and study abroad encouraged. The throne was to be freely memorialized even by the common people; annual financial statements of Government income and expenditure were to be published; and law-court reform inaugurated. Finally the question of a National Parliament was raised, and it was also suggested that the nation should abandon the ordinary Chinese dress, and the fashion of wearing a queue, imposed by the Manchus.

The Emperor, born and bred in absolute seclusion and knowing nothing of the world outside his palace except from books, revealed himself to his people as an earnest and radical Reformer, and the hearts of thousands leaped to meet his. But the millions remained untouched, for the customs of centuries are iron chains. It is a sad story. We cannot but wonder what would have been the history of the subsequent years had the Emperor and his advisers been more worldly-wise, content to "hasten slowly."

As it was, the old Empress-Dowager took alarm; it was not for this she had yielded the reins of power. There was a short, sharp struggle between Reform and Reaction, and Reaction gained the day. During the fourth week of September all the Reform Edicts were repealed, six of the most promising and enlightened of the young patriots of China were summarily executed, others fled to foreign lands, and the Emperor himself was immured in a living grave, from which he issued only at stated times to give mechanical outward support to the absolute rule of the Empress-Dowager. It was a beautiful spot, that grave, a quiet tree-embowered island in a picturesque lake, concealed in the very centre of Peking, with rockeries, and hidden paths, and unexpected rustic seats. What thoughts did he think there under

> "the insufferable eyes
> Of these poor Might-Have-Beens,
> These fatuous, ineffectual Yesterdays"?

It was long before any accurate knowledge of the *coup d'état* in Peking was allowed to reach the provinces. The

Reform Edicts had been received with consternation by the majority of officials, to whose advantage it was to keep things as they were, and their speedy repeal, before most people had heard of them, naturally gave satisfaction. The more enlightened of the reading men, especially in the cities, sighed bitterly over the postponement of their hopes, and resigned themselves to wait. Reform must come some day; for as one of the martyred Reformers had said: "They may cut the grass, but the roots remain."

The defeat of the Reform Movement did not leave things where they had been before. There was no standing still. With the execution of the Reformers on 28 September, 1908, began the reactionary movement which culminated in the Boxer outbreak of 1900.

The party which hated foreigners and foreign ways was now in the ascendancy, and the change of attitude showed itself very quickly. The metropolitan province of Chihli reflected with special readiness the feelings of those in power; on 23 October British railway engineers were attacked by soldiers on the railway line being constructed between Peking and Tientsin. On 4 November a missionary was murdered in Kuei-chou, far inland in the south-west. On 5 November an Edict recommended volunteer military organizations in all cities, towns, and villages, adding: "The whole country can then be turned into a great armed camp, to fight for their homes." Foreigners were not mentioned, but it was understood that the danger to be guarded against was from them.

Constant murmurings against foreigners were no longer discouraged. Their seizure of the three northern seaports, the French aggression in the south, Russian aggression in Manchuria, German aggression in Shantung, the Italian demand for a seaport, the extra-territorial rights at ports, the foreign control of the Customs, the foreign building of railways, the frequent mention in foreign papers of a possible " partition of China "—all these were legitimate grievances, and the Government in its present mood was only too willing to let them rankle in men's minds. The scattering of so many foreign missionaries through the country was also an irritant, the protection of Christianity by treaty exasperated the officials, and the meddling of Christians, especially Catholics, in law affairs, provoked much antagonism.

Shantung, the proud and ancient home of Confucius, was particularly bitter, because the Germans claimed it as their "sphere of influence," and obtruded themselves there. They had taken *Kiao-chou* and procured the dismissal of the Shantung Governor; they were insisting on making a railway through the province, and quarrelling over it with the next Governor, *Yü Hsien*. There was an ancient secret society long extinct called the "Righteous Harmony Fists," parodied by someone as the "Boxers." This was revived with the Governor's connivance, in connection with the local militia, in order to work the ruin of the foreigners whom he hated. He knew the Germans were seeking his downfall, and, as he expected, the Peking Government bowed to their will. *Yü Hsien* was degraded—temporarily—but he left behind him the dragon's teeth sowed in the soil of Shantung, which sprang up in that anti-foreign movement which was to cost China and the world so dear.

The original principle of this "Boxer" union was that its members were to be so possessed by patriotism that the gods would work through them, giving them supernatural powers, and invulnerability to sword or fire. Their motto, expressed in four comprehensive monosyllables, was "Exalt the Dynasty, exterminate the foreigner."

At first their influence was merely local. Not daring to attack the "foreign devils," they began with the "secondary devils," i.e. Chinese Christians, both Catholic and Protestant, looting and burning their homes, holding their persons for ransom, and sometimes killing them. Before long the movement spread across the border into *Chihli*, and here too the officials took no public notice. Gaining courage from their immunity from punishment, the Boxers, at the close of 1899, murdered a missionary, and all that winter the foreigners dotted over Shantung and Chihli, chiefly missionaries, were in daily danger of their lives.

Looking back, it seems strange how little it was realized what was going on. Those on the spot who gave warning were considered alarmists; for the Empress-Dowager and her Government continued to give fair words and promises to the foreign Ministers, while at the same time, as we now know, secretly encouraging the Boxers. In March, 1900, *Yü Hsien*, the degraded, was made Governor of *Shan-si*, and soon the Boxers began to be active in that province also. During the spring an Imperial Envoy was sent through the provinces, jokingly styled the " Lord High Extortioner," to raise money for the equipment of the local militia whose organization had been commanded, and wherever Boxers existed they and this militia were one.

What was lightly called " the unrest " was spreading. Boatmen and carters joined in large and vindictive numbers, because their living was endangered by steam-launches and the railway. There had been a bad harvest in 1899, and it was said that the foreigners had prevented the rain, so very many of the agricultural population joined also. There was no sudden outbreak, but outrages became week by week more common and more daring. Mission buildings were looted, telegraph wires cut, a Catholic village attacked by two thousand men, two Chinese preachers were openly murdered, railway stations were burned, the railway torn up, foreign houses burned. Still the Government made plausible excuses.

Then on 1 June two missionaries were deliberately murdered, and a few days later the railway service on the

Peking line completely ceased. At last there arose a consciousness that the danger was general and urgent, the Government not to be trusted. The missionaries in Peking took refuge in the Legations, and Admiral Seymour, with two thousand allied troops, left Tientsin for Peking on 10 June. It was supposed by most people that this was all that was needed to put things right.

In Manchuria all was quiet, and very little general anti-foreign feeling existed. For the most part, the people knew personally of only one kind of foreigner, the missionary, who was regarded as doing no harm but rather good. There were the Russians also, but they were distinctly different as they came from the north, while the missionaries came from the west by Shanghai. The railway had gradually taken shape, being built in sections, on some of which construction trains were running. Superstitious prejudices had prevented its coming closer to Moukden than about ten miles, lest the Imperial Tombs be disturbed and the prosperity of the dynasty destroyed. The Russian railway and the presence of Russians were sullenly accepted as facts which could be neither denied nor altered. The only thing to be done was to make the best use of them possible, and take one's journeys by train.

Little was heard of the Boxers, and no interest taken in their doings. There were floating rumours, and we read of them in our weekly Shanghai paper, feeling thankful that we had no such troubles here.

Our Annual Meetings were held in May. The Presbytery was composed of Chinese and foreigners, pastors and elders, to the number of about a hundred. The reports from all over Manchuria had never been more encouraging. The membership was increasing, schools multiplying, the education of women and girls developing steadily; several congregations wished to support ordained pastors of their own; and the subscriptions of the Church for its own ordinances, pastors, evangelists, etc., were $20,000, or about £2000 sterling, although $5 (10s.) a month was considered quite a good wage for a man. Plans for further development were discussed, and the members departed in high spirits to their various homes, little thinking that within a few weeks they would be hiding in the dens and caves of the earth, or laying down their lives for their faith.

Ten days later, about sixty merchants, many of them Christians, met in the hospital waiting-room to consider the question of supporting beds in the hospital. Nearly enough was subscribed and promised annually to support two beds, and plans were discussed for approaching the more wealthy merchants of the city.

On 30 May a terrible explosion took place in the barracks west of the city. An hour later, two riders galloped furiously to the hospital gate, bringing the cards of the Governor-General, His Excellency *Tseng Chi*, and the military commander, both of whom were Manchus of the reactionary party, who had hitherto had no dealings with the hospital. They now requested that we would receive and treat the injured men. Soon these arrived, eleven in all, and later on I went to the scene of the accident and attended to the injuries of about thirty more. The officers and the Government were most cordial over this matter. The Commander, or Lieutenant-General, sent a complimentary present, and the Governor-General himself a cordial message that he hoped soon to call and thank us in person. For about a fortnight streams of officers came to the hospital, to visit the men, see the place, and express their gratitude.

There now began to be much talk of the Boxers, but as an outside thing, in which Manchuria was little concerned. Then on 10 June the news was passed from mouth to mouth, "The Boxers have come!" A few Shantung leaders had arrived, and were seeking to gain recruits. They began their drill, but received little encouragement. All respectable people condemned them utterly, and they only made way in the lowest quarters of the city, where beggars, desperadoes, and outcasts congregate, who are at all times ready for any adventure promising gain.

Telegraphic communication with Tientsin and Shanghai was interrupted, and so unconscious of approaching trouble were foreigners and Chinese alike, that on the 14th—at the time when hundreds were being massacred in Peking, and Admiral Seymour was struggling in vain to reach that city—our little missionary community went for a picnic to the banks of the Hun River, where the children plashed in the water and played on the sand, and we had tea happily under the shady trees.

XVI

THE BOXER MADNESS, 1900

"Quem Deus vult perdere, prius dementat."
"Whom the gods would destroy, they first make mad."

"God is sad in Heaven
To think what goes on in His recreant world,
He made quite other."
Aurora Leigh.

MEN live peacefully, buying and selling, marrying and giving in marriage, working together in all amity, when suddenly there is a change. Human beings are hunted like partridges on the hills, a blind fury possesses men's minds, bloodshed, fire, and hate. What does it all mean?

The public injuries of China at the hands of foreigners were very real, but they are not enough to account for it, for this is a country which had always left thought of such matters to its officials.

The general contempt for and hatred of foreigners were also very real, and the resentment at the steady increase of those who "followed the foreigner" in religion was widespread. It is true that no religious fanaticism existed, which would be roused by any suggestion of replacing the gods to whom people were devoted by new objects of worship, for few were devoted to any god. The objection to Christianity was that it was foreign. Men holding to what was handed down by their forefathers were indignant that any alien faith should gain foothold. These feelings and prejudices, however, had lasted for decades, and were easily controlled. The very province where the Boxers had their origin, Shantung, was compelled by its new Governor, *Yuan shih kai*, to cease all open agitation, and no foreigner was killed within its borders.

Here in Manchuria the weakness of the resentment at these things was specially marked. Japanese conquest and Russian aggression had been submitted to with no thought of resistance. Anti-foreign feeling had died down almost entirely. Some forty thousand of the people of the two southern provinces were professed Christians, or in Christian families, or occasional attenders of Christian worship, besides as many Catholics. For the most part these people lived on friendly terms with all around, though here and there persecution still existed. It seemed impossible, alike to foreigners, to Chinese Christians, and to the general public in Manchuria, that any danger could threaten us and the Church and especially the hospital. Even the day before every foreign building in Moukden was burned, a high official said to my assistant :

" Why did the doctor leave ? He was quite safe here. No one would touch him or the hospital."

There were two features of the Boxer Movement which made it possible so to intensify the existing anti-foreign resentment as to cause deeds of fanatic cruelty to be done in province after province. One was the occult nature of the Boxer rites and claims ; the other the support given by the Empress-Dowager and her Government. Without these the Boxers would have prevailed nothing.

Their power over the people seems at first to have depended largely on mesmerism. Strange movements, passes, and contortions were practised until the devotee fell down in a fit or trance, sometimes uttering unknown words and uncouth sounds, said to be the language of the spirits which now entered into him. When he rose he was a true Boxer, and invulnerable. Superstition and imitation worked also on the susceptible nervous temperament of the Chinese, and many fell down because they believed they would, and because their neighbours did. There was a butcher who joined them, a big broad-shouldered heavy man. When he fell, overcome by hypnotism, hysteria, or excitement, he struck his head violently against a stone, fractured his skull, and never moved again.

At the beginning in Moukden the Boxer numbers increased very slowly in spite of their mysterious powers, for the Governor-General had personally no sympathy with their aims, and issued a proclamation against them. But the day after our light-hearted picnic, the news came of the destruction of the railways in Chihli and the burning of mission stations. Several Belgians were said to have been killed, and the worst was feared for the missionaries shut up in Pao-ting-fu and elsewhere. (They were actually massacred a fortnight later.) Uneasiness and fear began to spread through Moukden. Service was held on Sunday, 17 June, as usual, and opinion among the Christians was divided. Some laughed at the idea of anything happening, —what power could such impostors have? Many shook their heads and "doubted whereunto this would grow"— was not Satan himself the evil spirit who entered into these Boxers in their trance?

That night we heard of Admiral Seymour's advance on Peking of a week before. It was our last reliable news for days, and like foreigners elsewhere, we assumed that this would speedily make an end of the trouble.

The apathetic attitude of the Moukden Government to the Boxers now became very evident. The proclamations against them were openly scribbled on. Their drill was practised unchecked in open spaces in the city. Their emissaries were in all market-places and wherever men congregated. It was said that no beggars were left in the slums, all had become Boxers. Many young lads and boys swelled the ranks, eager for excitement, and they were joined by hundreds of members of secret sects such as the *Tsai-li-ti*, who had always been anti-foreign. In several of the many barracks the cursing of foreigners became open and violent, and there were loud boasts of what the Boxers were going to do. Gradually a spell of fear was laid on all the city. Level-headed men spoke of them with bated breath. Their aims and objects were not sympathized with, but their supernatural powers came to be believed in, and people were afraid.

Placards were posted on the walls and passed from hand to hand, telling of the evil doings of foreigners to China, from the introduction of opium to the seizing of seaports, including the poisoning of wells and the killing of little children. Many thought it dangerous even to possess foreign things. It was said that foreign buttons were bewitched, the proof being that they could burn, whereas true buttons were metal or bone. In our own kitchen our cook was found taking the buttons off his robe, while others in consternation watched them burn. They were harmless things of German manufacture, not professing to be metal. On Wednesday the 20th, vile posters were put up everywhere with horrible charges against foreigners, and all the loyal people of China were called on to rise up and sweep them out of the land. The 24th was fixed for the burning of the buildings, and rewards were promised to all who helped.

Next morning I wrote to the Governor-General, enclosing a copy of the placard and pointing out the danger of allowing this agitation to continue. His tardy reply was cold, formal, and altogether unsatisfactory, a remarkable contrast to his friendly message of three weeks before. We learned later the meaning of this. Although the public telegraph wires beyond Newchwang were cut, there remained a private Government line direct from Peking to Moukden; so the Governor-General knew what we did not, that the Taku forts had been taken by the Allied Fleet, that Tientsin was being bombarded

ENTRANCE TO MOUKDEN HOSPITAL BEFORE BOXER TIME

by Boxers and Imperial troops combined, that the German Minister in Peking had been killed, and that the Legations were even then being besieged. He had also received the Imperial Edict commanding the extermination of foreigners, and the Lieutenant-General was insisting on its publication and obedience to the letter. H.E. *Tseng Chi* was not a strong enough man either to disobey, as was done in some provinces, or to obey promptly. He did not wish to kill us, and he did not dare to warn us; so it was truest kindness to write in this callous, formal way, that we might be frightened into leaving while yet there was time.

We regarded the sudden change in his attitude as a serious matter, and discussed the advisability of ladies and children going away for a time. The same evening an official friend called in plain clothes, on foot, and after dark, to urge earnestly that we should leave without any delay.

"The Governor-General has news from Peking," he said, "which makes this necessary. I cannot tell you what it is, but the order has been given to-day that *two camps of Imperial troops in Moukden are to drill as Boxers.*" This was the most serious news we had yet heard. Still we were confident that the Government in Peking would speedily be compelled by Admiral Seymour to change its attitude, and that counter-orders would soon come and matters return to their old peaceful condition.

Friday was spent in making arrangements for the departure of our entire community except three men. By 5.30 a.m. on Saturday all had left, taking with them summer clothing and such things as could be hastily gathered together for what might be an absence of a month or two. It was a strange journey. The party consisted of two men, eight ladies, and five children. No regular trains were running, one might get one at once or wait a whole day, and there were no passenger carriages. The refugees were accommodated in empty covered trucks, where for over two days and two nights they lived, slept, and ate. At first there was a feeling of shame at having "run away." The burning of houses had been threatened so often and nothing had come of it, and it seemed absurd to think of China defying the world. Then news met them that Admiral Seymour's force was surrounded by tens of thousands of Boxers and soldiers, and its annihilation feared, that Tientsin was in ruins, and that the survivors of the foreign community there were gathered in the Town Hall where they were being shelled. (This was really a gross exaggeration.)

We were now only three in Moukden, but it soon became evident that we too must leave. When I returned from escorting the party to the station, the streets were already full of excited men, and the shops mostly remained closed.

"Why did you come back?" "How did you dare?" I was asked again and again, for it was now known publicly that the soldiers were to become Boxers, and groups of lads were drilling in every corner. On Sunday, the 24th, the day proclaimed for the burning, we went to church as usual, arranging that horses should await us in the compound for escape in case of need. A large crowd gathered at the church gate, among whom were a few soldiers, but there was no attempt at disturbance. Over four hundred Christians gathered, and earnest were the prayers that went up for strength, guidance, and protection. The last hymn sung was "Soldiers of the Lord, arise!" an adaptation of "Scots wha hae." Then the congregation quietly dispersed, to meet again no more for months, and then but a broken fragment.

During the day things grew rapidly worse. Inflammatory placards on Imperial yellow paper were boldly affixed on the city gates. A report was circulated that all the foreign ships near Tientsin had been sunk. One of our preaching-chapels in the city was sacked. The Imperial Edict for the extermination of foreigners was

THE BOXER MADNESS, 1900

at last issued, and 2500 taels were promised for every "devil" killed, 500 taels for every "devil's slave," or Chinese Christian. The hospital patients began to be alarmed, and many left. The news about Admiral Seymour and Tientsin reached us, and a telegram from Newchwang urging us to leave at once. We gathered some of our most trusted helpers to consult as to what should be done. They sat in silence with bowed heads for some time, then one said:

"If you remain, we will stand by you, and we'll all die together. If you go, your lives will be saved, and we can look after our families and ourselves."

On Monday morning at dawn we slipped away in closely curtained carts, and without delay got a truck in a train going south. I tried to warn the Russian stationmaster of the danger. He understood, but indicated that he could not leave his station. He was seized by the Boxers a few days later, tortured, and killed. It was well we left then, for next day a bridge was blown up, and no more trains went south. There were other parts of Manchuria where the missionaries did not get away so easily, but all did escape, some amid difficulty and danger. Several had their health permanently injured, and two died from the shock and strain.

Letters from my assistants continued to reach Newchwang for several days. Trade was at a standstill, all shops closed, patients diminishing, but still a few remained. On Wednesday the Bible Society premises were looted. On Saturday evening, 30 June, I received the following telegram:

"About four o'clock to-day the church was burned, and the hospitals and houses are burning. It is not known whether the Pastor is dead or alive, nor how many Christians have been killed."

Next morning came another, sent off two hours later:

"Men's and women's hospitals, dwelling-houses, Bible Society buildings, church, and chapels have all been burned to ashes by the Boxers."

That was our last voice from Moukden, then silence fell and darkness hid from us all that was happening there. We could not stay in Newchwang, but scattered to Japan, Shanghai, or home. In Japan we spent two weary, sad months, getting no news, indeed, from inland Manchuria, but hearing terrible stories of sufferings and martyrdoms elsewhere, and imagining only too vividly like trials for our own people. From the detailed accounts heard later, we can reconstruct the story of those days and months.

It was two o'clock on the afternoon of Saturday, 30 June. In the men's hospital several patients still remained; the last of the seventy or eighty out-patients who came daily had been seen by my assistant, Dr. Wei, and all was quiet on the Small River bank. Nearly a mile away, close to the church, was the Manse, where lived with his family *Pastor Liu*, for years the leader of the Moukden congregation. Hearing a rabble at the big gate, he went to it and " spoke reason " to them, reproving the many boys who had gathered. After he had shut the gate, sticks and stones began to fly, and he soon saw that matters were becoming serious. Returning home he got his wife, children, and grandchildren, with what things they could easily remove, over a wall into the house of a neighbouring Christian; while he himself proposed to go to the Governor-General to seek protection for the church.

As he dropped from the wall he heard the smashing of windows, then the crash of the big gate giving way, and the shouts of the mob as they poured in. From a spot where he could watch all that was done, he saw that this was more than a disorderly crowd. Two officials, wearing their official " buttons," were directing, and under them

THE BOXER MADNESS, 1900 141

were about a hundred soldiers. Realizing the uselessness of appealing to a Government which was itself aiding the destruction, he watched these two men enter his house, examine things there, and then let in the crowd to work their will. Large bundles of millet-stalk were brought and thrown into the church, among piled-up heaps of forms, a tin of kerosene oil was poured over all, and in a few minutes the flames burst forth, while from the great crowd in and around the compound went up a fierce yell of applause.

"Foreigners are done with now!" was the shout, but a few turned away, groaning that this was the beginning of the destruction of China. The quiet, law-abiding majority of the population were shut up in their homes that day, and the lawless minority had their way. This was their hour and the power of darkness. A little later came a terrible crash, and the great tower fell, some of the bricks striking the house where the pastor's family and their friends were huddled together in terror. Then there was a cry: "To the south suburb!" (the Catholic Mission). "To the east suburb!" (the hospitals and houses). And the great crowd divided, soldiers accompanying each part.

The Roman Catholic Cathedral and other buildings were surrounded by a high massive wall, and when the crowd began to attack the gate they were fired on from inside. A few were wounded, and the others quickly scattered.

Before the Small River bank was reached, most of the assistants and caretakers there and the few remaining patients had already fled for their lives; but Dr. Wei, hoping that the hospital might be spared, prepared to receive the unwelcome guests. While the women's hospital, the five houses, and the girls' school were being looted, a party came to the men's hospital also. Dr. Wei met them at the gate and spoke politely, appealing to them to protect the good work which was done there.

They listened and went away, but a few minutes later a larger company burst in. He invited them to drink tea, but they roughly thrust him aside, and more and more crowded in, smashing windows and bottles, and picking up anything they fancied. He soon saw it was hopeless, and was afraid to make himself conspicuous, but he hung about until he saw the flames, and then went straight to the telegraph office to send me word.

The whole premises were thoroughly searched before burning, and an articulated skeleton was found, bought in Edinburgh, also a valuable papier mâché model of the human frame, which had cost about £100, used for teaching anatomy to my students. These were taken away and were paraded through the city later as a proof of the evil doings of the foreigners, for the manikin was supposed to be the remains of a human being. In our house was found a mandarin's official "button," presented to me along with official robes when I received the Order of the Double Dragon. We had evidently killed an official, for "Here is his button, all that is left of him!"

That same evening the Irish Mission buildings at the west side of the city and the Bible Society premises were burned, and the six preaching-chapels throughout the city burned or looted. The Christians soon realized that their one chance of escape was while the Boxers were occupied in the destruction of property. When that was over attention was turned on them, but they were not to be found. Almost every Christian home in Moukden was empty that night, and by morning all were looted and many burned. Then began the Reign of Terror, which rapidly spread all over the country.

The Lieutenant-Governor, Commander of the army, threw himself with zeal into the task of exterminating all trace of foreign existence. The soldiers were employed to help the Boxers, who, however, remained a separate organization, their numbers being swelled by all who were eager for loot. The Russians were completely taken by surprise. Many of the railway men were killed. A party of engineers fought their way north from Tieling, generously escorting a number of Catholics and a Protestant missionary. All the northern missionaries were helped to escape by the Russians. Parties of soldiers and Boxers were dispatched to city after city, town after town, and even to villages and glens. One after another every church, hospital, school, and foreign house was burned, and many Christians were killed. In Moukden attention was for a few days concentrated on the Roman Catholics. The Governor-General did not want to kill the French priests, and offered them escort to Newchwang; but as the Lieutenant-Governor was eager to obey the Edict, it is unlikely that safe escort would have been possible. In any case they refused to leave, and strengthened themselves in their Cathedral compound, where it is said that they armed several hundred of their people.

Just at this time the Governor-General, *Tseng Chi*, in his heart disliking the Boxers, arranged with an enlightened military officer a plan to discredit them. He invited some of their leaders to a banquet, pretending to be very cordial.

"There are many," he said, after congratulating them on the marvels they could do, "who do not believe in your miraculous powers, and we must convince them that you are really protected by the spirits. Let us have a public demonstration of your invulnerability."

The Boxers agreed, and in presence of a vast crowd a row of a dozen stood up to be shot at. Their leaders had arranged blank cartridges, so not a man fell.

"That is wonderful!" said *Tseng Chi*. "But you have not the same guns as the foreigners. I have some brand-new rifles, the very kind they use; let us try these."

The leaders protested in vain, the new rifles were discharged, three men fell dead, the others fled. Immediately excuses were made: these men had not been sincere

Boxers; but from that day the angry leaders suspected the Governor-General. There was much talk against him, the report being even circulated that he was in secret a Catholic, so that he became afraid to assert himself on the side of mercy.

The Catholics were attacked again and again, but while suffering severely they held their own, and a good many soldiers and Boxers were killed or wounded. At last, by order of the Lieutenant-Governor, a determined assault was made, cannon were placed on the city wall which threw in shells and set some of the buildings on fire, the big gate was battered in, and the French Bishop, two priests, two sisters, a number of Chinese priests, and several hundred Christians were killed by shot, sword, or fire. All the buildings were burned, and at last Moukden was thought to be purged of the foreign poison.

Few Christians had been found in the city itself. One old evangelist was killed on the street. There was another, a marked man because his leg had been amputated. A number of Boxers met on the street an old patient, not a Christian, who also had lost a leg. "Here he is!" they shouted, and killed him without further question. One old widow woman did not attempt to flee. She was over eighty, absolutely penniless, and very stupid, but a Church member, supported by the Chinese Christians in the good old apostolic fashion. Near the smouldering ruins of the hospital she met some Boxers searching for Christians.

"I am a Christian, you can kill me!" she cried out. "You have broken my food-bowl (i.e. those who give me food), and how can I live? I believe in Jesus. Kill me!" The men laughed, chaffed the old lady, gave her food and money, and went their way.

But what of the Chinese Christians who had fled, and those in the towns and villages all over the country? Boxers and soldiers were out seeking them, having in many cases secured in the chapels the lists of members and inquirers. The months of July and August were a veritable "killing time"; and had there existed in Manchuria any widespread hatred of Christianity, many thousands must have died instead of hundreds. The general feeling was not hatred of Christians, but fear of the Boxers. There were cases where personal spite and long-standing grudges were satisfied by the betrayal of Christian families. On the other hand, large numbers of men, women, and children owed their lives to the silence of non-Christian neighbours, even when rewards were offered; many were housed and fed by heathen relatives and friends; many more given food and helped on their weary wanderings by comparative strangers.

One man lay for fourteen days between the ceiling and the roof of a Buddhist temple where a friend of his was a servant, and from his hiding-place saw Christians brought before the idols and killed when they refused to worship. Another was lingering about a village where he had friends. Hearing a crowd coming, he hid in some trees, and saw one after another of his fellow-members done to death. On one church door eighteen Christian heads were hung—the church was rented, so it had not been burned. In outlying districts many girls of Christian homes, Catholic and Protestant, were carried off to the hills to be the wives of robbers turned Boxers. Among the many miles of millet-fields thousands of fugitives crouched and crept, for tall millet forms a most perfect screen. Over and over again they would hear their persecutors on a path a few yards away, and the children were hushed into shuddering silence till the danger passed. They ate the raw grain, vegetables, roots, and wild berries, being afraid to light fires which would betray their presence. At night they would steal out to draw water from the village wells. The little ones pined with the unwholesome food and exposure, and many a grave was dug among that fatal unripe millet. The heavy rains came, soaking the fields and driving the fugitives to seek a precarious shelter in the villages for a few days. But even in those few days some were taken.

In the early vehemence of the Boxer fury, Christians who were caught were beheaded without question, but soon they began to be given a chance of life. The alternative usually was burning incense in a temple and renunciation of Christianity, or death often under torture. A good many, among them women, school children, and unbaptized "inquirers," chose death; but is it to be wondered at that others chose life? They were Christians of a day, and it seemed a light thing to tell a lie and say they gave up their faith. The forms of death varied according to the individual ferocity of the persecutors. The majority were beheaded; others were wrapped in cotton-wool steeped in oil and burned alive; one was given a "fiery crown," a thick ring of oily cotton-wool being placed round his head and set on fire; one or two were hacked to pieces bit by bit, being given a new chance to recant after each slice.

"Yes, I believe in Jesus," answered a man firmly when ears and eyes were gone. Then they cut off his lips, saying "That will stop you!" His little daughter also refused to recant and was beheaded by his side.

As the weeks passed on, a plan was devised by some more merciful minds to stop the killing. A form of certificate was drawn out stating that the holder had renounced Christianity, the wording in different places varying in the definiteness of its recantation. These were sold to thousands of Christians, or to their friends on their behalf, and often without their knowledge. Many a man who had spent suffering weeks in the fields and seen his wife and children languishing and dying before his eyes, hailed this arrangement as the merciful provision of the Heavenly Father to save their lives. He would have continued to refuse to worship in a temple or definitely to recant, but to pay for a document which was not true seemed to him very different. The great proportion of the Christians being men, it often happened that the family remained in safety with non-Christian relatives, while the man alone went into hiding. Now messages were sent to many of these wanderers that they could safely come home. Some, finding these lying certificates awaiting them, tore them up and went into exile again. Others reasoned that they could not be blamed for benefiting by them, as they had been bought and paid for without their authority.

The most prominent figure among the Moukden Christians was that of *Pastor Liu*, and a special reward was offered for his capture. He was never found, and for long not even the Christians knew if he was alive. After witnessing the destruction of the church and his house, he and his family escaped from the city and wandered about for some days, now with friends, now hiding in the millet, and again sheltering in an unused brick-kiln. Realizing that his presence increased the danger to his family, Liu decided to leave them. They found refuge with some non-Christian friends in the country, while he fled alone to the east. He had great difficulty in getting food and drink. The wells in that district were all locked for fear of Christian poison. More than once he was recognized and warned to go on. After nine days of this, he shaved his head, and passing himself off as a Buddhist priest who had lost his money, begged boldly for food. He found he was suspected, people said he did not look like a priest, so he continued his hungry wanderings, seeking for a place where he was unknown. One evening in an inn among the hills he met a Moukden Christian, but neither dared recognize the other. They slipped out separately and met in a gully where they stayed all night and exchanged tidings. Some days later Liu, still disguised as a priest, got work in a farmer's fields, remote from towns, and there he remained nearly two months. Once he was sent to a place five miles off, where he saw the chapel burning and was the reluctant witness of the killing of a Christian woman. It was late in August before he could send word of his safety to his family.

Throughout the summer there were incidents showing that the beneficent work of the hospital was not wholly forgotten. A dispenser met a band of soldiers, and one called out:

"That man's from the Moukden hospital!" He thought death was certain, but the soldier went on: "Don't you know me? I was wounded in that big explosion, and your people cured me and treated me well."

"Don't be afraid," said the officer in charge, "your hospital was very good to our men. You can stay with us for a day or two and you'll be all right."

Another student was led out to execution along with his father and brother, surrounded by a crowd of excited Boxers. One of these, shouting that no knife could wound him, stabbed himself with some force in the abdomen. The student, already on his knees awaiting the executioner's sword, instantly called out:

"I can save that man's life, and heal his wound, if you will set my father free!" So they bargained that he and his father were to be liberated as soon as the man was well; but they would not include the brother, who was speedily beheaded. The soldier recovered, and the bargain was kept.

Dr. Wei, my assistant, spent weeks in hiding; but early in August a band of Boxers and soldiers threatened to burn his village and kill his whole home, numbering some thirty souls, if he were not given up. So he returned and interviewed their officer, reminding him of the many soldiers who had been healed and helped in the hospital. This he could not deny, and Wei was liberated for the time. Soon afterwards he heard that the Lieutenant-

General, who was in Liaoyang on his way south to fight the advancing Russians, was looking for him to make him a military surgeon. It seemed to be the one way to save his family and village, so again he gave himself up. The General received him most courteously, apologized for not having called at the hospital to thank us in person for treating his wounded, and altogether ignored the fact that it had been burned down by his orders, and that he was speaking to a Christian. He proposed to appoint Wei as Surgeon-in-Chief, and he dared not refuse, but succeeded in delaying definite arrangements until he could get instruments and medicines. A few days later, when he was at home on a visit, the Russians occupied his village, and the unwelcome appointment was at an end.

After looting and confiscating all available Christian property, the Boxers had soon begun to seek new sources of gain. They blackmailed the merchants and wealthy men of city and country, levied taxes, interfered with trade, and took up an arrogant attitude to all. When the Governor-General's equipage met on the street some of their leaders with their mounted escort, he had to draw aside humbly to make room for them. Their claims for power and money grew till all Moukden trembled before them, and the country sighed for the old days of comparative prosperity and security.

At the beginning of August, their ally the Lieutenant-Governor went south with part of the army. During his absence very alarming news reached the Governor-General by the private Government wire from Peking. Tientsin had been taken by the foreigners, the Boxers and the Chinese army were being daily defeated, and a horde of foreigners were advancing steadily on Peking. The Boxer power had now lasted forty-one days in Moukden, and the Governor-General decided that this was long enough. A strong proclamation denouncing them was issued, which was received with relief by the people ; and at the same time, on 11 August, the soldiers were commanded to turn on them, and kill every Boxer they could find. A good many were killed, many more fled from Moukden, and the rest were absorbed in the ordinary population.

The Boxer Madness was at an end in Manchuria.

XVII

PAYING THE PRICE

" There shall never be one lost good ! What was shall live as before ;
    The evil is null is nought, is silence implying sound ;
What was good shall be good, with for evil so much good more ;
    On the earth the broken arcs ; in the heavens a perfect round."
Abt Vogler.

" 'Tis but to keep the nerves at a strain,
    To dry one's eyes and laugh at a fall,
And, baffled, get up to begin again."
" Life in a Love "—*R. Browning.*

THE Boxer Madness was at an end, but the price was still to pay, a heavy price. For the Empress-Dowager there was the humiliating flight, snatching from his quiet entombment the unfortunate Emperor, and hurrying west to unknown regions amid unaccustomed hardships and undreamed-of publicity. For Peking and other cities there was the occupation by the Allied Forces, with all that implied of humiliation and misery. For the whole nation there has been the long-drawn-out oppression in order to raise the indemnities, and the international complications whose end is not yet.

While the allies were marching on Peking and seeking to restore order in that unhappy city, it fell naturally to the Russians to re-conquer their railway area and drive back all opposing forces in Manchuria. Taken unawares by the outbreak, it was some time before they were able to do this. The first outrages were on 30 June. In August the Russians began slowly but steadily to move northwards, meeting with vigorous opposition from the

Lieutenant-General and his troops, very differently trained men from most of those who met the Japanese six years before. At the same time another Russian force was moving down from the north.

The missionaries were eager to get as early as possible into touch with the Christians, and learn how they fared, and in September Dr. A. Macdonald Westwater, of Liaoyang, accompanied the Russian army on its forward march, as a Red Cross surgeon. Knowing the country and people well, and having some previous acquaintance with the Russians, he was able to be of great use as an intermediary. When the army was encamped south of Liaoyang, he went forward into that city to represent to its authorities the hopelessness and suicidal folly of resistance, and persuaded them to open the gates and let the Russians enter quietly. Thus the city was saved.

Moukden was unfortunately occupied by those same soldiers whose passions had been roused by helping the Boxers to kill and loot. Many of them had at the command of their officers turned their weapons on their quondam allies and looted and killed them in their turn; others had returned angry and rebellious after being defeated by the Russians. There was open conflict between the Governor-General and the Lieutenant-General, who was very indignant at the massacre of his friends the Boxers. Fearing for his life, Tseng Chi fled on 29 September, followed by most of the officials, when the Russians were within a few miles of the city.

The consequences to Moukden were dire. The soldiers threw off all restraint, and all that night and all next day they pillaged and terrorized the defenceless merchants and people. The most prosperous banks and shops were sacked completely, valuable silks and furs being strewn on the streets and trampled in the dust. Thousands of pounds' worth of goods were thus lost. On the second evening they began to set fire to the shops they had looted; then hearing that the Russians were at the south gate, they fled precipitately by the north gates, leaving the most busy and prosperous streets of the city in flames, which were rapidly spreading. An advance party of three hundred Cossacks rode up to the south gate to reconnoitre, and finding it undefended, they entered and took possession of Moukden, their first work being to help to control and extinguish the fires. Had their arrival been delayed until morning, the soldiers would have continued their ruthless destruction, and half Moukden might have been burned.

Next day, 1 October, the main body of Russians entered, and with them Dr. Westwater. The burned streets were still smouldering, and everywhere were ruined houses and shops. The people, in dread of this new danger which had come upon them, hastened to hang out flags with Chinese inscriptions such as " Yield to the Russians," " Submissive People," " I am a Christian " (this being, of course, untrue). The Russian Commander was General Saboitisch, whose acquaintance I had made when he visited Moukden the previous year. He took up his abode at first in the Imperial Palace, unused for centuries, and set himself to restore order. Some days later the Russian armies from the north joined forces with those from the south, and through Manchuria there ran a line of Russian rule from Siberia to the sea.

The news soon spread, and Christians began to come out of hiding and venture back to the city. On Sunday, 7 October, fourteen weeks after the burning, a congregation of some hundred men gathered in the ruins of the church. A portion of the gable wall was still standing, and on it could be read the charred imprint of a part of the Beatitudes which once hung there. The words stood out distinctly, " Blessed are they that mourn." Many of the men were gaunt and haggard, some were starving, all were poor. They had neither Bibles nor hymn-books, but their hearts were full as they gathered round Pastor Liu, with his shaven priestly head, and prayed together, and sang together, and listened while he spoke to them in broken accents on this same old spot where they were wont to gather in peace to worship God.

Having seen my family sail for home in September, I returned to Newchwang and at once attempted to get up-country, but this was not easy. The principal towns on the main route all the way north were occupied by the Russians, but everywhere else the disorder was complete. Many of the Boxers and defeated soldiers had become brigands. Those well-to-do farmers who had not been ruined during the fighting were now mercilessly blackmailed, and none but the poorest could travel without a strong escort. At last three of us succeeded in getting passes by rail for Liaoyang, and from there after some delay we accompanied a Russian convoy by road to Moukden, the military railway being not yet rebuilt. The whole countryside was a scene of desolation; miles of millet-fields were uncut, trampled, and spoiled; the villages were in ruins, the houses either burned or gutted and wrecked; few Chinamen and no women were to be seen.

On the morning of 9 November, a bleak, chilly day, we entered Moukden, and drove through the ruined main streets. No attempt had been made to rebuild the burned buildings, there was little cart traffic, and few people were moving about. All the inns were closed, so we went into the least dilapidated empty one we could find, where one solitary old man was in charge. It had been sacked, first by Chinese soldiers, then by Russians, and was quite bare, but our servants soon lit a fire, and prepared food.

When we went over to the Small River bank, the scene that met our view made our hearts sink. Of hospitals and houses nothing remained but heaps of debris, with here and there a broken wall, a protruding gable. Even the trees and plants were gone, torn up by the roots or cut down. As we stood there with the wind whistling through the grey desolation, it seemed as if our life-work lay in ruins around us. The ruined walls were a symbol of the ruined Church, its apostasy, its falsehood, and of our ruined friendship with the Chinese people who after all these years had cast us out. We returned to our cold, cheerless inn, after seeing the remains of the church building also. Then, one after another, Christians slipped in to visit us, and all that evening and day after day our hearts were torn by their tales of suffering, till gradually there revived within us the consciousness that the Church was *not* ruined.

One old man of seventy came into our room and I did not recognize him. He was a colporteur, and had been noted for his flowing white beard, but this had been almost entirely torn out. Again and again he had been bound and beaten, and once he was hung up to a tree by his arms till he lost consciousness. He was taken to a temple where were two hundred Boxers, and saw dripping from their swords the fresh blood of some Roman Catholics who had just been beheaded.

"Do you follow the foreigner?" he was asked.

"No, I follow Jesus."

"Will you give up the false religion, and follow Buddha?"

"I worship the true Buddha. I believe in the One True God."

The sword was placed on his neck and he thought the end had come, but one interceded for him because of his age, so they beat him instead. Next day, to his surprise, he was liberated, after having his forehead well washed to remove the Cross which was supposed to be marked on every Christian.

"You cannot wash the Cross from my heart," he told them.

Tales like this, and of those who had died the martyr's death, made us realize that the Church's faith was greater than her apostasy, her truth more real than her falsehood. Even those who denied their Master with their lips were owning Him passionately in their hearts, and now that the iron hand of terror relaxed its grip, like a needle to the Pole they returned to their allegiance.

One of our preachers, a student for the ministry, told me how he had escaped and hid in the fields for several weeks till he heard that his mother was dying. Then he returned to his village, and while arranging her funeral he was taken. As he refused to recant, heavy chains were put on him and he was thrown into prison to await execution. He heard the soldiers discussing which one would cut off his head; they showed him the knife and sharpened it before him, then he was brought out to die.

"If they had only killed me then," he said bitterly, "I should have been all right."

But someone spoke for him, and instead of killing they beat and kicked him and put him into a filthy hole. The heat was suffocating, the vermin torturing, the chains on his ankles so tight that his feet swelled. For days he lay there and could neither sleep nor eat, then he was again led out for execution, and he longed to die. Some friends came and tried to buy his life, but the Boxers said they wanted his blood to consecrate a new flag. At last, after several days' delay, he was taken to a temple, more dead than alive. When he told me the story, he broke down here.

"Ah, doctor!" he said with tears, "it was there I denied my Lord."

Another told me how he hid in the fields with his wife and family till one child after another died of exposure and hardship. Then they heard they could buy exemption certificates.

"We knew it was wrong," he said, "but it was to save the lives of our children who were left." For among the many families wandering outcast that summer there was hardly one which did not lose a child.

We heard many expressions of thankfulness too. Over and over again was it said that the tall millet saved their lives. And the weather was too warm for sleeping out of doors to matter.

"We know now what that means," said one. "*Pray that your flight be not in the winter.* Had it been then, not one could have lived."

The chaos in Moukden was distressing. A large proportion of the respectable inhabitants had left, and the city was filled with the worst and lowest in Manchuria. The General commended himself to all by his justice and kindness; but the Russians could not, of course, discriminate as to who were trustworthy. The best class kept away from them; their interpreters were degenerate Chinese who cared only for their own gain, and many of those whom they employed even as policemen were ex-Boxers and deserted soldiers. Plundering and robbing went on nightly even inside the walls. Christian persecution continued, though not openly; and offensive things against foreigners, especially Russians, were continually written on the walls.

No direct mission work was possible, but we did what we could to cheer and advise the Christians, and to relieve their most pressing needs. It had been impossible to bring much money with us, but the head of the Merchant Guild advanced some. They were in terrible destitution, the tale of semi-starvation being legible in their faces. Their worldly goods were gone, many were living on the charity of relatives, trade was at a standstill, work not to be had. Some fortunes were indeed made that winter, but there was generally not much to be said for those who made them. Before the cold weather began, an unused theatre was rented for use as a church, and here on Sundays there gathered about two hundred men, and sometimes three or four women in men's clothes, for it was not safe for a woman to be seen in the street. Few Bibles and hymn-books were among them, and those few were tattered and stained, having been buried in the earth. Not a new one could be had in all Manchuria except in Newchwang.

Of our old possessions in hospital and houses we found few traces. Among the ruins we could recognize broken bits of crockery and ornaments, and an English book was handed me which a Russian soldier had found in one of the yamen buildings. It was an old copy of Hamerton's "Intellectual Life," valuable to me because it was presented by the author to an old aunt of mine in the Highlands. Strange that this shabby old volume should be preserved, when so much else perished! Our anatomical model was found in a dilapidated condition in one of the yamens, and I was informed that the articulated skeleton belonging to the hospital, after being paraded through the streets, had been deposited in a temple outside the city. I found the temple gate closed, and for a time knocked in vain. The priests were afraid of the soldiery, and pretended there was no one to hear. I shouted loudly, mentioning my name, and assuring them I would do them no harm, and at last the gate was opened. The priest professed to know nothing at all of the skeleton, but I insisted that it was there, and that if necessary the temple must be searched. Then he gave in, and ordered it to be brought.

"It's not my fault he is injured," he said, "that was done before he was brought to me. I have treated him well. I got a coffin for him, and have offered him food regularly."

A rough coffin was carried in, and there lay our teaching materials, badly broken, with parts missing, and in the coffin were also bowls with various kinds of food.

It was useless to remain long in Moukden, as hospital work was impossible, and there was little we could do; so after a few weeks we went back to Newchwang.

In January I returned for another visit, before going

home on furlough. The railway was now rebuilt, but travelling was still very difficult, as there were no regular trains. We obtained passes and started from Newchwang one afternoon, but about midnight we reached a junction and were suddenly informed that the train was now going south to Dalny. We and our baggage were hastily ejected on the snow, and we saw the lights of our comparatively comfortable quarters disappear in the distance. The station was not rebuilt, nor was anything visible in the dense, blinding snow. Knowing there must be Russians somewhere, we stumbled forward along the line, shouting as we went, till we saw a man with a lantern.

"Angliské!" he exclaimed in an excited tone, "Newcastle! Angliské! Newcastle!" and he led us away to a siding where stood a train without an engine. Out of the cold we gratefully climbed into one of the trucks, where was a stove. This he helped us to light, and then went off smiling in friendly fashion and reiterating with satisfaction, "Newcastle!" evidently the one word he remembered from some long-past visit to England. Thankfully we lay down to sleep. About daylight we became conscious that our truck had begun to move. Anxiously we peered forth to see which way it was going. It was *north*, so we settled down again and replenished our stove, and ultimately we reached Moukden. The railway now passed within a couple of miles of the city, the station being to the west. Here it remains to this day, the present Japanese station and hotel being close to the old Russian site.

Throughout the country, except along the railway line, there was still anarchy, brigands blackmailing and pillaging on all hands. There were constant rumours of expected risings, and it was said that the Lieutenant-General was gathering a large army in the north. The city itself we found more peaceful than before, and a few shops were open. The Governor-General had quietly returned to Moukden, and was living in a private house, where I had an interview with him. He received me in his official robes with much ceremony, most politely thanked me for all the hospital had done for his people and soldiers, and expressed regret for its unfortunate destruction. I reminded him that these very soldiers of his had a large share in the looting and burning. His face fell and he assured me that he had done his best to prevent it, but the Boxers were beyond his control.

"They said I was a Roman Catholic, and wanted to kill me," he exclaimed indignantly. He blamed the Lieutenant-General for everything, and said that when he returned to office he would protect the Christians. Some of my old official friends had suffered severely because of their association with the foreigner. The one who had warned us to leave lost everything and had to flee for his life. Now, however, he has received an appointment as magistrate of a city. At the present day he holds an important office in Moukden, under the Republic.

The political outlook at this time was most uncertain, and the missionary outlook no less so. The Russians were in possession of the principal cities, and in force all along the railway. Chinese officials held office in most places, and, it was said, would soon be reinstated in Moukden, but they were more or less under Russian control. The general fear was that all Manchuria would gradually come under Russia, for China was powerless to resist. It was impossible to expect that this would not affect mission work. The Russians had all along been most kind and helpful to us, and personally they were our very good friends. They would facilitate in any way they could the gathering together, relieving, and organizing of our Christians; but, knowing the official standpoint, we could not but fear it would necessarily be a very different matter when we and the Chinese Christians began once more to evangelize.

These gloomy forebodings, however, were not realized.

PAYING THE PRICE

Very gradually things returned to their former conditions. The Governor-General resumed his position and bit by bit regained his old power. Brigands betook themselves to peaceful avocations or re-enlisted; trade revived; a good harvest in 1901 worked wonders. Missionaries returned to their stations, living in temporary quarters, and helping to reorganize the rent and broken Church. Its membership was much reduced. Only about three hundred were definitely reported as killed, but hundreds more had disappeared. Of these many no doubt were also killed, others died, and many fled to other provinces. Of those who recanted, a number decisively abandoned Christianity, these being mostly new members who had come in on the wave during the year or two preceding the outbreak ; the greater majority still counted themselves Christians, though temporarily suspended from full membership. The former general friendliness to Christianity had quite passed away. Instead there were aloofness, avoidance, and fear.

"Who would want to have anything to do with a religion whose people suffered like that ? " was frankly said ; and resentment was harboured against foreigners and all who associated with them, for having caused the miseries of the Boxer summer, and also the Russian occupation. The *Tsai-li-ti* continued to be numerous and strongly anti-foreign and anti-Christian.

It was long before country work was possible for foreigners, partly because it was really unsafe, partly because the Russians considered it so, and refused to allow foreigners to travel. The Christians themselves were thus compelled to do much of their own reconstruction, and this materially increased their self-reliance and self-government. It is always difficult to engineer the transformation from dependence to self-support and independence. Looking back, we can see how largely this was wrought among us by events and influences over which we had no control. In the absence of any visit from a foreign pastor, and with hostile, suspicious, or contemptuous neighbours, the Christians in many a district drew together and ceased to depend on any earthly help outside their own circle for spiritual or temporal guidance. They put into practice the methods of Church government they had learned, and when at last the missionary could come among them, they had greatly advanced in self-dependence.

Another circumstance had a powerful influence, partly for good, partly for evil, on the development of the Christian Church. The Government decided to compensate Christians for their losses, to the extent of one-third of the total amount. This inevitably caused trouble, jealousies, and heart-burnings, and introduced into the midst of the Church, whose dross had been purged by fire, a new element which in many instances was most disastrous. To their credit be it said that a good many Christians devoted to the Church a large part of their indemnity money. The payment had been long delayed, they had already made themselves homes again, and though still poor were no longer in such urgent need. These subscriptions were chiefly used by them for the erection of chapels and schools, and in this way many a congregation started on its career of self-support.

The work of the next few years was very different from those preceding 1900. The condition of things was so uncertain that no one ever knew when war might break out between Russia and Japan. Men's minds were unsettled, so that new " inquirers " were few. There was much to do in consolidating the Church, teaching and training her members, gathering back those who had left. Those baptized, however, were worth having. They had gone through the persecution and come out of it Christians still, or else, in spite of contumely, they were drawn to this strange teaching for which some would even dare to die.

Education too received fresh attention. The Christians

were eager to have as many elementary schools as possible for both boys and girls, and Middle Schools were opened in several centres. An Arts College was started for our older boys, to train them for afterwards becoming more efficient pastors, evangelists, medical assistants, or school teachers, and the Theological Hall was reopened.

By the end of 1903 the work was once more in full prosperity, being only hindered by the uncertainties of the political situation and the fear of war. Hospitals had been early reopened in temporary premises. The Moukden Women's Hospital was rebuilt in 1903, and it was planned to build the Men's Hospital in 1904, when once more the war-clouds burst over us.

XVIII

WAR AGAIN, 1904

"My life must be lived out in foam and roar."
Sordello.

RUSSIA had long regarded Manchuria and Korea as part of her destined territory, her not unnatural ambition being to possess a seaboard free from ice. The conquest of Korea and part of Manchuria by Japan in 1894–5 was in her eyes an unpardonable impertinence which could not be tolerated. So Japan had to be content with Formosa, and to stand by and see Russia, within three years of the Chino-Japanese war, appropriate with China's sanction the ice-free harbour and fortress of Port Arthur she had marked as her own, establish a new ice-free seaport at Ta-lien-wan or Dalny, proceed to build a railway across her battlefields, and interfere in the affairs even of Korea.

The Boxer outbreak was a mere temporary set-back, which actually strengthened Russia's position, giving reasonable excuse for many an act of aggression. The unnecessary ferocity of her vengeance at Blagovestchensk and the military occupation cowed all impulse to resistance, though rousing bitter enmity. Manchuria was in the estimation of the outer world lost to China, in spite of the Treaty of 1902, whereby all but the railway zone was to be evacuated. A strongly guarded Russian military railway ran through the heart of the three provinces; a Russian Commissioner with a considerable military guard resided in each capital, in addition to consuls, and even the Governor-General in Moukden could do little with consulting this Commissioner. Harbin, that mushroom city with its thirty thousand Russian civilians and countless Chinese, had sprung up where in 1898 were but a few huts. Hundreds of Chinese had learned to speak a sort of semi-Russian jargon, and the lowest classes of the two nations fraternized with easy freedom.

Jealous Japan was watching closely all that went on, and steadily and silently preparing for a war on which she knew depended her very existence. If she allowed Russia to close her grasp on Manchuria, it meant that Korea would go too. And with Manchuria and Korea in the grip of the Bear, what chance would remain for Japan of that predominance on which she had set her heart, or even of independence and development.? When it became evident that the Evacuation was a mere name, she saw that the sooner the war came the better for her, before Russia began to take her seriously. She had spies everywhere, posing as Chinese, many of them in Russian employ; she knew all the Russian arrangements, and it was for her to fix the date for the opening of hostilities.

There were in Moukden a considerable number of Russians, and all, military and civilians alike, looked forward to the war with easy contempt.

"War?" said one loftily. "There will be no war worth mentioning. Peace will be signed in Tokyo within three weeks of the first shot."

"It is suicidal folly," said another, "for Japan to defy us, for now we shall wipe her name off the map." The sudden surprise attack by the Japanese at Port Arthur on the night of 8 February, 1904, and the torpedoing of warships while many of their officers were feasting and dancing on shore, was a severe shock to Russian complacency; but it was easy to make excuses for this "unfortunate accident," and complete confidence was speedily restored. To the last, many officers were always sure that Russia was about to gain a great victory.

It is not necessary to attempt to give any connected account of a war which is fresh in men's minds, and on which so many books have been written. Looking back, we wonder that its outcome should have been a surprise to anyone. Japan had made great advance since 1895, and profited by her mistakes and successes in the war with China. Her army worked with the precision of a well-oiled machine; there was provision for every detail and every individual, preparedness for every known contingency. More important still, there was universal personal enthusiasm for the war: nation and individual alike were determined to conquer or die; and they did not underestimate their foe.

The Russians, on the other hand, relied on their ancient reputation for valour, and on what they considered the contemptible size of their enemy. It was evident to the most casual observer in Manchuria that military preparations were carried out with easy carelessness and *laissez-faire*, that corruption and *graft* were rampant, that there were jealousy and lack of cohesion among the Generals and various branches of the service, that many officers cared more for their amusements than for serving their country, and that the rank and file of the men felt either indifference or dislike to the war. A Russian card was one day brought to me, and I was told that a foreigner urgently wanted to see me. He spoke English well, and after asking for medicine for some trifling ailment, he poured out his story. He was a Russian Jew who had gone to London years ago, and was in business near Blackfriars Bridge. He had returned to Russia to visit his old parents, and had been seized and compelled to serve in this war. He was comfortably dressed and evidently had some money, though but a common soldier.

"I am a Jew," he said bitterly, "so there can be no

reward nor promotion for me. I shall be sent to the front to die like a dog." Then turning passionately to me he exclaimed: "I don't want to kill these Japs! Will you save me? Get me a post as servant *any* where! I want to live, and get back to Blackfriars Bridge!"

It was natural, almost inevitable, that victory should be with the alert, the well-prepared, the keenly loyal; but at the beginning of the war few outside Manchuria knew the actual conditions, or were prepared to see Russia defeated.

For the third time within ten years it was now decided that all the ladies and children should leave Moukden. It had been officially stated that the Chinese Railway connecting Manchuria with Tientsin and Peking would shortly cease to run, so that our connection with the outer world would be cut. For this reason their departure was hastened, but after all the railway continued open throughout the war. Unfortunately I had to go to Tientsin later owing to illness in my family, and for a considerable time the way was blocked against my return, as the Russians allowed no foreigners to approach nearer to Moukden than Hsin-min-tun, the rail-end of the Chinese line.

During this time the Russian strategy aimed at delaying the advance of the Japanese until an army was ready with which to crush them. But the Japanese would not be delayed. They crossed the Yalu, they crippled the Russian fleet, they invested Port Arthur, and three armies moved steadily forward by three routes towards Liaoyang, beating down all opposition before them. By August they had retaken all their old conquests of the Chino-Japanese war, except Port Arthur. South of Liaoyang the Russians prepared to make a stand, and at last towards the end of August we heard that a great battle was taking place there. As this might be expected to cause a relaxation of the strictness of guard over the road entering Moukden from the west, another missionary and I decided to start at once for Hsin-min-tun, and attempt to get through the Russian lines.

At the beginning of the war I had received an official Russian pass for myself and family to leave Moukden. This I had used on my return, and though arrested by the way I was quickly released. When I left Moukden the second time I expected no trouble, my face being in the direction the pass indicated. Nevertheless I was stopped four times, a drunken Cossack keeping me under guard all one night in an inn. These Cossacks cannot read, but an official Russian document with an official seal and signature impresses them. Now I was to use this pass for the fourth time, and even this was not the last; it also served to bring my wife and family back through the lines the following February.

The Russian defeat at Liaoyang after eleven days' desperate fighting had, as we anticipated, thrown into confusion the guarding of the approaches. We left Hsin-min-tun without any challenge, and after covering seven or eight of the forty miles to Moukden came to the broad Liao River, which was considered the boundary of the war zone. As our ferry boat touched the eastern bank, some Russian soldiers came forward. The Chinese passengers were allowed to go their way, but we were arrested and taken to the camp, where for three and a half hours we were kept waiting. Our passports were taken away, and we much feared that if they were read we should be sent straight back. At last an officer came in, looked at us, glanced carelessly at our papers which he held, signed them, and we were free. To our Chinese inn that night, when we had just finished supper, a number of Cossacks came. They seemed to be starving, and gulped down the remains of our viands with great relish. Next day we passed some thousands of worn-out soldiers retreating from the Liaoyang battle, but we were not interfered with, and arrived safely home on the afternoon of 9 September, 1904.

Our life in Moukden that winter was a strange one. Around us raged a war, in which the Chinese with whom we identified ourselves were primarily little concerned. It was fought out on Chinese soil, and Chinese peasants suffered and died without suggestion of compensation, though it was not their quarrel. They wanted neither Russia nor Japan to overshadow them, the shadow of the Dragon Throne was preferred by all. They took no side in the struggle, though many of the people, groaning under Russian military rule, longed for the advent of the Japanese, in the mistaken belief that it would bring back freedom. They and we were neutral, yet we viewed from the inner circle the bloody strife.

Around us were tens of thousands of Russians who talked freely of all that happened. Their easy optimism was most striking, and their gaiety in the face of defeat and disaster. Most officers whom we met were very friendly, though we could not but surmise that there were many quite the reverse. The alliance between Britain and Japan made them suspicious, and the common soldiers, if they knew we were "Angliské," scowled at us openly. One officer told me frankly that the successes and generalship of the Japanese were easily explained, as they had a large number of British officers among them. This was generally believed throughout the army.

In vain the Russians had made their stand before Liaoyang, and when we arrived in Moukden it was to a panic-stricken city. During the summer, merchants of all kinds and nationalities, many of the lowest and most unprincipled type, had congregated in the city and battened on the needs of the army. Now hurried flight was the aim of all these, for the Japanese entrance was not to be opposed. Soon, however, it became clear that they were not going to advance, and the Russians took up a position midway between Moukden and Liaoyang, across and along a stream called the *Sha-ho*. Hospitals, bank, post-office, and other departments which had fled returned quietly. Reinforcements from Europe poured down steadily from the north. Kuropatkin completed the reorganization of his army, and prepared to take the offensive at last and to inflict a crushing defeat on his enemy before winter set in.

At the beginning of October a proclamation was issued congratulating the troops on their successful retreats, announcing that they were now strong enough to advance and "impose our will on the enemy," and urging them to "uphold the honour of Russia." The general opinion among war correspondents and military attachés, as well as among the Russians, seemed to be that there was good reason to expect a turn of the tide and a Russian victory.

On 7 October the *Battle of the Sha-ho* commenced, and we began to hear heavy firing, a sound which continued in our ears for five months. It was impossible to know what was happening from day to day. One evening a Russian officer told me that all was going well and they were successful; next morning there was an ominous silence, and we learned from the Chinese that the Russians were retreating. Towards midnight on the 17th we stood on our balcony and looked out on pitch-blackness in which a thunderstorm was raging. Between the peals we could hear distinctly the incessant rattle of rifles and machine-guns, punctuated with the sound of heavy artillery. This continued without intermission for an hour, then ceased abruptly. We learned afterwards that the Russians had made a night attack on an outlying hill occupied by the Japanese. After losing 1800 men they had wiped out the Japanese garrison, taken the hill, and captured fourteen guns which we saw later paraded through the city. The hill was thenceforward known as *Potiloff Hill*, from the name of the captor.

Soon after this it was evident to all that the great Russian attack, the first occasion on which they had taken the initiative, had failed. The *Battle of the Sha-ho* had been fought and lost, with terrible slaughter on both sides. The scenes in Moukden after the Battle of Liaoyang were now re-enacted, the hurried flight, the general stampede. But again the Japanese were unable to turn defeat into disaster. They did not press their victory. The panic was arrested. The fugitives returned, and camp-followers slunk back to their old haunts.

The armies settled down for the winter, facing each other on opposite sides of the Sha-ho. Many Russian officers lived in houses in Moukden, others in comfortable railway cars at the station, and some were with their men. For the remaining weeks until the ground was frozen hard, the entire Russian army were at work digging trenches, fortifications, and shelters, until the whole plain north of the Sha-ho was one vast, well-organized underground camp, extending east and west in parallel lines. All the trees in the countryside were felled to use as props, and the timber taken from the neighbouring Chinese houses, so that over that entire populous area the villages were destroyed and the inhabitants driven out.

During the four months between the battles of Sha-ho and Moukden there were constant skirmishes and some serious fights, and the boom of artillery continued at intervals day and night. Military attachés and war correspondents came and went. Some of these lived comfortably in Moukden, picked up what news and tales they could, and sent their dispatches promptly. Others risked their lives at the front, saw the realities of the war, and returned to Moukden to find themselves left behind by their less enterprising brethren in the race to supply what passed for news.

On one occasion a correspondent who usually stayed in the city decided to go out with a Russian company about to operate in a mountain district. With infinite labour some guns were dragged up a hill, from which some Japanese were seen not far off squatting on the ground smoking cigarettes. The Russians opened fire, but after a round or two found that by some mistake their ammunition had failed to arrive. While they were discussing the situation, a Japanese shell went over their heads, then a second fell close in front, and no one awaited a third. Down the hill they all tore, the correspondent with the rest. Suddenly he found that he was being pursued by two Cossacks. They attacked and knocked him down, and he realized with horror that they took him for a Jap, for he was dark and had closely cropped hair. In vain he protested. One of them lifted his rifle with its fixed bayonet, solemnly crossed himself, and was about to kill him when a Russian officer came up. To him the correspondent shouted, and in a few minutes his identity was established.

There was a strange friendliness between the soldiers on opposite banks of the Sha-ho. At stated times Russians and Japanese drew water from the same wells and holes in the river ice, and exchanged greetings and cigarettes; though the rest of the day they would " snipe " each other if given the opportunity. Thousands of Japanese picture-postcards were scattered through the Russian army, representing the happy time enjoyed in Japan by those Russians who were fortunate enough to be taken prisoner. No doubt these alluring pictures had their effect. Gradually with the postcards were circulated leaflets in Russian, which those who could read were glad to while away the weary hours in the trenches by explaining to those who could not. The Russian soldier at the front receives but little news from home; but in this way were circulated through the army stories which would otherwise have remained unknown, of the constant troubles and incipient rebellion in Russia over the calling out of fresh troops, of the naval mutiny at Sebastopol, of the unpopularity of the war, and finally the terrible tale of the shooting down of the petitioners before the Winter Palace in January, 1905. We may be sure these stories did not lose in the telling.

The most serious interruption to this friendly intercourse was in the last week of January. The Japanese had taken Port Arthur, the Winter Palace tragedy was filling the thoughts of all Russia, and it seemed a political necessity to win a battle just at this moment, though it was the coldest month of a specially cold winter. So the Russians to the south and south-west of Moukden left their cosy dug-outs, and drove back the Japanese outer line. For five days there was desperate carnage, and the large proportion of deaths among the casualties tells what terrible havoc the cold wrought. But the necessary victory was not won, and with thinned ranks the armies settled down again, apparently as before. Only it was noticed that there was less hopefulness among the Russians, they were beginning to regard the war as an unlucky one, foredoomed to failure.

Just as the year closed I had an interesting experience. On 29 December an urgent summons came for me to go to the medical aid of one of our missionaries in Kaiyuan, seventy miles up the line. At first the difficulty of getting there seemed insurmountable. None but troop trains were running, and no passes were given. At last, with the help of friends, I obtained a pass to travel on the Imperial Red Cross train, which was to go north with wounded that night. The train was the one presented by the Dowager-Empress, and was a revelation of the possibilities of comfort and luxury. I was given a large state-room, and dined and slept in royal style. The doctors in charge received me with great courtesy and kindness, showing me over the whole train with its perfect medical equipment. Next day we reached Kaiyuan; and, having done my work there, I returned to the station, some miles from the town, on the morning of the 31st. So far things had gone smoothly, but to get back to Moukden was the difficulty.

For twenty-six hours I waited at Kaiyuan station, with a very anxious mind. The railway had been cut by the Japanese once already, and it was expected to happen again any day, so that I might be stranded. The Red Cross hospital at the station was in charge of a Countess, who spoke English perfectly and had spent some time in Edinburgh. Among her staff of nurses were Princesses, Countesses, and other ladies, whose husbands were at the front. She and they were most kind, inviting me into the warmth and shelter of their hospital. I dined with them, and the Countess arranged that I should occupy a vacant doctor's room, with two Cossacks to attend me. One of them was to remain awake and call me when a train came. I slept little, but lay listening to the bursts of singing from the soldiers, full ringing unison, breaking now and again into rich harmony. Several times I was roused by the arrival of a train, and went out into the biting cold, but it was going the wrong direction, or it was already full and I was not allowed on it.

At last, about midday, I succeeded in getting away. The train was a marked contrast to the last I was in, consisting of filthy fourth-class carriages crowded to overflowing with soldiers for the front. It was cold, but the windows being hermetically sealed, the air was close and stifling. All that New Year's Day of 1905 I sat there crushed in a corner among men to whom I could not talk, but I was thankful to be there and to reach Moukden station by midnight. After considerable difficulty at the gates in getting past the Russian guard, I arrived home in the small hours of the morning.

Towards the end of 1904 some of the ladies returned to Moukden, and in February, 1905 my family came back also. One of our servants went to Hsin-min-tun to meet them, with our much-used pass sewed inside his clothes. From there they started in carts before daylight. The winter roads were hard and smooth, and good speed was possible, if only the Russians did not turn them back. The children were instructed to do their best, by laughing to the soldiers, to put them in a good humour, for Russians are all child-lovers. Several times mounted Cossacks roughly stopped the carts, but the official document which they could not read did its work, and the sight of nothing but a lady, an amah, and some smiling children. Each time the pass was thrown back and the soldiers rode away ; so the party went on without delay, reaching the Small River bank with thankful hearts long before dark, just the day before the great battle began.

XIX

IN THE MIDST OF THE BATTLE OF MOUKDEN

> " A sound
> As of the trailing skirts of Destiny,
> Passing unseen, to some immitigable end
> With her grey henchman, Death."
>
> *W. E. Henley.*

IT was now the middle of February, 1905, and the extreme cold was over. Occasional thaws might be expected, but there were still several weeks before spring would turn the hard roads and plains into heavy deep mud. A Japanese advance was daily looked for, and the Russians were well prepared to stand their ground. But whatever they said we had no doubt as to the issue: sooner or later the Japanese would certainly enter Moukden. We had little apprehension of any serious trouble. The Chinese Government was stable and had things well in hand, and the Japanese would certainly avoid shelling the city. There was some talk of turning our vegetable-pits into bomb-proof shelters, but nothing of the kind was done.

The battle, or rather the series of battles, called the *Battle of Moukden*, began on 19 February, and lasted until 10 March; and during all this time the roar of artillery, distant or near, was so constant that a silence attracted one's attention. It is estimated that about a million soldiers were engaged, perhaps a quarter of whom were killed or wounded. The Russians were constantly reporting victories, and confidently predicting complete success. With a line of battle extending in a curve of

IN THE MIDST OF THE BATTLE 177

over a hundred miles, there was opportunity for many minor victories at the same time as a general defeat.

To our east and south-east there was desperate fighting among the mountains with *Kuroki's* men and others, and General Kuropatkin was beguiled into believing that here was to be the main Japanese attack. South of us the Russians were so strongly entrenched and fortified along the Sha-ho, that it was believed to be impossible for *Nodzu* to drive them back. Here the cannonade was unceasing. Eight miles direct south of us, Potiloff Hill was taken and retaken in all eight times. I visited it afterwards, and the sight was appalling. For a mile round the ground was thick with broken shells, cartridges, and splintered stones. The hill was honeycombed with a network of trenches, underground stables, etc., all opening to the northern or Russian side. Its whole upper part had been blown away by the heavy Port Arthur siege-guns, which had been brought up by Nodzu, the heaviest artillery ever known in field warfare. It was this which broke the impregnable Russian defence in this region. We found traces of it in fragments of eleven-inch shells.

Farther west there was dogged fighting on both sides for possession of the plain where the fruitless battle of January had been fought, and here step by step the Russians were pressed back by *Oku*. At the same time *Nogi*, with another army, popularly supposed to have gone east to help Kuroki in the hills, was really going west behind Oku's men, and then north by Hsin-min-tun to turn Kuropatkin's flank.

In Moukden we quietly went on with our work among the many wounded Chinese and refugees who poured in upon us, and I had not a few patients among attachés, war correspondents, and Russian officers. With great interest we noted day by day the changes in the sounds of firing. We heard the new heavy Japanese artillery which seemed to come into play to the south on the 27th, the Port Arthur siege-guns, and the gradual creeping nearer and nearer of the cannonading where *Oku* was gaining inch by inch to the south-west. Then great fires were seen one night on the horizon, the burning of the Russian stores before falling back. Refugees poured in daily from villages which had been behind the Russian lines, but were now between the armies or in the hands of the Japanese. They told sadly of great Russian stores given to the flames, but one merciful commander gave notice to the Chinese still lingering round their ruined homesteads that he would give them four hours to loot. After that there was little left to burn.

Suddenly there was firing due west, and next day some refugees told us they had been stopped by *Japanese*, not Russians, on the Liao River near Hsin-min-tun. On that same day the Chinese Imperial Post, which had gone via Hsin-min-tun all winter, ceased running. This was our first intimation that the Japanese were in force so far north. Their semicircle was now complete, and this western wing began to curl round eastwards. Authorities say that as late as 6 March there was still a fair chance of success for Russia. A victory was reported with the capture of forty Japanese, and the attachés told us that the Russians were more than holding their own. Hearing Chinese reports, listening to the firing, watching the constant stream of Russian transport wagons heaped with baggage which rumbled away to the north along the road just outside the wall—we had our own thoughts.

One afternoon, as we walked on the plain and listened to the guns, trying to decide which were Japanese and which Russian, we suddenly became conscious that besides the loud booming we were accustomed to, there were distinct sharp reports from smaller guns from the *north-west*. This was *Nogi's* army, fighting its way towards the railway, to cut the Russian communications once for all. After three days of the fiercest fighting of the whole war all along the whole line of battle, on Tuesday, the 7th, the railway was cut to the north, *Nodzu* broke through the defence on the southern front, driving the Russians back on their entrenchments on the Hun River, and at the same time both east and west were hardly pressed. That evening Kuropatkin wired to St. Petersburg : " *I am surrounded.*"

This was hardly true, however. The railway was not yet taken, the breach was repaired, fresh reinforcements were hurried down from the north to hold *Nogi* in check, and in the night Kuropatkin gave secret orders for the orderly retreat on *Tieling* which was to save the larger portion of his army. The position prepared there was forty miles away, so time was needed. In Moukden nothing was heard of the order for evacuation, the Japanese must be held back for another day at all cost.

Next morning, Wednesday, the 8th, there was heavy firing due north of us, shaking the windows, the rush of the shells through the air being plainly heard. The Russians were occupying the North Tomb woods which he just beyond the railway, and here for two days there was sharp fighting. A little nearer, a captive balloon floated and watched. Just outside the wall a few hundred yards from us, a constant stream of cavalry and transport passed north, and we heard that the railway and the roads beside it were crowded night and day. When darkness fell, the sight from our attics was terribly grand. Four miles to the south the great Russian stores of fuel and grain were in flames. Bridges and villages were also burning, and the whole sky was ablaze. Close at hand were the fires of a large cavalry camp. High in the air the shrapnel were bursting into stars, and the roar of artillery was incessant from every direction.

On 9 March one of the worst dust-storms on record enveloped the armies, and fought against the Russians. There was a powerful warm south wind, bearing with it the fine loess dust characteristic of this country, so thickly that sometimes for five minutes at a time we could not from our windows see the brick wall eighteen yards distant. The Russians had this blinding tempest in their faces as they fought, and under its cover the Japanese crossed the Hun River on the rotting ice. One day later the Hun was broken up into great ice-floes, and crossing would have been impossible in face of Russian guns. " Verily Heaven is on the side of Japan ! " remarked the Chinese. The retreat was steady and methodical, and in this the dust-storm aided Russia. Trains ran constantly; every road and track was thronged; constant fighting kept the Japanese back and the way open; the Russian eastern and western wings were withdrawn, and gradually the front was retreating; pom-pom and rifle fire drew nearer us, sounding muffled through the thick dust.

From time to time for the past fortnight we had had serious difficulties with drunken Russian soldiers. They entered our Refuges, terrified the women, and threatened our lives when we expelled them. This culminated on the Tuesday night, when two fully armed artillerymen entered the Women's Hospital, threatening us with loaded revolvers and drawn swords, and were only got rid of after great difficulty. Again on this Thursday morning, the last day of the battle, a soldier tried to get into our private compound, and threatened to kill our watchman for preventing him. These were not mere idle threats. People wounded in this way came daily to the hospitals, and we heard of many killed. Just at that moment the Russian Chief of Police came to see me on purpose to offer us a guard. He promptly arrested the man, and insisted on sending us some Russian soldiers to prevent further trouble. In the evening they arrived, and we provided them with supper and a room for them to sleep in, in relays.

As darkness drew near the wind fell. The firing was close to us on the south and south-east, the rearguard action of the retreating Russians. The end could not be

IN THE MIDST OF THE BATTLE 181

far off. That night at 1 a.m. we were roused by loud shouting and knocking at our gate. A messenger had come to recall our guard in haste, for the order for the immediate evacuation of Moukden had been issued at 11 p.m. For a time the last thunder of the Russian guns was so loud that we could not hear ourselves speak, and the crackle of the pom-poms and the sharp rifle fire were incessant. We found afterwards that they had passed in the darkness, firing as they went, within a quarter of a mile to the east of us. Then for a couple of hours there was comparative quiet and we slept.

At dawn on Friday, the 10th, we were suddenly roused by deafening Japanese artillery fire. They had brought their guns forward and were shelling the retreating Russians, whose rifle fire we could hear in reply. The scream of the shells seemed almost overhead. One fell in the road close to us, but did not explode, several others in or beside the Small River. A shrapnel ball struck an earthen wall near by, and several bullets fell in our compounds, but no one was injured. Some Russians were killed on the Small River bank outside the wall, a couple of hundred yards away. Then the rifle fire ceased, and the battle passed on to the north.

During the forenoon companies of Japanese quietly entered Moukden, but the Russian evacuation was not yet complete. Several thousand had failed to get away in time, and in the afternoon some of these tried to escape by the northern of the two east gates. The Japanese outside opposed them, and there was a short, sharp engagement, some of the Russians sheltered inside the outer city wall, which they loopholed, firing east and south. We were surprised by the sudden patter of rifle bullets on the roof when in the midst of an operation, and looking out we saw our hospital coolies running for shelter with an arm over the head as if to protect it. A dropping rain of bullets continued in our compounds, and wild stories circulated of the many thousand

Russians in hiding in the city. In little more than an hour all was over. Those who had tried to break through the Japanese lines were killed or captured. The rest retired to the compound containing the Russian Church, where they surrendered later.

All that Friday cannonading continued to the north, gradually receding till it died away in a dull booming, and there was silence. The battle of Moukden was over. In the evening the Japanese cut off the retreat of many thousand Russians fifteen miles north of the city.

Throughout the war the sympathies of the Chinese were no doubt on the side of Japan. The Japanese had left a good record behind them ten years before; a Japanese occupation of which they knew nothing was presumably preferable to a Russian occupation whose drawbacks they knew; and finally, they were of kindred race, and this was the first time the East seemed to have a prospect of conquering the West. At the same time the Chinese took no side in the struggle. "It is not our affair," they constantly said. Villagers were coerced into giving information and acting as guides and scouts, but this was equally so on both sides. As far as the missionary body in Manchuria was concerned, absolute neutrality was observed, neither help nor hindrance being afforded to either side, except healing in the Red Cross hospitals.

The minute information possessed by the Japanese regarding the Russians was due to their own spies, not to Chinese. For several years before the war, secret service officers and men had been scattered throughout Manchuria, disguised as Chinese. They let their hair grow, wore queues, spoke Chinese with what passed for a southern accent, and, of course, the type of face is somewhat similar. They took service with Russians, learned their language, and when war began were ready to be of use to their country. The risk does not seem to have been counted. A "Chinese" barber who regularly attended the Russian headquarters staff in Moukden up to the evacuation was a Japanese spy, as were several of their table-boys and valets. They had in this way a thoroughly organized secret service throughout the Russian army, with runners via Hsin-min-tun to the Japanese headquarters.

One day, soon after the battle ended, I was told that a Chinaman wished to see me. From his appearance and accent I took him to be a Cantonese, but he soon undeceived me. This was his story. He was a Japanese spy who had lived in Manchuria for several years and knew the country well. To disarm suspicion he had an office in the city, where he carried on genuine business. He made friends with many Russians, who frequently visited him, and he had close business relations with the army. At the same time he had a staff under him, and sent dispatches regularly to headquarters. During the battle of Moukden he had a financial difference with a Chinese confederate, and had reason to fear he was betrayed. He barred his door securely while making preparations for flight. At midnight there was a noise outside. After some delay some Russian soldiers got in and began to batter the door of his room. He threw open the back window and, with a loaded revolver in each hand, awaited them. When the door was burst in, he fired repeatedly with both weapons simultaneously and saw several Russians fall. Then he jumped out of the window, and, in his own words, "never stopped until he reached Hsin-min-tun."

XX

THE SUFFERINGS OF THE INNOCENT

"Towns without people, ten times took,
　And ten times left and burned at last
And starving dogs that came to look
　For owners when a column passed."
Rudyard Kipling.

THROUGHOUT the war area all these months the distress among the Chinese was acute. Many of the well-to-do had fled with their possessions early in the summer to safer districts, and gradually large numbers of the humbler country folk brought their families into the cities, renting houses or lodging with friends. Still most of the inhabitants of the innumerable villages on the wide level fertile plain south and west of Moukden remained in their homes, hoping against hope that the fighting would not come near them.

When the Russians fell back from Liaoyang in September, many of these villages were occupied by troops, and during the next few weeks crowds of refugees flocked into Moukden in successive waves. On the main street of the south suburb might sometimes be seen a continuous heterogeneous stream, while the townsfolk looked on from the doorways and side-walks. Here were farm carts drawn by all the animals available—mules, horses, donkeys, cows, and laden with grain, millet-stalk, or household gear, women and children huddling among the bundles. There were lines of weary foot-passengers, most of the men bearing their belongings suspended from a pole across the shoulders, while the women carried the babies.

Where were such crowds to be housed ? Many found temporary shelter in temples, many more slept on the streets under the projecting eaves of the houses. House rents in the city ran up to fabulous prices, till the Governor-General issued a proclamation making it illegal to charge more than a definite sum for each room. Many who were Christians looked to their fellow-Christians for help, and for weeks several hundred were sheltered in the church compound and other buildings. Scores of homeless, knowing the benevolent nature of the hospital, gathered round our doors, and before long we opened a Refuge, admitting Christians and others indiscriminately.

Systematic aid was evidently necessary, for the misery must increase as winter approached and with each successive battle. This was not war on a small scale, like the Chino-Japanese war of ten years before, nor the march of a column through a limited area like the Russian conquest after the Boxer time. The whole breadth of the country from the inaccessible mountains to the Liao River was occupied by the armies, and as the fighting moved northwards the size of those armies grew ever greater.

In our extremity the Shanghai Red Cross and Refugee Aid Society came to our help, undertaking to supply us with funds and surgical requisites, and later on there was assistance from Tientsin and other places also. The Rev. James Webster was the Secretary in Newchwang, making known our needs, forwarding our supplies, and acting as a very necessary intermediary with the outside world. The Rev. James W. Inglis and I were asked to administer the funds and superintend the relief work in Moukden. At the same time the Governor-General, *Tseng Chi*, still the same as at the Boxer time, was arranging for similar Refugee aid from Government funds, and was anxious to co-operate with us. We had several interviews with him about it, and all through the winter we worked harmoniously, his representatives meeting with us in committee. One Refuge after another was opened for temporary or permanent relief. Sometimes, after a few days with us, a family would find a friend's house to go to. Frequently when the women and children had settled down in a Refuge, their men would return home to save what they could from the wreck, so that male inmates were always in a minority.

Before long we were faced with the impossibility of maintaining a supply of grain, as all carts were commandeered by the Russians; and indeed the city was threatened with famine. In this emergency the Chinese Government stepped in and made arrangements with the Russians to issue special permits for carts from the north with grain and fuel, and the danger was averted. The price of grain, however, remained at several times what was usual, and millet-stalk was six times its normal price. All food stuffs were dear in proportion, and coal which we used in our houses was £5 a ton.

When the battle of the Sha-ho began in October, the friendly attitude of the Russians to the villagers altered. They seem to have become soured, and charged the Chinese with betraying them to the enemy. Village after village was cleared of its inhabitants, who had to escape in haste for their lives, taking nothing with them. After the battle came the systematic destruction of villages to provide quarters for the Russian army. The posts and roof-timbers were all used as props for the underground shelters, so that nothing remained of hundreds of prosperous villages but fallen walls, isolated gables, and solitary chimneys. The inhabitants reached Moukden absolutely destitute, having lost their worldly all, and our numbers grew rapidly, sometimes as many as a thousand being admitted to our Refuges in one day.

During the first three months of 1905 we were supporting over ten thousand people, and the Government over thirty-eight thousand. It is estimated that there were

REFUGEES FROM VILLAGES RUINED BY WAR
"Where were such crowds to be housed?"

from first to last about ninety thousand refugees in Moukden, besides the thousands who fled to Hsin-min-tun and other places.

The housing of these crowds was no easy problem, but as one night without shelter in winter would have meant death to many, the most makeshift accommodation was thankfully accepted. We commandeered one or two large empty compounds whose owners had fled, paying rent if demanded. Our ruined hospital compound accommodated about seven hundred. Before the frost, the refugees themselves dug out dwellings about two feet below ground-level, making walls of the earth and old bricks from the ruins, without any mortar. A few posts were enough to support the roofing of millet-stalk and mud, with a light outer coating of lime. Inside, long *kangs* were built of the broken bricks, matting was spread, and they were ready for occupation.

One of the largest and best-known temples in Moukden opened its doors free of charge to our refugees. Here semi-dug-outs similar to those just described occupied the compound, and outhouses and temple tower sheltered some score. The long corridor called "Buddha's Walk," by which the invisible Buddha is supposed to transfer himself from one of his images to another, was also used for human habitation. A couple of stoves, strangely incongruous with the traditions of the place, raised the temperature a little above freezing-point. The main temple buildings were left untouched, and worshippers continued to visit them, and priests to burn incense as usual. The priests made not the slightest objection to the holding of a Christian service in their temple every evening, in fact it was an interesting variety in their life. The Guild-house of the Che-kiang provincials was also lent to us, and we occupied two theatres, a bank, and several other buildings.

In all these primitive or adapted dwellings the refugees lived contentedly, in spite of conditions and surroundings which we would consider misery. They cooked their own food and did all their own work; they had abundance to talk about and plenty of neighbours to talk to; they had food and shelter, and winter clothing and bedding were supplied to those who lacked them. The women did the necessary sewing; there was room in the compounds for the children to play in the sunshine, and every evening the monotony of their lives was broken by a Christian service with lively hymn-singing, which they could attend or not as they pleased. Naturally the oversight of these many refugees meant a great deal of hard work.

It can well be understood that the sanitary condition of Moukden at this time was not good. Epidemics were frequent. In our Refuges with their crowds of children, measles, chicken-pox, and scarlet fever were constantly present, and there was an epidemic of smallpox which carried away a number of little ones. Isolation was impossible except for typhus fever, for which we had a special compound. Fortunately there was no epidemic of enteric fever, though there were all the conditions likely to bring it about.

Throughout the war the general hospital work was very heavy. During my absence in summer it had been carried on in the women's hospital buildings by my assistants, and in autumn we arranged for four separate hospitals. The men, being far the most numerous, continued to occupy the new spacious women's hospital, which had been rebuilt the summer before the war, and here both men and women out-patients were seen. For the women in-patients we used an old temple almost next door to our hospital ruins, the San Yi Miao, Temple of the Three Righteous Ones. The priest was an opium wreck, glad to make a little money by renting it to us. The idols were screened off by matting, and the patients lay at their feet. There were also two temporary fever hospitals. Fortunately I had at this time a medical colleague, Dr. W. A.

DR. CHRISTIE   RED CROSS WORK, 1905   DR. WANG

DR. HSÜ   The sufferings of the Innocent.

THE SUFFERINGS OF THE INNOCENT

Young, and the ladies were able to return in December.

Not only were there the ordinary daily patients, and the many sick among our own and the Government refugees, but we had hundreds of wounded from the neighbourhood of the fighting, chiefly men. Many poor fellows, and some women too, lingered about their homes too long, and were shot among the Russians, or caught between the opposing fires. We heard of a hundred Chinese lying wounded in a village ten miles away, after the Sha-ho battle, and made fruitless efforts to send a Red Cross party to their help through the Russian lines. Just at that time a Russian Baron called, and on hearing our difficulties expressed much sympathy.

"If you can find a Chinese carter," he said, "who is willing to go, I will undertake to get him through and to give him a pass to bring back the wounded."

Chinese carters were most reluctant to be hired by Russians, as they did not know to what dangers they might be exposed; but we were well known and easily got a man who promised to do his best. We sent a hospital man with him, and handed him over to our friend the Baron, who was leaving Moukden at the same time. Then we patiently waited for the wounded to arrive. Some days later the carter returned in great indignation. The Baron and his friends had used the cart to convey their own baggage; he had not been near the village, nor was he allowed to look for wounded. Such heartless deceit, however, is far from characteristic of most of the Russians whom we met.

The times between the battles came to be almost as much dreaded by the Chinese as the fighting itself. In the early days of the war, the Russian common soldier and the Chinese peasant were very good friends, but the blood-lust of battle changes all things, and deeds were done too terrible to repeat. People were killed because they failed to understand what Russians meant, or because unwilling to give up their animals. A man was made to lead some Cossacks to a village, and because he could not run fast enough they bayoneted him. A party of eighteen farmers and labourers were accused of being brigands, tied with ropes to some Cossacks' horses, and made to run the forty miles to Moukden. Two fell exhausted and were killed on the spot. On arrival the remaining sixteen were acquitted, but several suffered long and sorely from that painful journey. A whole family were hiding in a pit when some Russians passed. Someone suggested that they were Japanese spies, and the soldiers fired down on them, killing all but one woman, who was left for dead. Some time later another Russian company passed. Hearing her groans, one of them had pity on her and had her carried into Moukden, where she came to our hospital. Such deeds of kindness and mercy on the part of the Russians were common, more so than the deeds of cruelty.

During the battle of Moukden very many Chinese were killed. Sometimes the line of firing would swing round suddenly and a village would find itself overwhelmed and cut off from retreat. Not a few were killed or wounded when fleeing from their burning dwellings. One of our Bible women remained in her home all the time, though it was in the very midst of the fighting, and bullets and shells rained around. The Russians occupied the village and loopholed the walls; they were driven out and the Japanese occupied it; still she and her old husband crouched and prayed, and then praised God for their deliverance. Their son was hired by the Japanese as a cook, and would only serve them if his mother was allowed to remain. When the Russian fire became very hot, the Japanese directed her to stand up against the northern wall between the two windows by which the bullets were entering.

When Moukden was evacuated and the fighting was at our doors, the wounded poured into the hospital. Early

THE SUFFERINGS OF THE INNOCENT

in the morning, that last day of the battle, they began to arrive, and soon we forgot the sound of the guns. Hearing that a number of Chinese and some Russians were lying wounded outside the city wall, we sent out Red Cross stretcher-bearers. By 9 a.m. the operating-room presented a lively scene, and all day long we were hard at work, as one after another Chinese and Russians were carried in. When these Russians who were left in Moukden failed in their last effort to escape, two of them seem to have gone mad. Just outside the northern east gate were large Chinese barracks, turned by Government into a Refuge where some two thousand people were housed. Into this these men ran, shooting off their rifles at anyone they met. A woman was nursing her baby a few weeks old, when one burst into her room and fired. The bullet passed through mother and child, killing it and wounding her severely, and then wounded her twelve-year-old daughter. In that one room two were killed and four wounded.

Our ministrations were not confined to Chinese and Russians. The same day a Japanese soldier, evidently worn out and ill, stumbled along our terrace. He was invited into one of the compounds, and after being refreshed with tea was directed to our hospital, whose Red Cross flag he evidently welcomed. Then another Japanese, seeing the flag, came to tell us that there were some wounded just outside the wall. Some hospital men were taken out to help them, and two carts full of Japanese wounded were brought in. We got a room ready for them with all speed, as it was manifestly undesirable that they and our wounded Russians should be together. During the next few days we admitted a good many Japanese and Russians, and did our best for their comfort and healing. The Russians were at first in terror that the Japanese would kill them, and grateful to be with us, but by the time they were removed as prisoners their fears had died away. The Japanese too left us when their own hospitals were in full working order. For our matter-of-course impartial Red Cross help, we received the generous recognition of both Russians and Japanese.

Outside Moukden the line of the Russian retreat was strewn with warm caps, heavy felt-lined boots, and other things which the Russians had cast aside in their haste and heat those mild spring days; and all the camps round the city, like the cavalry camp close to us, were littered with articles of value to the Chinese. The battle had hardly passed by when they stole out to pick up what they could, in spite of the risk of being shot as looters by the Japanese soldiers who were gathering in Russian transport wagons, hand carts, field guns, and many other articles.

Among the things picked up by the Chinese all over the countryside, there were unfortunately many unexploded shells, hand grenades, etc., which caused scores of deaths and many hundred wounds. One man near the North Tomb found a huge shell with part of the fuse left. Thinking it was a lamp, he took it home, placed it on a table to show to the household, and lit the fuse. Only one wounded man was left alive of that company. Another put his find into the fire to melt it, and the whole house was demolished and all in it killed or wounded.

During the succeeding months many children and others were seriously injured by playing with these dangerous explosives—eyes were destroyed, hands and legs blown off, and a good many were killed outright. When the cultivation of the ground began, ploughs and hoes exploded shells and cartridges by accident, with disastrous consequences. Even as late as two years afterwards such accidents continued to happen. In a few months we amputated in Moukden alone from this one cause over a hundred hands or parts of hands and many legs, besides treating other injuries.

The condition of the country round Moukden after the battle was most insanitary, though the Japanese, fully

THE SUFFERINGS OF THE INNOCENT

awake to the danger, used every possible means of remedying it. The dogs, left without homes and preying on the dead, became ferocious wild beasts. One actually entered our Refuge in the hospital ruins, and tore a baby from the *kang*. It was driven off with difficulty, leaving the child severely bitten.

The battle was no sooner over than men among the refugees began to slip away back to their homes; but women and children continued to arrive from north of the city where the bulk of the Japanese army now lay, so that for a time our numbers increased instead of diminishing. All the refugees were anxious to get home in good time to start ploughing, which is usually done in April. There were serious difficulties before these poor people. The homes of at least half had been destroyed, and the others wrecked and plundered, doors, windows, and furniture being burned as fuel. Their animals and farm implements were gone, and they had no grain for seed. We consulted with the Chinese Government, and approached the Japanese authorities on their behalf, and finally it was arranged that in those districts where the destruction had been most general the people were to be allowed to occupy the "dug-outs" used by the Russians and Japanese during the winter. The Governor-General made a small grant to the head of each household to buy seed to make a fresh start.

Gradually the people returned to their land, making shift as best they could for the summer. There was a very good harvest, and before winter most families had built themselves some sort of home. There were still many fields and great stretches of land uncultivated, and the rival armies faced each other farther north far into the summer. Even when peace was signed it was but slowly that the Japanese army was withdrawn, and the effects of the war were felt in Manchuria for many a day. In the aspect of the landscape there was one conspicuous change, the disappearance of trees. To this day there are long, bare, treeless stretches where formerly there were clusters of poplars, pines, or willows every few hundred yards.

Throughout the Japanese occupation our relations with their officials were most cordial. Their gratitude to us for receiving their wounded was the beginning of constant friendly intercourse. Marshal Oyama, the Commander-in-Chief, himself called on us, a most kindly and winning personality, of simple, unaffected dignity. We could only talk through our interpreter, and this was also the case with General Oku, whose decimated army occupied Moukden. But General Fukushima and others knew English, and they called frequently. Altogether we have a most happy recollection of our intercourse with the Japanese Headquarters Staff. Among military attachés and war correspondents with both armies we also made many friends.

At last Japanese military occupation came to an end, soldiers were withdrawn to the railway zone, which was now Japanese from Port Arthur to Kwan-cheng-tze, and only lesser officials were left in Moukden and other places. When the Chinese began to breathe again after the terrors and hardships of war, there was a general feeling of disillusionment and bitter disappointment. The justice and mercy of the Japanese at the time of the previous war had been extolled, and all excesses forgotten. The victors had now a great opportunity of making lasting friends of these Manchurian farmers, so often harried by war, who were eager to hail them as brethren and deliverers. Thus the way might easily have been paved for the permanent possession of the country, desired by many. But whatever their leaders and higher officials might aim at, the ordinary Japanese soldiers and civilians who came to Manchuria were incapable of realizing this position. A great nation had been defeated, Japan was exalted and supreme, China was nothing. They came not as deliverers but as victors, and treated the Chinese with contempt as a conquered people.

Then with peace came crowds of the lowest and most undesirable part of the Japanese nation. The Chinese continued to suffer as before, and the disappointment made their resentment the more keen. The deeds of soldiers, however brutal, they might readily condone, knowing what their own soldiery would do; but now that the war was over they could see no reason for the continued injustice and extortion of the many low-class civilians who remained. As one remarked :

"The Russians sometimes took our property for nothing, but more often paid four times its worth. The Japanese profess to pay for everything, but never give more than a quarter the real value."

Thus there grew and rankled in the popular mind an unfortunate dislike for the Japanese, a suspicion of their motives, an unwillingness to have dealings with them, which feelings are difficult to eradicate.

XXI

RECONSTRUCTION

H.E. Chao Er Sun, Governor-General, 1905–1907

> " The common problem, yours, mine, every one's,
> Is—not to fancy what were fair in life
> Provided it could be—but, finding first
> What may be, then find how to make it fair
> Up to our means : a very different thing ! "
>   " Bishop Blougram "—*R. Browning.*

WITH the close of the Russo-Japanese war Manchuria entered on a new era. Hitherto she had been left in a haphazard way to old-fashioned officials who were for the most part unenlightened and conservative, knowing nothing of foreign countries, looking upon the study of the Confucian Classics as the only education worthy of the name, and quite ignorant of the aspirations which were stirring the minds of a large part of China's youth. To give them their due, be it said that many among these officials were humane, unselfish, conscientious, seeking according to their lights to do their best for the people to whom they stood in the place of father.

H.E. *Tseng Chi*, Governor-General during both Boxer and war times, was one of these. He had not sufficient strength of character nor insight into the trend of events to make him hold out against Boxer influences, but the tragedies of that summer cut him to the heart, and when all was over he was very willing to atone. He was then for the first time brought into personal contact with foreigners, both the Russians and the missionaries. His attitude to the former was a helpless dignified aloofness,

H.E. CHAO ER SUN, VICEROY
"One of the men available, a notable financier . . . the future."

and to the latter an apologetic, courteous, but somewhat distant friendliness. The best of his kindly nature was shown in his treatment of the refugees. They were his children in trouble, and he strained his financial resources to the utmost to help them.

The Russo-Japanese war seems to have awakened the Central Government somewhat tardily to the importance of Manchuria. For the first time a Governor-General of outstanding merit was appointed, not a Manchu, as always before, but a Chinese Bannerman, *Chao Er Sun*, one of the ablest men available and a notable financier. He was not young, he had never been abroad, he knew no foreign language, his own education had been entirely on the old lines, and he was not in sympathy with the Progressive Party overthrown at the *coup d'état*. In spite of all this, he was a man of the future, not of the past. He saw what China needed, he understood what Manchuria had to fear, and he threw himself with energy into the task of introducing the most needed reforms. This he did in a quiet, gradual way which did not alarm the people. He was with us less than two years, but in that time Manchuria went far.

Chao Er Sun's watchword might have been expressed as " Progress, Efficiency, and Economy." Scores of paid officials had little or no work to do ; these he dismissed, and sought to gather round him men like himself, eager for good hard work. His personal expenses he cut down to the lowest point, living simply, with a small retinue and no pomp. He abolished the restrictions at his gate, which prevented any man from having access to him without first feeing heavily half a dozen underlings, and opened his ear to the appeal of all. He did his best to discourage bribery and to reward uprightness and faithfulness to duty. He frequently went out in disguise to find out for himself the true condition of things, and in this way visited courts of justice and other public institutions. His influence was consistently exerted in favour of elevating the moral tone of the community. Naturally he made many enemies, and it was some time before his sterling worth was generally recognized.

One of his most striking reforms was the abolition of *opium smoking*. This vice had never been so common in Manchuria as in some parts of China, still there were a large number of smokers, chiefly among the well-to-do and yamen employees, and many through its use had sunk to be the dregs of the population. Merchants would have no man in their employ who smoked, and it was everywhere regarded without qualification as a vice, though a fashionable one. The cultivation of the poppy was illegal, but very lucrative. During the years since 1900 it had rapidly increased, some of those officials whose duty it was to prevent it receiving a share of the gains. Year by year the poppies waved more unblushingly their beautiful alluring heads. We began to see fields of them close to the city, in inconspicuous hollows aside from the main road. Then they boldly crept nearer, till in Chao Er Sun's first summer we could feast our eyes on the exquisitely delicate tints of their loveliness within a few hundred yards of our doors; and when the opium harvest came, dozens of children would stroll about sucking the last juices from the wilted heads of the " withering flower of dreams " they had been helping to garner.

In accordance with the Imperial Edict which had hitherto been a dead letter, the Governor-General now issued his commands. Poppy cultivation was to cease. Opium dens all over the country, which had been increasing in number and prosperity, were given six months to close their doors. Opium smokers over sixty years of age might receive an official permit, but all others must give up its use within a given time or suffer punishment.

These laws were carried out. One by one opium dens ceased from our midst. Gangs of men could be seen mending the city roads under a guard—these were convicted opium smokers whose punishment was this open-air exercise instead of lazy confinement in a close prison. When summer came, not a poppy field was to be seen or heard of. Owing to this vigorous action, Manchuria was one of the first provinces closed to Indian opium.

Only once, a year or two later, did an opium poppy appear again among us. A farmer just outside the wall ventured to assume that as Chao Er Sun was no longer here, he might safely make some money. As the weeks went on, we sadly saw the poppies grow, till they bloomed in the hundred shades of their fatal beauty. Then just as the field was ripe for harvest, there came one morning a band of ruthless soldiers, who cut down and destroyed every bloom, while the farmer wrung his hands in vain.

Opium has gone, but unfortunately an illicit traffic in morphia has come, most of it from Japan. Tabloids and hypodermic syringes are sold openly, and pedlars go about the country charging a couple of cents for an injection. Patients frequently present themselves at our hospital with large patches of diseased tissue dotted with the marks of dirty hypodermic needles. The Chinese Government is awake to the new danger, and it is expected that international action will soon be taken to stamp out this evil traffic.

Education also received the new Governor-General's earnest care. Till now there had been no such thing as a Government school. Teaching was carried on privately, and was in the hands of old-fashioned schoolmasters, each having under him from a dozen to a score of boys, in his own house, a rented room, or the home of one of the pupils. In well-to-do households a teacher was engaged for the family, girls being sometimes taught along with boys. The instruction consisted of reading, writing, and memorizing the old classics, and, for advanced pupils, explaining these classics and writing formal essays on Confucian themes. The Empress-Dowager had issued what was in effect a repetition of some of the Emperor's unfortunate Reform Edicts of some years before. The old-fashioned Confucian examinations for degrees were to be superseded, and modern subjects introduced. To this end Government schools were to be established.

The time was ripe and more than ripe for such a change. Everywhere there was a keen desire for modern education, and a demand for instruction in the sciences and the English language. Manchuria had not been one of the best educated provinces. The large bulk of her immigrants were of the illiterate classes, and only a small proportion of the rural population could read. In the cities and towns the educated were more numerous. Our Christian Church had always emphasized the importance of its children learning to read, and had many village schools with old-fashioned schoolmasters. In a good many of the centres where missionaries lived, there were also Middle Schools of a more advanced kind, where modern subjects were taught. Girls' schools had early been opened, and had steadily developed and increased in number. The only institution in Manchuria of collegiate rank was the Christian Arts College, but its work, and that of all the schools, had been seriously hindered by the war. Manchuria more than any other province had been brought into close contact with foreign nations, and forced to realize the practical necessity for knowledge. But for this third war within her borders, she would have started her educational career immediately on the publication of the new Edict. Our energetic Governor-General now acted promptly.

Several large boys' schools and one for girls were opened, professing all the modern subjects, tuition, books, and stationery being free. As few trained teachers were available, the teaching was at first of the most superficial kind. A Confucian schoolmaster would buy an arithmetic, a geography, a history of China, a science primer, devote a couple of months to their study, and get an appointment to teach them. Much of the instruction was useless, but the best had to be made of the materials available, and year by year things improved.

The securing of teachers for girls' schools presented special difficulties, as it was decreed that they must be women, and where were sufficient of these to be found ? The first school was opened as a normal and elementary one, a large salary was promised to all who passed through the two years' free training, and an entrance examination was held of a very elementary nature. Tempted by the golden inducements, a good many Christian girls and young women applied, and they easily came out at the head of the list. The Moukden Christian Girls' School was thus deprived of most of its advanced pupils, but at the same time it became known that in it was to be had the real thing in modern education. Although fees are charged, and neither food nor books given free, it has always had more applying for entrance than could be admitted, non-Christians as well as Christians, and its numbers have risen to 160. To this day a large proportion of Government girls' school teachers are Christians.

With female education came a marked change in certain social customs. It had hitherto been considered improper for girls over ten or young women of good character to appear on the streets without an elder woman. Now they had to go daily to school. So all schoolgirls were provided with badges which they wore conspicuously and which protected them from insults. Gradually since then even this has become superfluous.

Soon after Chao Er Sun came to Moukden a Chinese daily paper was started, and later on another, and before long they had a large circulation.

Along with modern methods in education, material reforms were introduced. These were most in evidence in Moukden itself. The streets had been hopeless quagmires in wet weather and whirling dust in dry. The Russians had improved matters by forcing each merchant or householder on the main streets to level and mend in front of his own door, but now macadamized roads were made, steam-rollers and water-carts came into use. With change of roads came change of vehicles. Rickshas appeared in hundreds, the Russian drosky became common, and officials drove in foreign broughams.

Having had some years of contact with Russia, Moukden no longer went to bed with the sun. The formerly dark and deserted streets were now trodden in the evening by wayfarers, lantern in hand. This fugitive light being manifestly insufficient, street lamps had been placed at all Government offices and public buildings, and now it was ordained that householders should maintain lamps outside their own doors. A few years later electric light was provided by Government on all the main streets.

The need for police in the city was now beginning to be felt; the war had brought about many changes for good and evil, and the old simple ways were passing. So a strong force of semi-military police was organized, and little blue sentry-boxes appeared at street corners. Night and day these guardians of the public peace watched over the city, and before long were even stationed on the thoroughfares to control the traffic. A Board of Sanitation was also formed, very imperfect, but a beginning in the right direction, and for the first time in the history of Moukden laws were issued regarding sanitary matters.

So much was the need felt for increased medical help, that the Governor-General consulted me as to the opening of a Government Hospital and Dispensary. A compound in the north of the city was arranged for the purpose, and put in charge of two Chinese graduates of the Government Medical School in Tientsin. They became very friendly with us, and there has been ever since the most cordial intercourse between the two hospitals.

All these changes naturally meant expenditure, and it says much for Chao's financial ability, that he carried out his plans by means of economy, retrenchment, and reorganization rather than increase of taxation, and that he left a large balance in the Treasury when he was transferred to another province.

Our personal intercourse with His Excellency Chao Er Sun was throughout of the most pleasant kind. Soon after his arrival I called on him, and found to my surprise that he knew all about us and was quite familiar with the part we had played in the recent relief work. He inquired with great interest about our hospital, and from then on was our very good friend. He came frequently to see me, sometimes in quite an informal way.

The hospital was at that time in temporary and most inconvenient quarters in the tumbledown old *San Yi Miao*, the temple on our Small River bank. Its accommodation was ridiculously inadequate. Many of the patients had to wait in the open air. There was only one room for both consulting and dispensing, and the dispensers had hardly space to make up the medicines. Among the dilapidated idols which were partly screened off, the in-patients were uncomfortably housed, and in summer some were sheltered in a tent in the compound. The buildings were old, draughty, and insanitary, with damp floors and leaky *kangs* which smoked continually. In this hospital, such as it was, we were able to treat larger numbers than since the Boxer troubles.

The war had prevented our rebuilding, but in the spring of 1906 we were at last able to go forward. Colonel MacPherson, of the Royal Army Medical Corps, one of the British attachés with General Oku's army, and an expert in hospital construction, had guided us in laying out the ground, and we were now able to feel almost thankful that the Boxers had made such a clean sweep of the old patched buildings. Our great difficulty was money. Materials were several times their former cost, and wages had risen, so that the indemnity for the old hospital would not go more than half-way to building the new. We decided, however, to keep to our plan, and build as many wards as we had money for. Marshal Oyama, in recognition of our help to his wounded, had given orders that all wood for the building was to be conveyed by rail from Newchwang free of charge. This meant a great deal to us, for no seasoned native wood could be had at that time, and the American pine which we bought would have cost several hundred pounds to bring up-country, if, indeed, the Japanese railway would have undertaken its transport.

Some weeks before building began I was calling on the Governor-General, and he inquired minutely about the new hospital and how much money we lacked for the building.

"Leave it to me!" he said. "That will be managed all right."

Three weeks later he called and handed me Tls.4000, or about £600. With this we built a ward which bears his name. Other friends also came to our help. One carted all the bricks and tiles without charge, equal to a donation of £80. The director of the Imperial Chinese Railway ordered that our Portland cement and floor-tiles be conveyed free from *Tong-shan* to Hsin-min-tun. And there were many smaller contributions.

In the spring of 1907 the hospital was ready for use. It consisted of a two-story dispensary block, with accommodation for assistants and dispensers upstairs; a bright, airy, modern operating-room; three wards with accommodation for sixty patients; and outhouses. To complete the plan two more large wings were necessary, and some other buildings, but for these we had so far no funds.

Our good Governor-General agreed to perform the opening ceremony on 5 March, and for three days there was high festival on the Small River bank. The day before the opening, one cart after another arrived with gifts, bright silk scrolls and banners, a beautiful silk flag

CORRIDOR OF THE HOSPITAL: WARDS OPENING ON EITHER SIDE

with the Imperial dragon, a new Red Cross flag, lanterns, lamps, clocks, etc. Many of these were from the Christians. On the important day all was gay with flags and streamers, the Chinese dragon having the place of honour at the top of our tall flagstaff, above the Red Cross. Besides the Governor-General, the Consuls and all the leading officials in Moukden came, to the number of about 120, the most picturesque among them being the two Great Lamas, head of all the Lamas in Manchuria. Tables were spread in the large new waiting-room, and after seeing over the premises there were refreshments and speeches. We took care not to refer to the Boxer destruction, but the Governor-General himself alluded regretfully to the grief and loss we had suffered, for which, he said, " China is ashamed to-day." Before performing the ceremony he had presented me with an additional $1000 (£100) towards the building fund, and in concluding his speech he appealed to the wealthy men of Moukden to come forward and make up the necessary amount.

" It is my wish," he said, " that this beneficent institution be finished before the end of the year," and his wish was gratified.

The next day there was a solemn dedicatory service attended by several hundred Christians; refreshments were supplied, and they all saw over the premises. On the third day we had about 150 of the leading merchants in Moukden, with the President of the Merchants' Guild at their head, and during their repast one after another expressed a desire that whatever was lacking for the building should be made up. The fête days were concluded by an exhibition of fireworks, provided by the merchants, on the river bank in front of the hospital, viewed by a dense crowd on both sides of the river, numbering from forty to fifty thousand men, women, and children. The thoughts of many went back to the last great gathering there seven years before, when the hospital buildings went up in flames. This was a very different crowd, peaceful and good-natured, needing not a single policeman to keep them in order.

The following day the Chairman of the Merchant Guild called on me and said : " I am authorized to tell you that you are to go on with your building, and to come to me for money as you need it." During the summer I again and again proved the sincerity of this promise. Whatever I asked was given, and by November the whole hospital was complete, providing accommodation for 110 patients.

The old temple, the San Yi Miao, which the hospital had temporarily occupied, had been bought by Government some time before we left it, but we were allowed to remain in it rent free till our new building was ready. A few days after our opening ceremony, workmen arrived to pull down and to build up, in order to fit the place and some adjoining open ground for a Government Industrial School. They were immediately faced with the difficulty : What was to be done with the idols ? All the other Buddhist temples in Moukden were invited to accept these homeless gods, but only one was considered worth removing. The rest were, amid laughter and mockery, carried out to the narrow terrace before the temple and left for some days exposed to the elements. Even there they were in the way of the workmen, and one day a man seized a huge broken limb and threw it over the edge of the terrace towards the water. A shout of laughter went up, a crowd soon gathered, and with much merriment and jeering the old gods were one after another smashed, and heaved piecemeal into the river.

XXII

SPIRITUAL UPLIFT

"We cannot kindle when we will
 The fire that in the heart resides.
The spirit bloweth and is still,
 In mystery the soul abides.
But tasks in hours of insight willed
Can be through hours of gloom fulfilled."

R. W. Emerson.

A CHRISTIAN community which had been subjected to such a series of devastating wars and searching persecutions as had the Manchurian Church, might reasonably be expected to settle down thereafter to quiet development and rest, and for some time this was so. The Boxer bitterness died out, the refugee aid work going far to obliterate in the public mind the line between Church members and outsiders. Churches and meeting-houses dotted the land anew. Two Moukden churches were built, not in Chinese style this time, for foreign buildings were now the aim of all. When the church for the older congregation in East Moukden was opened in 1907, it was crowded to the door, and next day there was a sympathetic gathering of officials, merchants, and others, to express the goodwill of the non-Christian public to the Christian Church. Numbers were again on the increase, slowly but steadily. Those who had been suspended for recanting in one form or another had been gradually readmitted. There was specially rapid development in education, the standard aimed at being markedly higher.

Below this outward smooth prosperity there slowly rose in the heart of the Church an undercurrent of dissatisfaction, a wholesome though as yet unrecognized discontent with herself. The Chinese are not given to self-analysis, and the standards of the ordinary Christian are of the simplest. A man either *believes* and is a Christian, or does not *believe* and is not. Into this child-like involuntary division of the world into two classes had broken the Boxer summer with its many varieties and degrees of apostasy. It was sometimes the best man, the most truly spiritual-minded and upright, who had failed to stand in the evil day; while the easy-going and shallow, from force of circumstances or occasionally from pure physical pluck, had come out of it unscathed. An undefinable consciousness stirred in the minds of many that there were questions they had never thought of, heights and depths in the Faith hitherto undreamed of.

A change in the mental view-point of the Manchurian Christian was inevitable in this time of political and social change, even apart from all inward stirrings. The change seemed for a time not unlikely to take the form of an aggressive propaganda to extend the borders of the Church, while more or less relegating to the background that need felt so keenly by the missionaries and by a growing number of individual Christians—the need of intensifying the personal Christian life of the Church. At the annual meetings of Synod, especially that in 1907, there was a great enthusiasm for pressing forward. A Missionary Society was formed; the unevangelized northern province of Tsi-tsi-har or Hei-lung-Kiang was chosen as the first field for its operations; two men from the Theological Hall were ordained as missionaries, and, supported by their compatriots, were sent forth to break new ground. A small Christian Church is now growing there, which has never had anything to do with foreign missionaries or foreign money. In the older districts one pastor after another was ordained over self-supporting congregations, and the spirit of self-assertion and independence was most encouraging.

At the same time there was a general consciousness that for the Christians themselves something was needed, and this took form in special meetings for the building up of believers, which were held in most churches for a week early in each Chinese year, when business was slack. These were well attended. Into these regularly organized quiet meetings in Liaoyang and Moukden in 1908 came a new element, which caused that mighty stirring known as the Manchurian Revival. The detailed story of that wonderful movement has already been written,[1] and would be out of place here. Humanly speaking, it was a sequel to the Korean Revival. Stories of the evangelistic fervour of the roused disciples in that downtrodden land had been sounding strangely in our ears for months past, and a Canadian missionary, the Rev. Jonathan Goforth, after visiting Korea, had been asked to tell of what he had seen to the special meetings in both Moukden and Liaoyang. All were interested in the subject, and it was hoped that the churches might be roused to greater zeal; but any general movement such as took place was far from the thoughts of any. One evident reason for the story coming home with special force to the Manchurian Christians was that the Korean had always been looked down upon with marked contempt, as of an inferior race.

"The Koreans have gone forward like this, why is it that *we* are left behind?" was the question which struck home to many a conscience.

Such, then, were the various streams of influence converging on the minds of the Christians at the time of these meetings, but they are far from sufficient to explain the wave of intense spiritual impulse which moved the Manchurian Church to its very foundations from south to north and from east to west. The only adequate explanation is that "Here is the finger of God, a flash of the will that can." The Church was in serious danger of becoming a somewhat worldly institu-

[1] "Times of Blessing in Manchuria," by the Rev. James Webster.

tion, seeking for mere increase of numbers, prosperity, education. Here she was arrested as by a lightning flash, which revealed her complacent corruption, and by contrast the high calling to which she was called.

The Chinese sense of sinfulness has always been dull. There is no real translation for *sin*. The same word is used in such phrases as " a *criminal*," " I am to *blame*," " He has *offended* me." As words both reflect and suggest thoughts, the ideas of the ordinary Christian regarding *sin* were as loose as his phraseology, and he was slow to grow into the realization of the vital importance of an upright personal character. Yet the most prominent feature in all this movement was the confession of personal individual sins.

It is easy for a large meeting to be moved by an eloquent address and carried away by sympathetic emotion, till many weep for their " sins." This was not what happened. It is a different thing when a man of established respectability stands up before a company of his own friends and acquaintances, owns that he has swindled, and proceeds to pay back the money; when a prominent church leader convicts himself of secret immorality; when a man who has borne the reputation of having stood firm at the Boxer trial, comes forward voluntarily to confess with distress that he had really saved his life by worshipping idols; when another who had been tortured in vain in the *yamen* to make him acknowledge his guiltiness of a certain crime, now pours out the confession with cries and tears. Perhaps even more convincing were the quiet sorrowful confessions in prayer of minor sins which had heretofore been regarded as unimportant; such as lying, petty dishonesty, anger, refusal to forgive an injury. The outburst of thank-offerings all over the country, filling the church treasury to overflowing, was also very striking, though more transient.

In all this there was inevitably a certain amount of

unconscious imitation and hysterical excitement, for a nervously susceptible people like the Chinese are peculiarly open to such influences. Besides, the great majority of them had but recently emerged from heathenism with its ignorance and superstitions. In looking back over the five years that have elapsed since then, we see, as we might expect, that where the excitement, the extreme experiences, the physical "manifestations" (such as cataleptic fits) were most common, there the spiritual and practical results were least permanent. It is also noticeable that it has usually been the Christians of some years' standing who have profited most deeply by this new experience.

With every possible discount for all extraneous impulses, the number of Christians must still have been very large, who from the depths of their hearts confessed and turned from sins hitherto concealed or thought lightly of, and whose eyes were opened to new possibilities of communion with God. Were there no other result, those months burned into the consciousness of the Church the exceeding sinfulness of sin, and raised the standard of upright Christian living once for all to a higher level.

Among the thousands who thus caught a glimpse of an unforgettable ideal, and realized their own distance from it, were some—scores or hundreds, we know not—to whom the heavenly vision meant a complete revolution in their Christian life. We judge not by their words but by their continued life and actions. The vision passes, the life goes on.

There was in Moukden one of my trained assistants, the son of Pastor Liu, who since the Boxer year has been in practice for himself. He was a good Christian, a good son, a good husband, a good father. To him the new light came with illuminating force, transforming his whole existence. While others saw in him little need for repentance, he realized his shortcomings before a higher tribunal. The first result was a public confession, the next the dedication to God's service of one-tenth of the capital he had amassed. He had in all $7000 (about £600) invested in his medicine shop, and $700 was paid down as subscriptions to hospitals, schools, Bible Society, Missionary Society, and congregational funds. He then set himself to consider how best he could serve God, and decided to remain in self-supporting practice, while giving part of his time to voluntary medical missionary work. Since then he has made a number of medico-evangelistic tours, healing and preaching in the villages. Often has he been asked : " How much do the foreigners pay you for this ? " and the discovery that he was travelling and working at his own expense and at his own initiative made a marked impression. In Moukden his presence and influence are of permanent value.

In Moukden the lasting results of that time have been specially prominent among the women. The uplift of Christian womanhood among us has been a gradual thing, but in looking back we realize how far we have come and what an upward impulse was given by that " Revival time." The ordinary Chinese woman of the early days was illiterate, ignorant, often stupid, bound by custom, without inclination to learn anything. In the country it required almost bribery to get a young woman to attempt to learn to read. Even in the cities, for years it was taken for granted that none but former schoolgirls could use the hymn-book and Testament. All this is changed. In Moukden to-day the women are as prominent in the church as the men, though still fewer in number. Most of them have their books at service and use them, for a certain knowledge of reading is made a condition of baptism, except for the aged. They elect their own deaconesses, who take round the collection-plates to them on Sunday, receive and keep accounts of women's subscriptions, arrange women's meetings, and manage all their affairs.

The energy and zeal of these women was manifested recently when it was proposed to make a new departure and open a tent for Christian preaching in the women's part of an annual temple fair. Under the direction of a lady missionary a band of women was organized, and preaching was continued by about a dozen of them in turn from six in the morning until dusk for six consecutive days. This was repeated at two subsequent fairs. The temple authorities were most cordial, in one case giving the use of a building free, and in the others charging no ground-rent for the booth. They regarded the women's preaching as a "meritorious action" on their part, and possibly as a fresh attraction to the fair. Crowds of women listened, and the words of these simple Christians, most of whom had spent their youth in heathenism and illiteracy, were evidently acceptable.

The development of this independent Christian activity and sense of responsibility among women has been very gradual, and the general standard of intelligence has still a long way to rise. Chinese women, in Manchuria at least, have never been, properly speaking, "downtrodden." They have to bear the yoke in their youth in serving their mothers-in-law, they are legally in complete subjection to their husbands all their lives, and for very many this is a practical as well as a legal actuality. But wherever a strong woman of character is found, and they are not few, she will as years go on inevitably assert her individuality and find her kingdom, be she never so ignorant and uneducated. In hundreds of homes the manager and leading spirit is a middle-aged or elderly woman, to whom all the men of the household defer as having the best judgment among them. When such clever, capable minds are educated in girlhood in our schools, or trained in middle life in a Bible Woman's Training Home, they become an irresistible force in the forward march of Christianity.

Girls' schools have been and are a most important

factor in the development of a wholesome Christian home life, as from them issue streams of girls to be the mothers and heads of the Christian families of the future. Government schools cannot take their place. In the Christian atmosphere, especially where the foreign lady throws her personality into the work, character is built up; whereas in the Government schools there is usually a lack of definite principles, a laxity of discipline, an absence of high ideals. The same is true of boys' schools. There is a great future before the educated and trained women of China. In the capable young women dispensers and school teachers we have glimpses of what the future holds. They and the Bible women, so keen to learn and make up for the blankness of their youthful years, so eagerly glad over any new insight into hidden knowledge, make us certain that when New China enters fully into her inheritance, her women will be in the forefront of the highest and truest progress.

The general education of the Christian youth of both sexes has continued to advance during recent years. A Girls' Normal School has been begun in Moukden, and seems likely to furnish teachers not only to Christian girls' schools, but to many a Government school also. The Christian Arts College (for men only) entered on a new era of its usefulness when it was established in a new building at the west of the city in 1910, the Viceroy *Hsi Liang* and other officials cordially assisting at the opening ceremony. One of the most encouraging features of this institution is that most of its graduates seem determined to devote themselves to the Christian advancement of their country rather than to their own personal enrichment.

The character of the Theological Hall seems for this reason on the verge of change. Hitherto our pastors, now sixteen in number, have been men who have spent years as evangelists, who have had little or no " modern " education, and who have passed through the theological training when no longer in their youth. A new type of pastor is now needed and will soon be provided, men who have been through our schools and colleges, and who, after a time of practical work among the people, return for a scholastic training of a very different type from that which the former theological student could assimilate. Thus we have good hope that the Chinese Church will have men well equipped to lead the thought of the China that is to be.

XXIII

THE PRINCIPLES OF MEDICAL MISSION WORK

"Go, and do thou likewise."
The Parable of the Good Samaritan.

IN 1907 there was held in Shanghai the "China Centenary Missionary Conference," a hundred years after the arrival of the first Protestant missionary in China. I was asked to be Chairman of the Committee on Medical Missions, and to prepare a paper on the subject. Part of this is given here, as it expresses my strong convictions as to the place Medical Missions should occupy in the world-work of the Christian Church. The principles here laid down were unanimously adopted by the Conference in the Resolutions passed.

" From the very beginning of Medical Missions, this form of work has been notably blessed of God. Its success as a pioneer agency has been very marked, and healing the sick has everywhere been found the best way of overcoming suspicion, dislike, and opposition, breaking down prejudice, and removing misconceptions. Especially in Mohammedan lands, practically no advance has been made except in conjunction with medical work. And among all peoples and in all parts of the world, it opens the way for the preaching of the Gospel. In China it has been more difficult to gain an entrance than in most lands, for between our missionary agencies and the life of the people there is a great wall of anti-foreign prejudice. It is now about seventy years since the missionary societies began to realize that to win the hearts of such a proud and hostile people, something more than preaching and literary work would be needed; and that the wall on which the force of arms and the influences of Western civilization could make no impression would best be broken down by those acts of kindness and love which lie at the heart of the Gospel. Medical Missions were no sooner established in the principal ports by Drs. Parker, Lockhart, Hobson, and others, than crowds flocked to be healed. And ever since they have been recognized as the best way to begin work in a new or hostile district.

" The unique advantages of this method of pioneering are so obvious and have been so notably exemplified, that this side of the work has perhaps gained undue prominence. It has been concluded by many that this is the *raison d'être* of Medical Missions,—to open new ground, and provide audiences for the Gospel. The logical conclusion of this view is, that they should only exist when there is a measure of difficulty in gaining a hearing for the Gospel in other ways, when there is active hostility, proud aloofness, or dead indifference. Once these are overcome, and there is a general openness of welcome, and large numbers are ready to listen to the preaching of the Word, the medical missionary might reasonably withdraw, and press forward once more to virgin soil. If he still remains, it is often assumed that the most important part of his work is now over.

" As an evangelistic agency Medical Missions have been so fruitful, that this alone would be sufficient reason for their establishment, and for their continuance. Nowhere can such miscellaneous crowds be regularly preached to as in the dispensary waiting-rooms, and many are reached who could never hear the Gospel in any other way. Those who are admitted to the hospital have unique opportunities of hearing and receiving systematic instruction in Christian truth, and that at a time when many are moved by the uncertainty of life, when their hearts are softened by the unwonted kindness shown them, and when they have leisure and rest from their accustomed labours.

"The hospital and dispensary are valued also as giving an object lesson in Christian love and mercy. They are a practical exemplification of the parable of the Good Samaritan. They convince the heathen that Christians do good deeds and have kind hearts; and they are a constant reminder to the native Christians of our obligation to love our neighbour. There is special need for this in China, where the whole system of law and literature encourages each man to consider himself, and to look with indifference on the sufferings of others. The Chinese are a very practical people, and they are quick to perceive and appreciate the practical side of Christianity. 'It must be a good doctrine,' they often say, 'that produces such good deeds.'

"It concerns the Church vitally, to find out if this view of medical work as a threefold aid to missions is an adequate one, or if we are warranted, from the revelations of God in Scripture and history, in placing it on a higher plane. Our entire policy and methods will be influenced by the view we take of its essential standing in the whole scheme of Christianizing the world.

"Let us look at the life of our Master. It is evident that, during the three and a half years of His public ministry, He spent at least as much time in healing the crowds as in preaching to them. He seems to have turned none away, and expended time and strength freely in dealing individually with each case of bodily need. This was not done to combat hostility; indeed many of His miracles were the cause of hostility. It was not done to attract audiences; Christ's preaching seems to have been always enough to draw a crowd, and several were forbidden to make their healing known in order to avoid the pressure of numbers. It was not done to prove Messiahship; indeed Christ definitely refused to work any miracle to this end. Neither is there any sign that His object ever was to produce faith either in the one healed or in the onlookers, though this was the natural result of His works. Nor were the acts of healing done from didactic reasons. Each miracle contains the germ of a parable, and may well be used as such, but that is not why they were worked. And certainly they were not done casually, by the way, as a side thing, which might be done or not without materially affecting Christ's life. It would be a very different Gospel, were the works of healing left out. What then were these works of healing? And why did Christ spend so much of His short earthly life in the relief of mere physical distress, which, in the nature of things, must before long be ended by death?

"Christ came as the Revelation of the Father, the Word of God to man; and it is evident that a very vital and important part of that revelation concerned men's bodies. From the very beginning, God in His dealing with men had regard for their temporal well-being. In the earliest times His promises and commands were primarily for this world,—those to Abraham for instance,—and the very existence of a soul and a life to come is implied only, but never stated. The Mosaic law, in many particulars, was dictated by considerations of public health and sanitation, and it concerned itself minutely with personal details of the bodily welfare of the private individual. Along with the most highly spiritual passages in the prophetic writings, are promises of temporal blessings, and warnings of earthly disasters, and the redemption of the body is part of the hope of the Messianic kingdom. For when sin entered into the world, the whole man suffered, physically, mentally, morally, spiritually, and the message of God Incarnate is to the whole man, mercy for the body as well as for the soul. So when Christ came, He was not wholly concerned with spiritual matters, men's souls and salvation, leaving their bodies to suffer, and die as soon as might be. He spent Himself on their bodies. He was careful, not so much to preach to men of what God is, as to live the Divine Life before them, showing them by deeds what God's heart is. Whenever Christ met with sin and suffering, He put forth against them all His power, and by so doing He revealed God. In His answer to John He appeals to His deeds of mercy, side by side with or even before His preaching, as a manifestation of His spiritual identity. It seems as if He could not restrain the love and compassion of God within Him, which welled up and flowed forth spontaneously in acts of healing of the body.

"Now the principal function of the Christian Church on earth is admittedly to act as the channel of the revelation of God to man. And the revelation which we make known must be entire. We must bring to men all that Christ brought, we must show to them the same God that He showed. If He, who spake as never man spake, found deeds necessary as well as words, in order to manifest His Father, we cannot expect adequately to make God known to the heathen by preaching alone, even where crowds are willing to listen. If He, who is the express image of the person of that God who is a Spirit, yet addressed Himself to save men's bodies as well as their souls, we also must inevitably concern ourselves with the whole man, and relieve bodily suffering while leading souls into light. Only so can we be as He was in this world, only so can we offer to men the whole Gospel.

"In this light, Medical Mission work is seen to be no mere adjunct to the work of preaching, but an essential and integral part of the Mission of the Church. Can we imagine Christ ignoring the suffering around Him, while directing Himself to put away the sin? As unnatural and one-sided are Christian missions without healing. Miraculous gifts are indeed no longer ours, but in their place we have all the resources of modern science, which are equally the gift of God. As the years advance, the discoveries and inventions of medicine and surgery reveal more and more of the wonderful provision for healing, which God has made. All these are ours to use in His name and for His glory, and they manifest His power and mercy scarcely less than did the miraculous healing of old.

"The Church of modern days has been marvellously

slow to recognize the fullness of her high calling. Among the primitive Christians, bodily and spiritual healing were intimately associated, and everyone was expected to do his best to alleviate the sufferings of those around him. No line seems to have been drawn between miraculous powers and the natural ministrations of loving gentle hands and prayerful hearts. In medieval times the principle that the Church should care for both body and soul, seems to have been dimly grasped and instinctively acted upon, without any theorizing on the subject. When the missionaries of the undivided Church went forth to heathen lands, they healed the sick and preached the Gospel.

"But with the Renaissance and the Reformation, medical science in large measure parted company with the Church. When the great Protestant missionary movement began, it was directed wholly in the line of preaching, teaching, and translating the Bible. It was assumed that the whole message of God to man could be conveyed in that way; and even to those earnest and rare souls among the missionaries of that time, who stand out as examples to all ages of devotion and sacrifice, it does not seem to have occurred, that a more complete Gospel would have more power in winning the souls they were hungering for. In very many cases, individual missionaries have done their best for the suffering ones around them, feeling that they could not do less, and still represent their Master. Dr. Morrison, first Protestant missionary to China, though not a medical man, opened and for some years superintended a dispensary, with the help of a friendly surgeon, and there have been many instances of Christian doctors freely giving their services to help on missionary work. Still, it is not until comparatively recently that the Church has realized her great power lying unused, and has called upon her sons and daughters to go forth to heal as well as to preach.

"In Christian work as in other fields of labour, we are not likely to reach beyond our aim. The aim of the Church hitherto, in sending healing to the heathen, has been too much limited to the three points,—Pioneering, Evangelistic work, and Philanthropy. The success of any particular work, apart from its pioneer aspect, has been too largely estimated according to the number whom it attracted into the Church. But let us now aim higher. Let us consider the place which deeds had in our Master's life-work, and the place they should therefore have in the life-work of the Church. Let us realize that by healing a man we are letting in a ray of Divine Light on the darkness of his surroundings, even if he takes absolutely no interest in the Divine message. Let us seek to let the heathen and hostile world read more plainly in our Christianity, the same Gospel as it finds in the Gospels. Let the whole work of Medical Missions be lifted to this higher plane, as a necessary and fundamental part of missions, not a mere aid to them. Let this be our practical aim, and so shall we hasten the time we are all longing for, when the whole world shall stretch out its hands to God."

Medical Missions being thus regarded as an integral and permanent part of the mission of the Christian Church, it is evident that that Church must do her best to ensure not only the establishment but also the continuity of such work. Our own presence here is not for always; the propagation of Christianity by means of foreigners can be but a temporary expedient; China must be Christianized and educated ultimately by her own sons; so that the way to perpetuate our work is evidently to train those who in their turn will carry on what we are beginning. It is not enough to give a smattering of practical knowledge to a succession of dispensers and assistants. We need well-educated Chinese Christians who can adequately and worthily stand forward as fully equipped medical men.

This has been increasingly realized during the past six years, and one medical college after another has sprung up in various parts of China. There have always been

PRINCIPLES OF MEDICAL MISSION WORK 223

some who have opposed the movement, believing that this is not the legitimate work of Christian Missions, but should be left to the Government or people. This, however, would inevitably result in the development in China of a medical profession apart from Christianity, and in the ultimate cessation of Medical Missions. We are responsible for making provision that this shall not be. We must see to it that Chinese Christianity shall be in a position to continue to proclaim her message to the whole man, body and soul. The conviction is growing that in Christian medical education lies the important part of our Medical Mission work for the next few decades, and it is agreed that such education must be of the highest standard.

The responsibility of the Government of the country for providing for medical education is also acknowledged, and the Chinese Government and the Board of Education are awake to the necessity, especially in connection with the public services. Government medical colleges already exist, and there is a strong movement to establish training on a much higher standard.

The question naturally arises: How can these two responsibilities be brought into harmony? Some colleges have already been established on a purely foreign and missionary basis, but the desirability of co-operation with the Chinese is more and more strongly felt, and the necessity for Government recognition of medical diplomas is realized. We are laying the foundations of what will one day be purely Chinese work, and we want as close union with them as possible. If the Christian ideal of service is to permeate the ranks of the Chinese medical profession, there must from the outset be co-operation and friendly relationship between the various medical schools, and also between the Government and those who are responsible for conducting them.

At the triennial meeting of the China Medical Missionary Association held in Peking in January, 1913, this whole subject of medical education was discussed, and a definite line of policy was adopted. It was decided that the urgency of Christian medical education is such that it should take precedence of advance in any other branch of Medical Missionary work. The following resolution was passed, and was published in Chinese :

"*Resolved :* That the Medical Missionary Association of China met in Conference, let it be known :

" 1. That, in establishing medical colleges and hospitals, their sole object is to bring the blessings of healing to the bodies and minds of the people of China, and to give a thorough training in medicine and surgery to young men of education and intelligence, enabling them, as fully qualified doctors, to be of the highest service to their country.

" 2. That they have no desire to create permanently foreign institutions, and that their aim and hope is that these medical colleges will, gradually and ultimately, be staffed, financed, and controlled by the Chinese themselves.

" 3. That the Association is desirous of bringing its teaching work into line with the regulations of the Ministry of Education, and in all ways to co-operate with and assist the Government of the Republic in Medical Education, so that a strong and thoroughly equipped medical profession may be established in this great land.".

XXIV

THE BEGINNINGS OF MEDICAL EDUCATION IN MANCHURIA

H.E. Hsü Shih Chang, Viceroy, 1907–1909

> " Let a man contend to the uttermost
> For his life's set prize, be it what it will ! "
> *Statue and Bust.*
> " Who keeps one end in view, makes all things serve."
> " In a Balcony "—*R. Browning.*

IT is unfortunate that in dealing with Manchuria the Central Government did not see its way to a continuity of policy. From the Russo-Japanese war until now, eight years, there have been five Governor-Generals or Viceroys, no one remaining longer than a bare two years. It has been a remarkable succession of notable men, but it has not been the custom to arrange that the new official should consult with the old except in a formal way. Each one has had his own policy and his own plans, and two years were not sufficient to develop them.

In 1907 it was decided to bring Manchuria into line with the rest of China and make it a Viceroyalty, and *Chao Er Sun* was succeeded by another fine man of a totally different stamp, the first Viceroy, His Excellency *Hsü Shih Chang*. The political importance of Moukden was now well recognized. It had been thrown open to the trade of the nations, and Consuls from various countries were now in residence, besides a Commissioner of Customs, Postal officials, and some merchants. The new Viceroy, one of *Yuan Shih Kai's* right-hand men, set himself to maintain before the world the dignity and importance of the Chinese Government. In this and in all his forward policy, he was ably seconded by H.E. *Tang Shao Yi*, who was appointed Civil Governor of Moukden. Mr. *Tang* and Mr. *M. T. Liang*, who was associated with him later, were American graduates speaking English perfectly, and were eager to bring China into line with the most advanced Western nations. Tang Shao Yi came to Moukden with the reputation of being " anti-foreign," but I saw no ground for this. Pro-Chinese he was, keen to uphold the rights and liberties of his nation, and to resent any infringement of them, but in all our intercourse I found him a fair-minded man, ready to meet more than half-way any foreigner who sought the good of China, and sympathizing with everything which would tend to uplift his country.

During the couple of years of this regime a good many changes were made in Moukden, the most striking being the handsome modern building now so conspicuous. The old-fashioned, one-story, inconvenient Governor-General's yamen, and various lesser yamens throughout the city, passed away. In their place rose fine, large, roomy, two-story Government offices, where the various departments work in convenient proximity, with the Viceroy's residence in their midst. In keeping with these, a stately pomp was maintained. Official banquets were given in the most approved foreign style, at which a Chinese military band played, with much spirit, foreign music on foreign instruments. When the Viceroy made an official visit to the hospital, a regiment of cavalry lined the roads as he approached, and a numerous mounted escort rode in front and behind. The horses and carriages of Viceroy and Governor were well known as the finest in the city.

Education was further developed in these and the next few years. Elementary schools were established in every large town and many small ones, and at least one Middle School in each city. Moukden was provided also with a

H.E. HSU SHIH CHANG, VICEROY
"He maintained the dignity of the Chinese Government."

large Normal School, a Science College, a Law College, a Military College, an Agricultural School, an Industrial School, a School of Foreign Languages, besides the Women's Normal School, two Girls' Schools and Kindergartens. For most of these, as well as the Government Bank, Library, etc., large imposing buildings were erected.

A telephone system and exchange were inaugurated, and with this our hospital was connected free of charge. This has been continued ever since, and proved specially invaluable at the time of plague, Red Cross work, etc. Electric works were established to supply light to all Government offices and buildings. Later on the benefits were extended to the public, the main streets were lighted, and now very many shops and houses have electric light. The hospital and medical college are supplied at half price by Government order.

Local enterprise was also active. A tramway company was formed, and a line of horse-tramcars run from the imner west gate of the city to the railway station three miles away. By this time the Government railway from Peking had been extended from *Hsin-min-tun* to Moukden. The Japanese railway ran south and north, with a short branch east to the coal-mines thirty miles away; and a new Japanese line was projected south-east to the Korean border.

His Excellency *Hsü Shih Chang* had not been long in Moukden before I became well acquainted with him and with Mr. *Tang;* and their appreciation of the importance of our work was shown by the donation of Tls.3100 (£440) to the hospital, from the Viceroy, Governor, and nine other officials. I had many a talk with Mr. Tang, especially about public health and the urgent need for medical education.

It had from the first been manifest that foreign missionaries, however liberal the supply, could not hope even temporarily to meet the medical requirements of the fifteen or more millions of people in Manchuria, once they awakened to a consciousness of these needs. I had not been long in China when I began to have dreams of Christian Chinese medical men dotted here and there all over the land, a Christian medical profession. It seemed Utopian, and there was nothing for it but to begin by devoting oneself to the immediate requirements of the hour, and to limit teaching efforts to training the assistants and dispensers wanted for the daily work.

As time went on, the wider need became increasingly apparent, and equally clamant with that of assistants for mission hospitals. The appalling amount of preventable suffering and death came home more and more to our consciousness. Confidence in Western medicine was steadily increasing, the demand for Chinese doctors who could practise it was very great, and it was distressing to have this met only by quack remedies, and by such dispensers and assistants as left our hospitals with a smattering of knowledge. In addition there was the growing Government desire for medical officers, civil and military.

Before the Boxer time I had been able to bring a limited number of men through a fairly complete medical course, and had given them diplomas. Two of them continued to assist me in the hospital; others went into private practice, where they are still doing well and exercising a good influence. There are two settled in Moukden, one of them Dr. Wei, who have always been ready to help us in any way without remuneration, and have often assisted with the out-patients when my assistant was ill or on holiday. These men were well known, and requests poured in from Government, the Army, Christian congregations, the Missionary Society of Manchuria (native), and towns throughout the province. " Give us one of your men ! " they all asked.

I had more than once laid before our Conference of the United Missions proposals for the establishment on a small scale of an efficient medical school. Neither men nor money were available, and the scheme had to be postponed; so I arranged to continue to train assistants single-handed as before. Then came the destruction of our work by the Boxers, the political unrest, the war. When peace was established, the Governor-General, *Chao Er Sun,* invited me to take up medical education, and promised his ardent support; but I was then about to rebuild the hospital, and much to my regret it was impossible even to consider it. It was not until now, at the beginning of 1908, that our medical work was once more in full swing with adequate equipment.

Still it seemed hopeless to think of the missions establishing a medical college. A modest scheme had been planned to meet pressing needs by gathering together dispensers and assistants annually for short courses of lectures. The Union Medical College in Peking had been opened two years previously, and we were urged to unite with it, and give up all idea of a separate institution for Manchuria. I was convinced that though Peking might supply us with some qualified assistants, it could never meet the growing needs of our Three Provinces. Yet the door seemed closed to us, and reluctantly I acknowledged that I must give up the hope cherished so long.

Just when the prospects for Christian medical education in Manchuria seemed most dark, suddenly the way opened clearly before us.

It was May, 1908, when one day a distressful piece of news was brought us. Next door to the hospital was a compound which we had previously tried in vain to buy. Its owner was absent; it was mortgaged and not for sale, though we had rented its poor dwellings more than once— for a hospital long ago, and for a Refuge during the war. Now we were informed that it was sold. That was disappointing enough, and a breach of Chinese custom, which ordains that the next-door neighbours shall have the first option of purchasing any ground ; but there was more. The new owners were the Guild of a southern province, who were about to build a large two-story Guild-house, with a hall for theatricals, banquets, etc. This would closely overlook the hospital ; and the noise and clanging of native musical instruments, which after modern fashion would continue far into the night, would be most serious for our patients.

I was in despair. I saw member after member of the Guild, but they could do nothing. The transaction was completed, the money paid, the plans made, the contract signed. Soon workmen came, the houses were pulled down, bricks and wood arrived, and the foundations were being dug. Meantime word of our sad plight reached the Viceroy, and at once he came to our aid.

" If the hospital," he said, " which has done so much for Moukden all these years, wants this ground, it must have it. Let the building be stopped."

Negotiations took some time, but ultimately the materials were all taken over by Government, the purchase price paid by them, and the title-deeds handed over to me, the money for it being made up by Chinese subscriptions. While these negotiations were still incomplete, we had a visit from some friends travelling in the East. We were then talking of the possibilities of the future, and what an ideal site this would be for teaching purposes. Impressed with the importance of the developments here, these friends offered £100 a year towards whatever work should be carried on on this new ground.

Shortly afterwards I had a long talk with Mr. *Tang Shao Yi* about the crying need in Manchuria for men trained in Western medicine. He expressed himself as anxious that I should undertake medical education, and that a college should be established with Government help. A few weeks later, just before Mr. Tang left for America, he called, along with the Viceroy and others. I showed them over the hospital premises, and they

A WARD IN THE MOUKDEN HOSPITAL

MEDICAL EDUCATION IN MANCHURIA 231

seemed greatly surprised to see so many patients, and all so clean!

"We knew you were doing a good work," said Mr. Tang, "but had no idea it was like this." Then the Viceroy told me that if I could arrange for medical teaching the Government would undertake to give Tls.3000 (£420) a year for ten years. Mr. *M. T. Liang* was appointed to make all arrangements with me, and we felt that a medical school, however small, was now secure.

During the following months a scheme was drawn up, and laid before our Mission Council and the Conference of United Missions, as well as discussed with Mr. *Liang*. The next spring (1909) I went home on furlough, empowered to bring the matter before our Church and the home public, and to raise funds. It was a rather large undertaking. We had only an empty site, local subscriptions from Chinese and foreigners amounting to £112, and promises of about £520 a year. We wanted buildings, equipment, and at least two new men. For most of my time in Moukden I had been single-handed; but as the number of foreigners increased, it was impossible to attend to them in addition to other work. So it was arranged that their fees, along with money received from the Chinese Railway, Post Office, and Customs, should go to the salary of a second Medical Missionary, to be associated with me. This was carried out before I left, so that we had now a staff of two, as a nucleus.

It was decided that the college should be a union one, the three missions on the spot sharing in its management, and provision being also made for full representation of the Chinese. It was to be supported entirely outside ordinary mission funds; but the United Free Church of Scotland, to which I belong, recognized it as an important part of their mission work, and gave every encouragement in raising money for it and in appointing its staff.

In October, 1909, a short appeal was printed, and over 4000 copies were sent out, chiefly in Scotland. From this I quote : " The object of the college is to give young men a thorough training in the knowledge and practice of medicine and surgery, and to prepare as many of them as possible for Medical Missionary work. It will be essentially a missionary institution, run on Christian principles, permeated by Christian influence. . . . It is proposed to draw up a plan for the entire building, and to erect at once as much as our funds allow. . . We shall not go into debt."

Four thousand pounds was asked for buildings for immediate use, besides enough to make up the salaries of two men. The response to this appeal showed that we had made out our case. In little more than a year we received £4889, and had secured the services of two specially qualified and eminently suitable men. Our first large contribution gave us special pleasure. Our old friend Mrs. Bishop (Isabella Bird) had left some money, for a lady friend to dispose of as she thought best, for Medical Missions. I had long ago been introduced to this lady by Mrs. Bishop, and now she was greatly interested in our college scheme, " Just the thing Mrs. Bishop would have supported," and she gave me £1000 with which to erect a wing of the college as a " Bishop Memorial."[1]

Soon after I left Moukden the Viceroy *Hsü Shih Chang* was withdrawn. This was no doubt owing to the death of the Empress-Dowager, with whom he was a great favourite, and the subsequent downfall of *Yuan Shih Kai*. The nominal Emperor had not survived the Empress, in popular belief was not allowed to survive her. The Prince Regent, who was to rule during the minority of the little Emperor, had his own personal feelings towards various officials. *Yuan Shih Kai* was only retained long enough to ensure the peaceful acceptance by the country of the new ruler ; then he was politely dismissed, and

[1] The subject of Medical Education is continued in Chapter XXVIII.

with him went most of those men in whom he had placed trust, including *Hsü Shih Chang, Tang Shao Yi,* and *M. T. Liang.*

It is tempting to speculate on what the difference in the course of China's history might have been, had the Prince Regent been far-seeing enough to make a friend of *Yuan Shih Kai,* and give him a free hand to carry out his own plans for the development of China, and the gradual enlightenment and enfranchisement of her people. Would the Revolution ever have taken place?

XXV

THE BLACK DEATH

H.E. Hsi Liang, Viceroy, 1909–1911

> ' Contented for my part
> To give this life up once for all,
> But grant I really serve."—*Sordello.*

> " ——Pity me ? . . .
> No . . . greet the unseen with a cheer !
> Bid him forward. . . . ' Speed,—fight on, fare ever
> There as here ! ' "—"Epilogue," *Robert Browning.*

DURING the winter of 1910–11 Manchuria was swept by an epidemic of pneumonic plague, of such a virulent and deadly type that it recalled the traditions of the Middle Ages, the Black Death which decimated Europe, the Great Plague of London. Its origin is still shrouded in uncertainty. It was at first believed that men were infected by the *tarbagan,* a species of marmot, but bacteriological investigation has not confirmed this theory. It is only certain that the disease showed itself in the autumn among marmot-hunters and others, crowding in the villages on the railway line on the Siberian side of the border ; but as it had been known before as a local visitation, no special notice was taken. The desert mountains of the Tsi-tsi-har province might have proved an effective barrier in former days, but the Siberian Railway now runs through them, and the infection was thus brought to Harbin and neighbouring towns in November. Towards the end of the year we heard terrible accounts of the awful mortality in the Chinese part of Harbin, but the spread of the disease southward was not anticipated by the general public, as many an epidemic rages in the crowded hovels of Harbin, and comes no farther.

This was not *bubonic* plague, and its spread had no connection with rats and fleas. It was communicated directly from man to man, and was *pneumonic* in character. Small outbreaks of a similar nature had been met with elsewhere in combination with bubonic plague, but they had not spread. This was the first time for centuries that there had been in the world a serious outbreak of *pneumonic plague,* independent of the bubonic variety. Its specially marked feature was its unvarying fatality : 43,942 cases are recorded, and 43,942 deaths. There was no authenticated case of recovery. As this inexorable deadliness became known, it seized on the public imagination, and the general terror of the forward march of the disease was quite out of proportion with the actual mortality. This was well, as it made it possible to combat that advance in a systematic and scientific way.

Our Viceroy at this time was H.E. *Hsi Liang*, an official of Mongol race, regarded at his appointment as one of the more or less reactionary party who surrounded the Prince Regent after the fall of *Yuan Shih Kai*. Personally he proved to be progressive, welcoming gratefully any proposal that would be for the good of his people. He had the warm heart of a father to those over whom he ruled, was moved by their joys and mourned with their sorrows—a fine example of the best type of the old-fashioned Chinese official.

He had little direct responsibility for combating the epidemic in either of the more northern provinces ; and in Harbin the doctors who gathered from Peking and elsewhere to fight it were for a time handicapped by the incapacity and dilatoriness of some of the leading officials. In Moukden it was very different. The Viceroy seemed to have the gift of choosing men, and there were in office some of the most practically capable Chinese I have had to do with. Specially notable was Mr. *Han*, the Commissioner for Foreign Affairs, on whom fell most of the responsibility for taking steps in plague prevention. He knew no foreign language, nor had he a modern education; but he had read much and was thoroughly up-to-date, he had considerable organizing powers, was prompt in action, and always ready to adopt any fresh suggestion.

I was in close touch with both the Viceroy and Mr. *Han*, and at the beginning of 1911 was asked officially to become Honorary Medical Adviser to the Government. The Viceroy had learned of the deadly nature of the pneumonic form of plague, and was keenly anxious to save Manchuria from its grasp. A Plague Prevention Bureau was organized, the principal members besides Mr. Han being the Commissioner of the Interior, the Tao-tai, the Chief of Police, and Dr. Wang, the head of the Government Hospital. With these men I consulted constantly, both privately and in committee, and steps were taken, slowly it is true according to Western standards, but far more rapidly than I had ever known in China, to prepare for the coming fight.

Before, however, any preventive measures could even be discussed, a sick man had been taken to the Government Hospital and had died there of plague. Within a few days the alert police reported several other cases, all being men who had just arrived by rail from the north. It was evident that the railways were the most urgent source of danger, and that if the traffic continued, not only would Moukden be infected, but the disease would be carried by the Chinese line to Tientsin and Peking, and introduced among the closely packed millions of the provinces of China. Unfortunately the necessity for limiting or stopping the traffic came at a specially difficult time. Chinese New Year was approaching, and crowds

H.E. HSI LIANG, VICEROY
"He had the heart of a father to those whom he ruled."

of coolies were on their way home from the far north. A thousand a day were being brought south by the Russian and Japanese lines, and cheap tickets were advertised by special trains on the Chinese line, for the two days' journey from Moukden to Tientsin. The Government had no authority over the railways from the north, but on their own line they arranged to stop first the coolie trains, and then all general traffic. Some time later the Japanese also stopped their third-class and coolie traffic.

There were at this time three British doctors on our staff, Dr. A. R. Young, Dr. A. F. Jackson, and myself. We were all anxious to do our utmost in this fight, but it was necessary to divide the work. I had to devote myself specially to the general organization and direction of anti-plague measures; Dr. Jackson volunteered for the work at the Chinese railway station; Dr. Young took charge of the hospital and attended on foreigners.

Dr. Arthur Jackson had only arrived in Moukden in the middle of the previous November. After a distinguished career at home he had been appointed to our college staff, for which work he was very specially fitted, both professionally and personally. He was a Cambridge graduate in Arts and Medicine, had taken the diploma of Tropical Medicine, had wide experience in home hospitals, and was of exceptional ability. Personally he won the hearts of all with whom he came in contact. We have known many new missionaries, but none who became popular with the Chinese so rapidly. He seemed just the man for college work, and was looking forward enthusiastically to a life among our Moukden students, in that new college building whose planning so keenly interested him.

The spectre of Plague was now daily stalking nearer. From the 2nd to the 12th of January twenty-three deaths were reported in Moukden. On the 13th there were ten. On Saturday the 14th it was arranged to close the Moukden-

Peking Railway, and that morning the last special train of coolies was sent off, most of whom had come down by the Japanese line. They were medically inspected, but one of the difficulties in checking pneumonic plague is the frequent absence of premonitory symptoms, and consequent impossibility of detecting the disease in its earliest stages. Two deaths occurred in that train, and from Shan-hai-kwan it was sent straight back to Moukden, with its 478 souls.

On Sunday afternoon, a cold winter day, Dr. Jackson 'phoned from the Chinese station, six miles away, that he would be late back, as these coolies were returning, and he must stay to look after them. It was a difficult situation. Not one of the isolation stations was ready for use, and no empty building was available. Some of the authorities wanted to let all those coolies who seemed well go free, but that meant carrying infection broadcast through Moukden. Others proposed to make them remain in the trucks till morning, but the temperature during the night had fallen to 25° Fahr. below zero, and many would certainly die of cold. "We must do our best for the poor beggars," said Dr. Jackson. The Chinese station was but a temporary one, with scanty accommodation and few sheds, but near by were a number of large Chinese inns, and in these the 478 arrivals were hurriedly housed, with a military guard to prevent their leaving.

During the night several died, and next day Dr. Jackson began the hand-to-hand fight which lasted until he himself was struck down eight days later. A small building was set aside for those who had plague, a hospital it could not be called; it was a comfortably warm place to die in. Another house was used for suspicious cases, most of whom were removed to the plague-house one by one. An entire inn was kept for those who had been in close contact with the stricken, and so far as possible the inmates of the various inns were kept apart. In all these

DR. ARTHUR JACKSON

arrangements I was able to help Dr. Jackson, and he had willing assistants on the spot. At the same time we were pushing forward the preparation of a place to which these coolies could be removed, for the inns were as unsuitable as could be—filthy, dark, damp, low-roofed, huddled close together, veritable traps for infection.

As much as possible of the inspection of the men was done in the open air, all having to turn out twice a day. More than one poor wretch, unwilling to own to the illness he felt creeping over him, struggled into line with the rest, only to collapse at the doctor's feet, and be carried away to die. Inspection inside the inns was also necessary, and many times a day suspicious cases were reported and seen promptly. On the Tuesday Dr. Jackson went to live at the station, in order to be close to his work; and morning, noon, and night was unremitting in his efforts to save from contamination those who still had a chance of escape. The dying too received his attention, and every man in the whole camp knew that no one appealed in vain to the foreign doctor. His energetic and sympathetic personality made an impression on all who saw him at work there, and the Chinese minor official who had been appointed to act along with him for Government, carried his good report even to the Viceroy's ears. All the railway men swore by him, and those who came nearest to him in helping him day by day have before their inward vision for all time a fadeless memory of whole-hearted unselfishness and devotion.

At first it seemed a losing fight. Day by day men saw their neighbours fall by their side; in five days seventy died. Panic seized the remainder, the military cordon was not very strict, and a number escaped one night, carrying infection into the city. But by that time the worst was over. There was one inn with no deaths; and its sixty occupants were liberated on Monday, the 23rd, being first shaven and bathed, provided by Government with new clothes, and having their train fare returned by the railway. Next day the remaining coolies, who were not yet out of danger, were removed to a roomy compound in an airy situation eight miles outside the city, from which most of them were liberated later on. The battle at the station was won, but the same day Dr. Jackson was taken ill.

He had always realized the risk he was running, and had been most careful in taking every precaution. When unavoidably in close contact with patients, he would say to his assistants : " Keep back ! keep back ! Don't take any risks ! " But for himself he did not reckon danger where there was service to do. He rejoiced in his work, taking the most lively interest in its scientific aspect. " Not many fellows get such a chance as this," he said, on his last working day. He was in full vigour that Monday, in great spirits over the discharge of his sixty men, looking forward to the removal of all the others the following day, and talking of his speedy return among us and the share he would take in the superintendence of isolation camps. But it was not to be. Already Plague had marked him as its victim. We do not know the fatal moment. Was it when he supported a poor staggering fellow to the Plague-house, or when giving a cup of water to the dying ? He had been inoculated against Plague, was closely masked, and, as we thought, well protected from infection ; but it found entrance to his lungs somehow.

Each morning we consulted together on the telephone, and on Tuesday he mentioned casually that he was not feeling up to the mark. I went straight to the station and found that he was feverish. Not liking his look, I persuaded him to go to bed, though he insisted there was really no cause for anxiety. All that day, as his symptoms developed, we held our breath with fear, saying little, and Dr. Young and I took it in turn to be on the spot. In the evening the unmistakable Plague sign appeared, the bloody spit. He was alone at the moment, but his unselfish courage did not fail. When Dr. Young returned to the room he was met by the warning not to come near, and as long as consciousness lasted his concern was for the safety of those attending him. Every known method was used by Dr. Young and myself, but in vain. The disease ran its rapid course, and he died in little more than twenty-four hours.

Dr. Jackson's death came as a terrible shock to all who knew him. He was so strong, athletic, reliable, full of fun and vivid personality, that it seemed impossible he should be so suddenly cut off. We had not realized till then what a hold he had gained on the affections of the Chinese who came in contact with him. Their grief was sincere and deep. Still more marked was the impression made by his death on the officials and the general public, who had never even seen him. When it was known that he was ill, the Viceroy stationed special messengers outside the house where he lay, to convey constant news of his condition, and on hearing of his death was deeply moved. During the six succeeding days, which Dr. Young and I spent in isolation, many telegrams, letters, and messages of sympathy were received from Chinese and foreigners, and appreciative articles and letters appeared in one Chinese paper after another. What seemed to strike home to the Chinese heart was his youth, his willing service, his death for their sakes; and recognizing him as a Christian they also saw clearly that in his death he was but following in the footsteps of Another.

> "Now he has given his only life for the lives of others, we see that he was a true Christian, who has done what Jesus did thousands of years ago."

> "His death in labouring for our country was actually carrying out the Christian principle of giving up one's life to save the world."

"He was able to do what he did because he held firmly to the great principle of his religion, to sacrifice one's own life for the salvation of others. Dr. Jackson has not died of plague, he died for duty, and he is not truly dead."

"He did the will of God, to die for all. He came to China to be a teacher in the Medical College, but all that he had learned he offered up, to save men. His work is not finished, and his death will not destroy it."

Strange words these, from four different non-Christian pens in non-Christian Chinese newspapers.

A week after his death a Memorial Service was held at the British Consulate, attended by the Viceroy, about twenty of the leading officials, and almost all the foreigners in Moukden. At the end the Viceroy read the address which has been so widely circulated:

"We have shown ourselves unworthy of the trust laid upon us by our Emperor; we have allowed a dire pestilence to overrun the sacred capital.

"His Majesty the King of Great Britain shows sympathy with every country when calamity overtakes it; his subject, Dr. Jackson, moved by his Sovereign's spirit, and with the heart of the Saviour, who gave His life to deliver the world, responded nobly when we asked him to help our country in its time of need.

"He went forth to help us in our fight daily, where the pest lay thickest; amidst the groans of the dying he struggled to cure the stricken, to find medicine to stay the evil.

"Worn by his efforts, the pestilence seized upon him, and took him from us long ere his time. Our sorrow is beyond all measure; our grief too deep for words.

"Dr. Jackson was a young man of high education and great natural ability. He came to Manchuria with the intention of spreading medical knowledge, and thus conferring untold blessings on the Eastern people. In pursuit of his ideal he was cut down. The Presbyterian Mission has lost a recruit of great promise, the Chinese Government a man who gave his life in his desire to help them.

"O, Spirit of Dr. Jackson, we pray you intercede for the twenty million people of Manchuria, and ask the Lord of Heaven to take away this pestilence, so that we may once more lay our heads in peace upon our pillows.

"In life you were brave, now you are an exalted Spirit. Noble Spirit, who sacrificed your life for us, help us still, and look down in kindness upon us all!"

Our hearts were torn with the sense of disaster and grievous personal loss, but there rose within us the consciousness that he had done more by his death than could have been accomplished by a long life, even such a life of usefulness as we had anticipated for him. He had been preparing for it for many years, and then he was but ten weeks in China. The consummation of his lifework was pressed into those last busy days, and the greatest part of all was his death.

He is buried in a quiet country spot about a mile distant from the college, outside the city. The Government gave the ground and built a wall round it, and his fellow-missionaries have erected a memorial stone.

The Viceroy had at once sent me a letter of sympathy to forward to Dr. Jackson's mother, along with $10,000 (about £900) "for the use of his family," saying: "His heart was in the saving of the world, and he brought an incalculable benefit to this land, which I hold in grateful remembrance." This money Mrs. Jackson immediately gave to the Medical College, that a part of the building might form a memorial to her son. The Viceroy was deeply moved on hearing of this. "What a mother!" he exclaimed, "and what a son!" and he said he would like personally to add to it, that the building might be a really worthy memorial. For this purpose he gave $4000.

In the hall of the college hangs a tablet with this inscription :

IN MEMORY OF

ARTHUR FRAME JACKSON

B.A., M.B., B.C., D.T.M.

Who came to Moukden to teach in this College,
Believing that by serving China he might best serve God,
And who laid down his life in that service
On January 25th, 1911

AGED 26

While Striving to stay the advance of Pneumonic Plague
The western half of this building is erected

BY

MRS. JACKSON, HIS MOTHER

AND

HIS EXCELLENCY HSI LIANG

Viceroy of Manchuria

Opposite there is an enlarged photograph of Dr. Jackson which was unveiled by Dr. Mott early in 1913.

Soon after Dr. Jackson's death a movement was set on foot to raise a fund for the endowment of a " Jackson Memorial Chair " in the college. The Viceroy headed the list with $5000, and the Board of Communications gave $2000. The contributions from many Chinese who did not know him show how the death of a foreigner " for China " was regarded. The list ranges from Prince Su and our two ex-Viceroys *Chao Er Sun* and *Hsü Shih Chang*, down to humble employees, some of whom subscribed ten cents, or twopence. The sum raised in China amounted to over £1000, but little was done to make the matter known at home, so that the response there was meagre.

For the students of the Medical College Dr. Jackson is

DR. JACKSON'S GRAVE

the modern embodiment of the Christian Ideal to which they are striving. "He being dead yet speaketh." His truest memorial will be found in the lives of young men whose thoughts and aspirations have been lifted to a higher level by his example, and who seek to live the life he lived of service and sacrifice, following the Master whom he followed so closely.

XXVI

FIGHTING THE PLAGUE

" Our interest's on the dangerous edge of things."
" Bishop Blougram "—*R. Browning.*

PLAGUE prevention measures were early taken in Moukden, and the Plague Bureau faced its work with energy and determination. As the disease was spread by direct infection, it might evidently be possible to stamp it out altogether. Effort had to be directed firstly towards keeping new Plague cases out of the city, and secondly towards the complete isolation of the inmates of contaminated houses, until the period of danger should be over. Unfortunately the former was impossible, for as fast as those in contact with one case were isolated, fresh cases were imported from the north. We could only hope to limit the extent of the epidemic, and we directed our plan of campaign accordingly.

Between the railway stations and the city a temple was set aside for a Plague hospital, repairs being begun at once. Six isolation camps were arranged outside the city in different quarters, three of which had to be built on purpose. A bacteriological laboratory was established. A burying-ground was selected, and a force of grave-diggers hired, who were set to the hard task of digging deep graves in the frozen ground where any who should die might immediately be buried. The city was divided into districts, over each of which was placed a man with some medical knowledge, fully qualified doctors not being available, and under him were an assistant, a staff of sanitary police, disinfecting coolies, and bearers. House-to-house visitation was decided upon, that all

Plague cases might be promptly discovered and removed, and contacts taken to the isolation stations. These arrangements took some time to perfect, but were brought into operation as speedily as possible.

Meantime the wildest stories began to circulate through the country regarding Plague and its origin, many of which are firmly believed by some to this day. The Japanese were credited with encouraging or even causing the epidemic in order to destroy the people and possess the land. The old slanders, formerly directed against all foreigners, were now revived and applied to them alone. It was universally stated that they were poisoning the wells. Where the idea originated no one knows, but there was hardly a well in city, town, or country that was not safeguarded by a padlocked wooden cover; and the well-cleaners were kept so busy that they charged four times their usual rates. At first, though most people believed the story, no proof was given; but after a time we began to hear circumstantial statements about a white powder found round the mouths of wells. Men were arrested in various villages with this powder in their possession, who were reported to have said that they were paid by the Japanese to put it in the water. At last I succeeded in having brought to me for analysis one of these mysterious packets, picked up by a policeman beside a locked well in Moukden. It was found to contain a harmless mixture of naphthalin and a white powder used in preparing Chinese pork for the market. This only increased the mystery. Who scattered these meaningless powders over the country? and why?

In the struggle against Plague, the Moukden Government was faced with many difficulties, not unlike those which hampered our British authorities in their efforts to stamp out cholera in England seventy years ago. At the beginning there was general disbelief in the necessity or usefulness of preventive measures. It was an absolute novelty to the Chinese mind to attempt to check the spread of any infection, and apathy naturally accompanied their fatalism. " This is the scourge of Heaven," said many. " All will die whose time has come, and no others. Then why take people away to isolation stations ? Why burn good clothes and bedding ? "

Interference with personal liberty was strongly resented, and still more the disturbance of trade and business. When a shop was forcibly closed and disinfected, and twenty-nine persons removed from it to an isolation station because of the death of a thirtieth, the merchants were highly incensed. The co-operation of the general public could thus hardly be expected. When the house-to-house visitation began it caused much fear. It was said that every sick person was to be removed, and those who had been ill for weeks struggled to rise and present a cheerful front to the unwelcome intruders. As days went on and no terrible results followed from the police inspection, it came to be welcomed by many as a kind of official certificate of health and protection from Plague. The inspection was, of course, far from complete, being carried out by untrained men ; but it worked well, and to it is largely due the fact that Moukden was saved from being swept by Plague, as were Harbin and other northern cities.

The isolation camps were at first a source of great dread. Many threw out their dead and concealed their sick for fear of being taken there, and Plague cases were thrust out to die on the streets, especially from inns and lodging-houses. It was said that everyone who went there would die, that people were sent from them to the Plague hospital who had not Plague, and that some were buried before they were dead ; and many other groundless calumnies were repeated. Gradually this feeling died down. A warm *kang* was provided, and plenty of good food, and there was no need to work. The members of each household were encouraged to keep by themselves, and when they returned home after their ten days' holiday, they found that their houses had been well guarded, and that they received full compensation for anything burned by the police.

Another difficulty which greatly hampered the Plague Bureau in its operations was the lack of trained assistants. In looking back we cannot but wonder at the efficiency of the work, considering that hospital students had to act as doctors, and that there was no time to give much practical instruction to the inspectors and police corps. They were helped by the fact that pneumonic plague is usually easy to recognize, once it has declared itself. Early every morning the Sanitary Police staff, in the clean white overalls and masks, started on their rounds, each party to its appointed district. Inns, lodging-houses, and tea-houses were visited daily, as well as any locality where Plague cases had occurred, other districts every second day. If a policeman found what seemed a suspicious case, he called in the chief of his party. If it was doubtful, a note of it was taken and another call paid some hours later. If it was clearly Plague, bearers were summoned and the patient taken straight to the hospital. The district police-station was notified, the inmates of the house conveyed to the nearest isolation station, the bedding of the sick person and other articles burned, the house disinfected and put under guard.

One day a foreigner saw a sudden stir and excitement in a restaurant on a main street; a man had fallen down ill, and quickly became unconscious. The police were called, and within two hours all was complete, the premises empty, disinfected, and closed, with a cordon of soldiers round them. When the day's work was over each member of the Plague staff visited a disinfecting station, where he had a bath and left his outer garments to be disinfected.

When the isolation stations were ready for use, there was a call for men to superintend them. I asked our dozen assistants and dispensers for four volunteers, and every man of them stepped forward. This was shortly after Dr. Jackson's death, so that they knew the danger. A little later another of our medical missionaries undertook the charge and inspection of all the isolation stations, and found them being well worked and efficiently superintended.

It was some time before opposition to Government measures altogether ceased. The most serious resistance was on the part of some merchants, who determined that their business should not be interfered with. They combined to have a Plague hospital of their own, and came to me about it at the outset, asking me to take charge and to place one of my assistants over it. I tried to convince them that this could only be done in co-operation with Government, and under the same strict regulations as were laid down by the Plague Bureau, else it would be worse than useless; but they would not listen. They opened their hospital. On one side of the compound were isolation quarters, and on the other rooms for undoubted Plague cases, who were treated by needling and other methods, all under the charge of two native doctors. No proper precautions were taken, no masks were worn. Rapidly the disease spread. Those on the isolation side became infected, and almost all died, including the two doctors. Then in consternation the merchants allowed the police to disinfect and close the place. It had been in use for twelve days, and 251 had died, most of them in the last week. It was a costly experiment, but it taught Moukden a lesson.

Owing to the effective measures taken, the mortality in Moukden from Plague did not actually rise high. Most of the deaths were in the western slums of the city where the migratory coolie class congregate, for the bacilli seem to thrive in darkness, dirt, and overcrowded rooms. The strong and vigorous seemed as susceptible as the weak, and the infection often passed over the aged and the very young.

READY FOR PLAGUE WORK

One important aid in the fight was the posting up of placards all over the city, explaining in the simplest everyday language the dangers of the epidemic, how it spread, and the measures taken against it. A small paper called the "Plague Bulletin," giving a daily official report, was also widely circulated. Fresh placards were issued almost daily. One of these told circumstantially how Plague was introduced into a particular village. Two carts, laden with tobacco leaf and other things, arrived one day at an inn. On one of the carts, hidden among the goods, and wrapped in tobacco leaves, were two bodies, which the carter had been well paid to convey secretly to an ancestral burying-ground at some distance. He seemed for some reason to have taken fright, for early next morning he left with the other cart, abandoning this one with its load. After waiting a day or two, the innkeeper proceeded to confiscate the tobacco to pay the carter's inn bill, and discovered the bodies. Fearing to have his inn closed by the authorities, he said nothing, but secretly had them buried. Within a short time he and about twenty others of his household and inmates of the inn died of Plague.

Chinese New Year drew near, the great time for visitation of friends, when every man pays scores of calls. In one proclamation the Viceroy urged his people, in fatherly fashion, to refrain from these calls for the sake of the public good; in another he strictly commanded all to remain at home that day. On New Year's Eve snow began to fall, and continued all night and all day, till it was fourteen inches deep, a more effective hindrance to moving about than many proclamations. During the next two months we had a most exceptional amount of snow, two of the falls being over a foot, and several four or five inches. Many of the streets were often almost impassable, and there is no doubt that this helped greatly to lessen the spread of infection.

The snow brought a new danger—it made easy the

temporary concealment of bodies in the heaps shovelled into the corners of the yards. The city authorities employed hundreds of carts to remove it, first from the streets and then from compounds. One of the Government placards announced that a carter had been discovered to have made large sums of money by carrying out Plague corpses hidden in the snow. Ten times he did this, then Plague seized him, and every member of his household died also. The name and address of the man were mentioned, and the public warned against such action. These tales and many others like them were told in every home in Moukden.

The Government concerned itself with other places besides the capital. Every city and town received copies of placards, instructions for guarding against the entrance of Plague, and stringent orders as to the carrying out of these measures. In one town of about twenty thousand people Plague had appeared, and the officials were doing nothing, neither isolating, disinfecting, nor even burying the dead. I received word from a foreigner that the disease was beginning to spread rapidly. An intelligent official who had seen something of Moukden methods was promptly sent by the Viceroy as special Plague Commissioner with full powers, and in three days the whole situation was changed, active preventive measures set a-going, and the city thereby saved.

Plague did not confine itself to the railway lines and large towns, but soon crept along the country roads and into the villages. At first the ignorant people exposed themselves blindly to infection. A man in a small hamlet came home ill from Moukden and died, his family attending on him and performing the usual rites. A few days later the entire household of seven died within twenty-four hours, except one infant who was found wailing beside the dead mother. The neighbours buried the bodies and helped themselves to the contents of the house—clothing, bedding, etc., even the matting on which the stricken had lain. Another few days, and one after another was attacked, until the whole of that village, about 150 souls, had died, except an old woman of over seventy, and three infants.

Tragedies such as this were reported in the villages far and near, till there arose in men's minds a terror of Plague, such as the most fatal epidemic of cholera had never produced. The instinct of self-defence triumphed over fatalism ; the placards and leaflets sent out by the thousand from Moukden were read in every village and homestead ; and the people themselves instituted wonderfully effective anti-plague measures. In very many places the inns were closed, and no visitor, however intimate, allowed to spend a night in a house. The approaches to the village were guarded, and carters warned to go round outside. Frequently the villagers combined to send in their goods in carts to the city and purchase supplies by the hand of reliable men, who were not allowed to enter an inn there or come in touch with any but those absolutely necessary, and who returned home the same day. There were scores of villages round Moukden which in these ways prevented the disease from entering.

One afternoon there arrived at a hamlet some fifteen miles away a young man from the city to visit his father. To his dismay he was stopped and refused entrance. It was too late to get back to Moukden that night, so the father pled for him and promised he should leave before daylight, and the village elders at last yielded. In the night he became ill, and in the grey dawn the father himself supported him away to a distance, and left him to die in the snow. The sacrifice was in vain. In due time the father too died, and every member of the home. By cutting off all communication with this house from the first, the rest of the village was saved.

A Korean and his wife, medicine-sellers, arrived one bitter cold night at a village where the restrictions were less severe, but no one would receive them. At last, as they were turning away in despair, a kind-hearted Christian had pity on them and took them in. In the morning the Korean woman died of Plague, and her husband fled. The whole of that household died, and several inhabitants of the village.

The battle with Plague in Manchuria lasted over three months, and taxed to the utmost the resources of all engaged in it. The earlier half of the struggle was the most strenuous, when the number of deaths per day was rising and rising in successive waves, and no one knew how high it would reach, or whether we should succeed in controlling it at all—when the subordinates of the staff had not yet learned their duties and were constantly making mistakes—when the opposition of the merchants and the apathy of the people gave rise to a feeling of despair of any good results. The fatal venture of the merchants was the turning-point. Fitfully and slowly the deaths reported fell during March, until at last there was, for the first time since the beginning of January, a day without any. Scientific methods were telling, and the milder weather helped; but it was not until well on in April that the last case was reported. For the last few weeks we had the valuable assistance of several foreign doctors from other parts of China; but the brunt of the battle in Moukden was borne by the Chinese themselves, who worked intelligently and heartily, shoulder to shoulder with their foreign colleagues.

While Plague was still raging its fiercest and spreading fast, and when there seemed reason to fear that it would be difficult to stamp it out, the Chinese Government invited an International Commission of specialists to meet in Moukden to investigate the nature of the disease, and to confer as to methods for its eradication and prevention. Thirty-three delegates were appointed by eleven different countries, and I had the honour of being asked to be one of the Chinese delegation. It was a remarkable gathering, and was accommodated and entertained in a unique manner.

Next door to the site where we were about to build our Medical College was an extensive compound belonging to Government, used as an Industrial School, but now closed on account of the Plague. It was decided to utilize part of it for the Conference, and all March workmen were busy preparing it. Four long, one-story buildings, one behind the other, lent themselves easily to this purpose. The front block was transformed into Conference Hall, secretaries' rooms, drawing-room, and dining-hall. The other three were used for bedrooms, of which there were about fifty, as there were secretaries and others besides delegates. Each room was comfortably furnished, and all were lighted by electricity. No expense was spared, and I was frequently consulted as to how to make things convenient for the foreign guests. Immediately to the east was the old temple which we had used as a hospital during the war, the *San Yi Miao*, now a part of the Industrial School. This was turned into laboratories. The hospital being so conveniently near, I was asked to allow part of it to be utilized as an overflow, and the Government installed electric light throughout the entire buildings. The most striking part of all the preparations was the Conference Hall itself, got up with perfect taste— rich green carpet, curtains, and chairs, and round the wall instead of a cornice a beautiful trailing device of pale wistaria.

From first to last the Conference and all its members were regarded as guests of the Chinese Government, and many of the delegates remarked that never in their experience of Conferences had they been treated so handsomely. Not only were they entertained as if at a private hotel, but there were carriages at their disposal whenever they had time or occasion to use them, and their very letters were stamped for them.

The Conference was summoned for 3 April, 1911, by

which time there were very few cases of Plague in Moukden. The delegates and other guests, including members of the various diplomatic corps, were received in the Conference Hall by H.E. Hsi Liang, Viceroy of Manchuria, and the Imperial Commissioner, the Hon. Alfred Sze. The Chairman of Conference was Dr. *Wu Lien Teh*, a distinguished Chinese medical graduate of Cambridge, who had spent the previous months in Plague work in Harbin. He presided over the gatherings with a dignity and ability which called forth the admiration of all. The language most used was English, but Chinese, German, and French were also recognized as official languages, and Russian and Japanese were sometimes employed and translated into English.

From the opening day until the closing ceremony on 28 April, the Conference had constant meetings, and every aspect of the pneumonic plague problem was discussed—its origin and spread, clinical data, bacteriology, pathology, measures employed to combat the epidemic, and its effect on trade. A complete report of the proceedings has been published, with a résumé of the conclusions arrived at, so that if ever a similar epidemic visits this earth, it will find the medical profession much more fully prepared to meet and combat it.

The Conference delegates were invited to spend one week-end in Port Arthur and Dalny as guests of the Japanese Government, and another in Harbin as guests of the Russian Government. At the conclusion of the Conference we were invited by the Chinese Government to visit Peking, where we were fêted royally for some days, and shown the sights of the capital in a way vouchsafed to few. We were received in audience in the Winter Palace by the Prince Regent along with several other princes. At some of the gatherings we met notable historical personages, a conversation with the famous Prince *Ching* being of special interest to me.

The Plague Conference was over, and the epidemic a

thing of the past, but those months could not be quickly wiped out from men's memories. The value of modern methods was burned into many a mind, and a knowledge of Western medicine, always valued, was now regarded in Manchuria as a possession of supreme importance. Some apprehension continued lest there should be a recrudescence of pneumonic plague in the following winter or later, and I was asked by the Moukden Government to secure an additional man for the college staff, whose salary would be paid by Government, and who would be ready for special service in the case of an epidemic of Plague or any other serious emergency. A most important step was taken by the Imperial Government, in establishing at Harbin an Anti-Plague Bureau, under the able and energetic direction of Dr. *Wu Lien Teh*. He has organized a staff of fully qualified doctors, and established well-equipped hospitals, laboratories, and investigation centres at important points from Harbin northwards. Provision being thus made for detecting and dealing with the disease near its sources, we have every reason to hope that Manchuria will not again be visited by this terrible scourge.

XXVII

MOUKDEN AND THE REVOLUTION

H.E. CHAO ER SUN, Viceroy, 1911–12

> " 'Tis time
> New hopes should animate the world, new light
> Should dawn from new revealings to a race
> Weighed down so long, forgotten so long.'
> "Paracelsus"—*R. Browning.*

ONCE more the head of Government in Manchuria was changed, and this time the man who had started these provinces in their career of progress was brought back as Viceroy. *Chao Er Sun* held the reins for about a year and a half at what proved to be the most critical time of Manchuria's history. It was well for China and for Manchuria that at this juncture there should be in charge of affairs in Moukden a man of such mental grasp, moderation, firmness, and political insight—a man who was willing to sink private opinions and feelings in the effort to preserve peace and secure the good of his people. While here as Governor-General some years before, *Chao* had lived down opposition and prejudice, and by sheer honest work had convinced Manchuria of his worth. People looked back to his time as the beginning of advance, and he was enthusiastically welcomed on his return. He had many plans for the development of Manchuria, and we looked forward hopefully to his term of office, but his work during that year and a half was very different from what was expected.

Ever since the defeat of China by Japan in 1895, and the suppression of the Reform Movement at the *coup d'état* of 1898, there had been a growing unrest among the youth of the educated classes all over China The enlightening education in Christian schools, taken advantage of by ever-increasing numbers, prepared the minds of many for emancipation. Thousands of young men went to Japan and elsewhere to study, and returned with their old ideas overthrown. The teachings of *Kang Yü Wei, Sun Yat Sen,* and others bore fruit. Those who as impressionable boys glowed with anger at the killing of the Reform Martyrs, were now men, and could read the modern literature which issued in a constant stream from the Christian Literature Society, the Commercial Press, and other enterprises. Newspapers all over the country were doing their best to lead public opinion in new channels. In very many hearts there had developed a burning desire for freedom and self-government.

The standpoint of Reformers had changed since 1898. Though one progressive decree after another had been issued by the Throne and most of the points in the repealed Reform Edicts had been conceded, and though the Prince Regent's Government was committed to a nominally constitutional policy, Reformers were not content. They now wanted more than this. Like the sibyl of old, they demanded the price of delay. It was no longer enough that the Imperial Power should graciously grant reforms to the people, it was claimed that the people themselves were the supreme power who should impose their will on the Government.

In the provinces farther south this was associated with intense hatred of the Manchus and determination to be done with Imperialism. The blind folly of the Government in supporting the Boxers and thus bringing upon the country the heavy burden of the Indemnity, and the loss of prestige involved in the Imperial flight from Peking, had now their natural consequences. As long as the Empress-Dowager lived, no one cared nor dared to take action; but her despotic hand was removed in 1908. When the Prince Regent showed himself willing to yield slowly to the pressure of the forces of progress, but unable to devise any bold policy as a leader of those forces, discontent and disloyalty began to seethe more openly. There was no strong man at the helm of State to guide the ship safely through the storm, for the one man who had shown himself capable, *Yuan Shih Kai*, had been dismissed. One mistake was made after another, both in home and in foreign policy. Government yielded where it should have been firm, was obstinate where it should have yielded. And so came the Revolution.

Manchuria had somewhat different feelings, interests, and fears from the rest of China. In southern cities Manchu garrisons reminded the people of their conquest, and these Manchus dressed with a difference, spoke with a difference, and lived apart from the Chinese. Here in the north the racial distinction was well-nigh obliterated, and there was no antagonism. For some years Manchuria had been fairly well governed, so that she had less cause than most to complain of the existing state of things. Her great and ever-present fear was from without. Few men in South Manchuria in 1911 were so ignorant of political movements as not to realize the danger of being absorbed by Japan as Korea had been. "Empire or Republic, what does it matter?" was the general feeling of the ordinary country farmer; "only let us remain a part of China." It was therefore some time before the revolutionary movement made itself prominently felt among us, and when it did it was in the cities, and chiefly among the student class.

The standard of revolt was raised in *Wuchang* on the Yangtze on 10 October, 1911, and events moved quickly. The Chinese newspapers in Moukden gave full details from day to day, and crowds gathered round the stands where these papers are exhibited on the streets. The greater part of the city people looked upon the Revolution with more or less favour, but few cared sufficiently to be willing to fight for it. In November emissaries from the south began to move about, and there was a general feeling that something was about to happen. On the 9th a written notice was handed in to the Chinese pastor at the church, saying that the Manchu rule in Moukden was about to cease, but that Christians need not fear, as the People's Army would protect them and the foreigners, if they did not side with Government. A session meeting was hurriedly summoned and a dignified and discreet answer written, saying that the Christian Church loved peace, and existed for the highest good and progress of the whole people of China. Next morning the same messenger, a young lad, called for this reply.

There was much excitement throughout the city and great fear lest once more we were to have war. It was generally felt that a great deal depended on what attitude the Viceroy took up. He was known to be an Imperialist; and as perhaps half the army would be ready to support that cause, while the other half were eager to don the revolutionary badge, Manchuria would certainly be plunged into war if he decided against compromise. Something more than mere bloodshed was feared, the general apprehension being as to what action Japan and Russia would take.

On 10 November it became known that the police, a well-armed force, had received instructions that in case of any revolutionary outbreak they were to be neutral, devoting themselves to keeping order and preventing looting. The same day a meeting was summoned of all the leading officials, merchants, and gentry, and a Committee for the Preservation of Peace was proposed, with the Viceroy as President, which would seek to prevent any disturbance, to maintain the neutrality of Manchuria in the strife, and to mediate between different parties. It was generally believed that *Chao Er Sun* had promised to offer no resistance when the Revolution took place, but had urged its postponement until the rest of China should come to a decision, in consideration of the special circumstances of Manchuria.

This, however, did not suit the more keen revolutionaries, among whom was one of the leading generals of the Army. On the afternoon of the 11th the generals met in council, and the story is that he advocated following the example of other provinces, killing the Viceroy, and proclaiming independence of the Imperial Government. It was a critical moment for Moukden and Manchuria; but fortunately the others, especially General *Chang Tso Lin*, opposed him and carried the day, so it was decided to stand by *Chao Er Sun* and the Peace Committee. The Viceroy had knowledge that this meeting was to take place, and so had his devoted bodyguard at the Government House, who were prepared to defend him to their last breath. When after dark two officers arrived and demanded to see the Viceroy, the worst was feared, and they were politely told at the gate that he was not at home.

"We must give him our message in person," they said insistently. "Where is he?"

"At the Provincial Assembly Hall."

The officers and their escort rode off hurriedly there, and in great alarm the guard told the Viceroy what had happened.

"I must follow them at once," he said, and ordered his horse. His man prepared to accompany him, but he stopped them. "I go on this errand alone. It may be that I shall not return."

When he reached the Assembly Hall, it was to find himself received with acclamation as President of the Peace Society, and to receive the assurances of the support of the Army. On the 14th the Committee for the Preservation of Peace was formally announced, some well-known revolutionaries being among its officebearers, and *Chao Er Sun* President. After this the excitement subsided for a time, for the Viceroy was trusted and liked by all classes. Moukden recognized how much it owed to his wisdom, tact, self-effacement, and pluck.

As the winter wore on the wisdom of *Chao's* waiting policy became manifest. Manchuria declared herself neutral. All went on as usual, though with a constant leaven of excitement and expectation, secret plotting, and an occasional threatening of serious trouble. There was no bloodshed, and no excuse was given to any foreign Power to step in to "pacify the country." *Yuan Shih Kai* had been recalled to power by the trembling Imperial party, after wonderfully little bloodshed the fighting in the Yang-tze valley had come to an end, and the Revolution was being carried on by negotiation rather than by the sword. Just as the year closed, an Imperial Edict announced that the Throne would abide by the decision of the People between a Limited Monarchy and a Republic. 1912 had not gone far before it seemed likely that abdication would be only a matter of weeks.

Under these circumstances it is difficult to see what the revolutionary party in Manchuria expected to gain by further plotting against the Viceroy and his Government. There was apparently a feeling among them that things were going too slowly, that the Revolution would be of no account if the same officials were allowed to remain in office, and that the murder of some was necessary to inaugurate Republican rule.

The general who had been so prominently against *Chao Er Sun* in November had left Manchuria, and the one who had now the most important command was *Chang Tso Lin*, a man of only thirty-six years of age, but already experienced in fighting and an avowed Imperialist. As a lad he had served under General *Tso* at Ping-yang in the Chino-Japanese war. When the Russians dominated the land he had headed a band of banditti and conducted a systematic guerilla warfare. Later on the

Government, recognizing his military powers, had invited him to return to the service of the Emperor and bring his men with him. His natural gifts found a place for him, and he was now practically Commander-in-Chief. To a man of his training, absolute power naturally seemed the only right method of government. It was not to be expected that he should sympathize with the idea that every peasant and workman had the right to say how the country should be governed. His soldiers worshipped him, for he treated them well, justly, and generously; but they feared him too, knowing that he had the power of life and death, and would never hesitate to use it. So while *Chao Er Sun*, as President of the Peace Committee, was using every diplomatic means to keep the two extreme parties quiet, and to delay action until the Central Government should come to a decision, *Chang Tso Lin*, as custodian of the public safety, was watching events with an alert army.

No man was better hated by the revolutionaries, and a plot was set on foot for the murder of these two men, Viceroy and General, and the immediate proclamation of the Republic. Many fine men among the Republicans were implicated, specially one who was an old friend of the hospital and who had been prominent on the Peace Committee. General *Chang* seems to have had secret information as to the treasonable nature of the meetings of a " Society of Progress " which had been started, and without informing the Viceroy he set himself to find out and frustrate their plans.

On the night of 24 January, a little more than a week before the day they had fixed for the Moukden Revolution, the General took action. He struck decisively and without warning. Formal arrests, accusations, and trials seemed to him superfluous. A number of the leaders of the revolutionary plot were seized as they left a secret meeting and killed on the street by his soldiers. The member of the Peace Committee above mentioned was

GENERAL CHANG TSO LIN
"He was watching events with an alert army."

one of these. His house was also entered and searched, and his brother was killed there. Many incriminating documents were found, his own commission from the revolutionary leaders further south, letters regarding help promised, details of the plan for the rising to take place simultaneously in various parts of Moukden, a list of those to be killed including the Viceroy, *Chang Tso Lin*, and another General, a note of moneys received, and, most serious of all for those concerned, a list of fifteen hundred names of Moukden supporters.

When morning dawned it was whispered that General *Chang Tso Lin's* men had entered compounds and killed people in the night, but no one dared to criticize or ask questions. The next few days were a time of terror. Reports were naturally exaggerated, but several score must have been killed, mostly in the night-time. It was said to be unsafe to be out after dark, and certainly soldiers were at every turn, and challenged all passers-by. As the wearing of a queue was originally a Manchu custom and a sign of submission to Manchu rule, almost every student in Moukden had cut his hair; but now not a queueless man was to be seen on the streets even in broad daylight. The Viceroy was said to know nothing of what was happening until the third day, and then he ordered the Black List of revolutionary names to be instantly burned.

During this time there was much fear among the assistants and dispensers in the hospital. Some days previously we had had a call from a young man, who had once been a hospital student, but had not proved satisfactory and had left under a cloud. He now returned, dressed very smartly in up-to-date foreign garb, and with great importance announced that he had come from the Red Cross Society of the Chinese revolutionaries in Dalny, to ask me to be their President. There was a rich Chinese gentleman there, he said, who would give a large sum to the society if I agreed. He invited all the hospital men to join also, and they would all work together when Moukden was " taken " ; but the assistants agreed with me in refusing to have anything to do with his so-called Red Cross Society. I counselled him to get away as fast as possible before he was arrested, and to leave Moukden alone, and he escaped just in time to save his neck. Then my assistant, Dr. Wang, was privately informed that his own name and those of two others were on the Black List found in the conspirator's house, having no doubt been given in by that unwelcome visitor. It was several days before any of them dared to leave the compound.

A fortnight later was issued the Imperial Proclamation of Abdication, and China became a Republic.

During all January and February and on into March General *Chang Tso Lin's* men patrolled the city every night. A band occupied our own *Bund*, or terrace, and challenged us if we happened to cross to the hospital after dark. One night a man attempted to slip home from the next-door house under the shadow of the wall without disturbing them, but suddenly a bayonet was at his chest and he was summoned to stand. They were quite friendly to us, and indeed were placed there to ensure our safety. The absence of any attack on foreigners in any part of China during the Revolution is remarkable. No less so is the fact that no member of the Imperial House suffered in any way, and that the Republic was actually proclaimed by Imperial Edict.

Before the Revolution began, *Chao Er Sun* was a strong, vigorous man, sixty-nine years of age, but youthful for his years, with a bright, cheery purposefulness which gave one confidence in the years of usefulness before him. Six months later he was an old man. The terrible strain, personal and diplomatic, broke him down. He never knew when his life would be attempted, and lived immured in the Government Buildings. He was separated from his family, who had been sent away out of danger.

The fate of his brother was always before him, murdered by his own soldiers in his Viceroyalty of Szechuan. The deposition of the Imperial Family, to whom he cherished a strong personal loyalty, was a sore grief, and he was convinced that the people were not able to govern themselves as a Republic. Yet he stuck to his post and remitted no effort to save Manchuria from the threatened anarchy which would be fatal to her. It must have been very bitter to him to lower the Dragon Flag—how much easier to resign and get away from it all!—but on the appointed day in February he was loyal to the Peace of Manchuria as he had been loyal to the Emperor, and the five-colour flag of the Republic waved over the Government Buildings.

Strange to say, the fighting which took place in Manchuria in connection with the Revolution was mostly after the Republic had been proclaimed. To many ardent young Republicans peace was of little consequence, they wanted a REVOLUTION, an overturning of Government. The Republican flag, indeed, gradually replaced the Dragon over every yamen, and officially all magistrates were now in the employ of the "People's Realm," as the Chinese call a Republic. Some of these magistrates were certainly slow to acknowledge the change.

"They are all false!" denounced hotly the revolutionary bigots; "they are not at heart loyal to the Republic. Turn them out!" So here and there local rebellions took place, bands calling themselves "The People's Army" were raised and officered by hot-headed youths, and with the help of local brigands fought against soldiers in the pay of the Republic.

Early in the year I had been asked to take steps in forming a branch of the Red Cross Society. A meeting of the leading men in Moukden was summoned, to whom were explained the objects and methods of the society. The Viceroy consented to be Patron, and placed a considerable sum of money at its disposal. A small Executive

Committee of Chinese was formed and I was appointed Director. In this connection I had an interesting interview with General *Chang Tso Lin,* and found him most cordial. A number of his wounded soldiers were in hospital at the time, and he knew personally each individual, and inquired about them by name. He welcomed the Red Cross Society, promising to give every assistance and facility. "For," he said darkly, "much blood is about to flow in Manchuria." This gloomy forecast was not fulfilled. The Viceroy's conciliatory attitude prevailed, and there were but skirmishes and risings which came to nothing.

One of these was at Kaiyuan, where a company of the "People's Army" entered the town and overpowered the yamen. We were wired to for assistance for the wounded, and the Red Cross Society was able to arrange that Dr. Westwater, of Liaoyang, and some of our Moukden assistants should go up at once with a military guard. Officials and soldiers were much impressed with this prompt Red Cross aid. Fortunately it was not needed for long, the revolutionaries dispersed, their leaders escaped south by train, many of the robbers in their pay enlisted as Government soldiers, and the wounded were conveyed to various mission hospitals.

While the people throughout China, with the exception of a few young zealots, were thankful that the Revolution had been comparatively so bloodless—being in this respect a contrast to all other Revolutions—there were many in the Army who felt themselves defrauded thereby of their rights. According to the most ancient customs of all nations under the sun, loot was the privilege of a conquering force. An army may be organized on modern lines, but it is not easy to eradicate that idea, as was proved by the amount of loot taken by the Allied Troops at the Boxer time in Peking and elsewhere. As there had been little fighting, there was little loot; but this omission some of the regiments proceeded to rectify. It began in

Peking within a fortnight of the Abdication, when a regiment mutinied and looted boldly. During the next six months similar risings took place in one city after another, some being occasioned by non-payment of soldiers' wages. Moukden's turn came in June, when over a thousand men mutinied, not of General *Chang Tso Lin's* command. The authorities were warned in time, and had the city gates hurriedly closed, so that the looters had to content themselves with banks and shops in the north suburb. The prompt action of General *Chang Tso Lin* saved the situation, for he called out his men against the mutineers, and quelled them after a short, sharp fight. A good many of the wounded were brought to our hospital.

In the autumn, when the Republic was an established fact, a Red Cross Conference was held in Shanghai, each province being invited to send representatives. I was asked by *Chao Er Sun* to represent Manchuria. During my absence his resignation, which for some time he had been pressing on the Central Government, was at last accepted. He was worn out; Manchuria had been safely brought through its most critical time; and now he might well retire. So passed from the stage of public eye one of the most valuable servants China has ever had.

XXVIII

THE MOUKDEN MEDICAL COLLEGE

" If you are planning for ten years, plant trees ;
If you are planning for a hundred years, plant men."

Chinese Saying.

IN the spring of 1911 the building of the Moukden Medical College was much delayed by the Plague epidemic, but at last it was possible to begin it as well as houses for the staff. The Viceroy, *Chao Er Sun,* was greatly interested in the progress made during the four years since he had opened the hospital, and cordially agreed to be patron of the College, promising to open it also when the time came.

During the autumn the unfinished building was accidentally threatened with destruction. One night in November we were roused about midnight by the unaccustomed sound of a loud blowing of policemen's whistles, and the racing of feet down the road beside us. Learning that fire had broken out in the Industrial Buildings used for the Plague Conference, I lost no time in reaching the spot. A strong south wind was blowing, and the fire raged unchecked, so that soon all the four blocks, unfortunately united by a covered way, were in flames. There were some pumps and fire apparatus, but they were rusty and would not work, so buckets had to be used. We got the men to centre their efforts on isolating the fire and thus saving the surrounding buildings. A double line was formed down to the river, and a constant though limited supply of water furnished by bucket in the old Chinese fashion. The well in the compound

THE MOUKDEN MEDICAL COLLEGE 271

was also kept busy, and at last, when the danger was almost over, the pumps began to work. For a time it seemed as if nothing could save a building used as an office, just to the west of those already burning. If that went, then close by was a wooden outhouse. Separated from the outhouse by a narrow road was the College with its wooden scaffolding still standing, and its joiners' shed full of shavings and wood. Close to the College was the hospital. For a couple of hours that office roof was drenched with water from the line of buckets, and again and again flames were put out where they had taken hold. In the College compound our own men worked with desperate eagerness, soaking the woodwork and extinguishing repeated small fires among the shavings. Had the wind veered round even slightly, our position would have been most precarious. Gradually the danger passed, the fire ceased to spread, and at last died down.

The College is a compact and substantial building, consisting of three stories and basement, on a commanding site conspicuous from some distance. The western half with the tower forms a Memorial to Dr. Jackson, the eastern to Mrs. Bishop, the distinguished traveller. The steam heating, electric lighting, water installation, fittings, furnishings, laboratory, and other equipment were supplied directly from the College funds. It was arranged that all the students, not to exceed fifty, should sleep on the premises, the top story being devoted to dormitories, until such time as a separate block could be erected.

Accommodation was thus prepared for the Medical College, which was announced to open its doors early in 1912. A more important point still lay in doubt : what supply of students would there be ? We knew that large numbers wanted to study medicine, but could they face the Entrance Examination ? All the years of my life in Moukden I had dreamed of the time when medical education worthy of the name. *Christian* should be carried on here, when we would train our colleagues and successors and make sure that our work would not die with us. Now a building stood ready to realize these dreams—what was to be the outcome?

Intimations of the Entrance Examination were sent to all the Chinese newspapers and Mission and Government schools, giving details of the subjects and conditions of examination, length and cost of the medical course, and asking candidates to send in their names in November. All the papers refused to charge for insertion of this intimation, and the principal Chinese daily in Moukden called attention to it in an appreciative leading article. Before November came, however, the Revolution had begun, and the student class, especially in Government institutions, were greatly agitated; and it was from Government Middle Schools that we expected to draw a large proportion of our candidates. It was therefore with some anxiety that the month of November was entered upon. As the days went on, applications came in by dozens and scores, and 270 names were received before the lists were closed. There is no doubt that in normal times the numbers would have been much larger.

During the winter the unrest increased so much that there was great uncertainty as to how many of these candidates would be able actually to come forward to the Entrance Examination, to be held on 25, 26 January, in thirteen different centres all over Manchuria. All Government schools had been closed in December owing to the political situation, and the young men scattered to their homes. Business was almost at a standstill, so that many who formerly could easily afford a College course were now uncertain what the future might hold. Brigands were numerous, making the country roads unsafe and communication difficult. In spite of all this, 142 men were examined. Five of the following subjects were required: Chinese, Arithmetic, Geography, History,

THE MOUKDEN MEDICAL COLLEGE

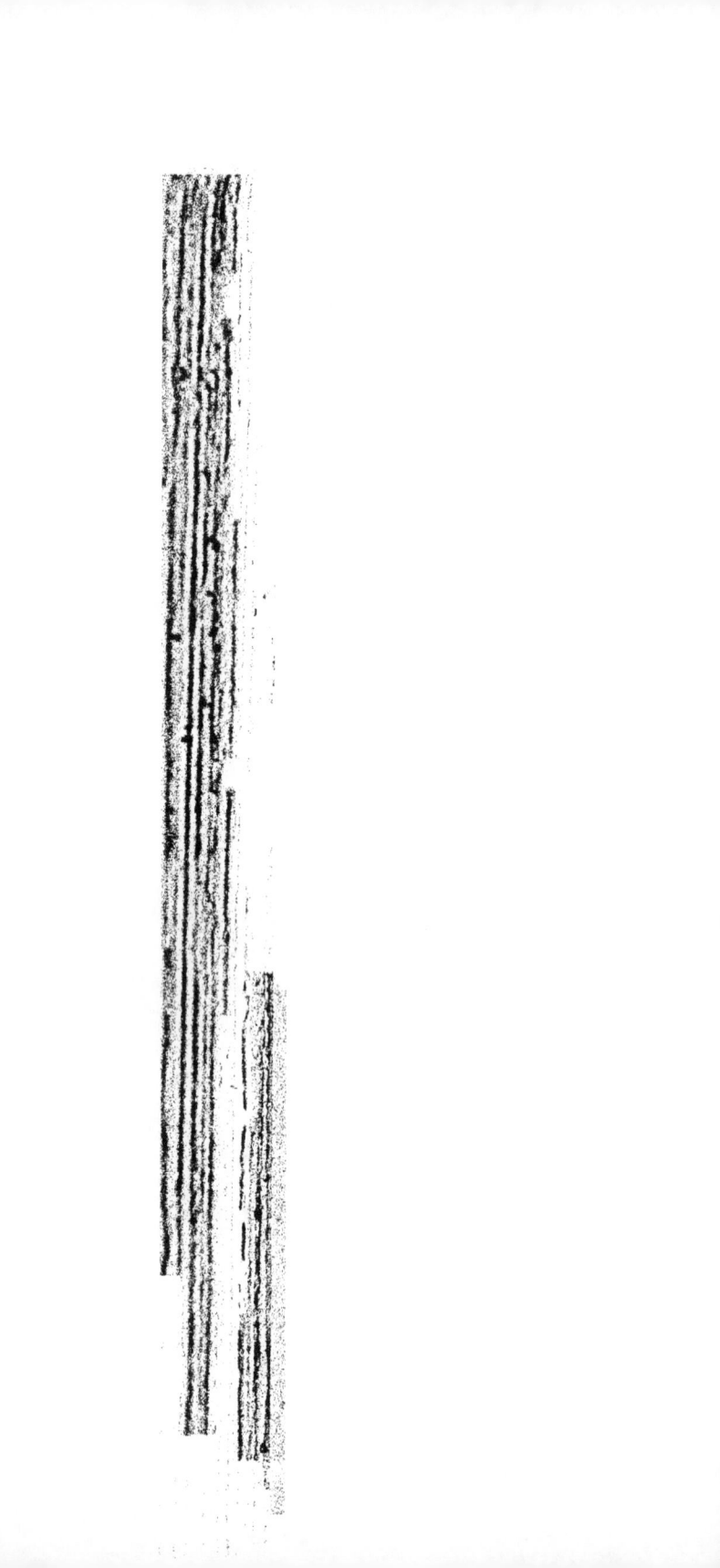

Higher Chinese, Algebra, English, Chemistry, Physics. All these except the Chinese Classics have been introduced into the curriculum within the last six years.

In Moukden alone seventy-three men came forward, and it was interesting to observe that more than half had discarded the queue. It was while this examination was going on that the sudden blow was struck at the Revolutionary plot in the city. On our second morning the students were excitedly discussing the summary executions of the night. By the time the examination was over a general terror was abroad, no one knew who was suspected, and those without queues were afraid to show themselves. Had it been held two days later, but few of the men would have dared to appear.

Of the 142 men examined, the fifty highest were admitted, nearly three-quarters of whom were Christians. A formal opening of the College could not be arranged, the political situation making it impossible for the Viceroy to appear at any public function; and the beginning of teaching was postponed until things were more settled. On 28 March, 1912, the students were gathered into the College, classes were quietly opened, and work begun.

About the same time as we were organizing this Medical College, the authorities of the South Manchuria Railway (i.e. Japanese line from Dalny to Kwanchengtze) also arranged to begin medical teaching in connection with their Railway Hospital near the Moukden station. Since then a building has been erected, and is being added to. The teaching is in Japanese, the students being largely Japanese, with an admixture of Chinese. A school is associated with the College, to teach Japanese and German to intending Chinese students.

Our teaching staff at the outset was somewhat limited. It had been arranged in the previous year that Dr. D. D. Muir, of the United Free Church of Scotland, who had been fifteen years in Manchuria, should be associated with me in all the work of the Medical Mission and College.

His presence and energy were of vital importance, both in the carrying through of our plans and in the opening and conducting of the College. We were also joined by another man of experience and skill, Dr. Ellerbek, of the Danish Mission. Now, in the autumn of 1913, our staff numbers eight—seven medical men and a qualified chemist, besides medical missionaries in other centres, who will give courses of lectures. More are needed, both foreign and Chinese, before we can consider ourselves fully manned.

The close proximity of College and hospital is most important for clinical teaching, and also enables the same staff to work both institutions. We have now 110 beds, but this is quite inadequate for teaching purposes, as well as insufficient to supply the demand for indoor treatment. A couple of years ago we were much concerned that the hospital, hemmed in by College, public roads, and Government ground, had no possibility of expansion. I brought the matter before Government, and they presented to the hospital a strip of ground directly behind it. Here we planned to erect a two-story building which would accommodate at least fifty additional patients. Part of this is being built during 1913 with the help of fees received from foreign patients. The Moukden hospital has always held to the principle of giving healing free in our general work. This has stimulated voluntary giving much beyond anything we might have gained by charging, and has maintained the purely benevolent character of our Medical Mission work. Now, however, there is a demand from well-to-do patients for treatment in private wards, for which they are ready to pay. We are making provision for these, and in this way we shall be helped to meet our ever-increasing expenditure.

We aim at having a lady nurse as matron of the hospital, to superintend the entire nursing organization, and to train male nurses. Only so can we hope to raise the standard of our nursing efficiency.

THE MOUKDEN MEDICAL COLLEGE 275

Our out-patients are more numerous than ever before, forty-five thousand visits having been paid to the dispensary in the last twelve months, and this affords a valuable field for clinical instruction. The accommodation and arrangements, however, which were suitable when all was under one man, become utterly inadequate when there are several doctors and many students. Extensive alterations have therefore been made, and we have now three consulting-rooms, surgical, medical, and ophthalmic, besides a large surgical dressing-room and an electrical room, so that four doctors may see out-patients simultaneously, and students may attend in relays to learn their work practically. Our one operating-room too was insufficient. We have now two bright, modern operating-theatres, with galleries for students, expense being met by a legacy from an old friend.

The College course is a five-years one, comprising all the ordinary subjects of the medical course in our home Universities. Our Class and Professional Examinations are as near as possible equal to the home standard, and the diplomas given on graduation will have the Government Imprimatur upon them. English is also taught throughout the course, as our men must be able to read English medical text-books, if they are to keep up in their profession after graduation. At our First Professional Examinations, the Board of Education in Moukden at our request sent a representative to be present, and the Government are very ready to further the interests of the College in every way.

With our limited staff, it is impossible to take in a new class of students each year. Our second group of men will be admitted in January, 1914, the standard of entrance being considerably raised. It is expected that a new dormitory block will be built in spring, so that the present building may be devoted entirely to teaching purposes.

The training of fully qualified medical men has thus

begun in Moukden, and prospects open out before our students of lives of rich usefulness. My experience convinces me that the Chinese are specially adapted to make good physicians and surgeons. Their mental powers are of a high order, they readily assimilate scientific teaching, they have remarkably retentive memories, they are accustomed to observe such details as are of the first importance in diagnosis, they are neat-handed, and they make good operators. Our Western methods of study are, of course, foreign to them, and one of our chief initial difficulties is that many of our students have yet to acquire the habit of steady concentrated thought and continuous application.

Among Chinese graduates there is an unfortunate tendency to rest content with what they have learned, to allow themselves to stagnate mentally, to become more absorbed in money-making than in scientific advance. It remains for us to create among our men that pride in their profession, that readiness to sacrifice much for it, that altruistic desire to serve, which are so conspicuous in our own land.

The pronounced Christian character of the College is no drawback in the eyes of the general public. It is recognized that Christianity and Healing have a natural affinity, and the crowds of non-Christians who have applied and are applying for admittance prove that our religion is regarded with friendliness, or at least indifference. When our first men graduate in 1917, there will be many careers open to them. We hope to retain several on the staff of the College, and expect that in time their usefulness will be equal to that of the foreign teachers. Some will become house physicians and surgeons in our own and other hospitals. Others will enter the Government services, where there is now a great demand for fully qualified men. The Chinese Christian Church has already expressed a desire for medical missionaries of her own. And there are endless openings for far more men than we can hope to supply, in private practice all over the country.

If our men go forth to live and to heal, realizing that they do both in the service of God as well as man, they will do much to hasten the growth of the Kingdom of God in Manchuria.

XXIX

AFTER THE REVOLUTION

H.E. Chang Hsi Lan, Governor, 1912

" Leave thy low-vaulted past !
Let each new temple, nobler than the last,
Shut thee from heaven with a dome more vast,
Till thou at length art free."
O. W. Holmes.

WITH the Republic come new titles and new regulations in Government affairs. Our Viceroy becomes a Military Governor or *Tu-tu*, and his power is much limited. *Chao Er Sun's* successor is a very old friend of mine. During my second year in Moukden I was called in to see a child who was dying, of the family of *Chang Hsi Lan*, a minor official in the city. I could do nothing for the little patient, but the simple fact that I said he could not live till morning and that I was right, established my reputation in that household. We soon became friendly, and Mr. Chang and members of his family used to drop in to tea in quite informal fashion. Afterwards he held office in various places, and for years I would lose sight of him, but whenever he returned to Moukden we renewed our friendly intercourse. In all his appointments he approved himself to the people, and when his nomination as *Tu-tu* was known, it was a popular one. The Governor in this frontier province holds no easy post, but peace has been maintained and entanglements avoided.

Manchuria has her own special hopes and fears which the other provinces hardly realize. In her eyes " the integrity of China " means her own inalienability. Thibet and Mongolia are a different question. Manchuria is one in language, one in interests, one in loyalty, one in government with the rest of China; and no greater blow could be struck her people than to allow any foreign power to dominate them. The casual traveller by rail receives quite a false impression. From the Siberian border he travels by Russian train through a barren and sparsely populated region, and concludes that this is practically Russian, lost to China. Then he changes to a well-appointed Japanese train and becomes still more convinced that it is only a matter of time, that indeed the whole of Southern Manchuria is already Japanese in all but the name. The railway does not follow the line of population, and few Chinese live in proximity to it, so he sees nothing of the populous villages and towns, mile after mile, where neither Russian nor Japanese influence or authority is known; he hears nothing of the civic life of cities, the educational developments, the far-reaching activities of Government, with which foreign countries have no touching-point. As a matter of fact, Manchuria since the Revolution is more intensely Chinese than ever.

Next to the *Tu-tu*, the most powerful man in Moukden at present is General *Chang Tso Lin*, whose well-known severity towards those who oppose him has done much to preserve peace. By the people he is at once feared and trusted to save the country from any real danger. As long as the Emperor was on the throne, he strenuously resisted any attempt to raise the standard of Revolution, and would have fought against it even had no other General sided with him. Now that the Republic has taken the place of the Empire, he stands loyally by it, recognizing *Yuan Shih Kai* as a man whose lead it is possible to follow.

In consequence of what he had seen in the hospital, General Chang resolved to organize a medical service in his army, and made known that he wanted a number of doctors. Applications of all kinds poured in, but one day in spring he came to me in some exasperation.

"Will you get me a foreign-trained Chinese doctor whom I can *trust* ? " he said. " I'll give any salary, but I want a good man. I don't believe these fellows know anything about it, and I can't trust one of them. If you could get me a man like your own Dr. Wang, I should be well satisfied." I promised to do my best to secure one, but it was not easy.

Dr. Wang had been my right-hand man for years. He had come to me straight from school, twenty-one years before, and since the Boxer time had been my chief assistant, on whom I relied in all things. Indeed, he had been doing as much and as important work as a foreign missionary, and his quiet, consistent goodness had a powerful influence. After the Russo-Japanese war the Government had conferred on him an official " button " of the fifth civil grade, for services rendered to the Chinese wounded, and throughout Moukden he was well known and respected. He had been repeatedly pressed to go into other service with a large salary. A few years ago an offer was made him through myself which meant £150 instead of the £45 a year which we were able to give him. I left it entirely to himself to decide, but he would not even take an hour to think it over.

"Doctor," he said, "you have been my master and teacher since I was a child. All I know I owe to you. As long as you need me I will never leave you."

Since then, however, circumstances have changed. Now that there are so many foreign doctors in connection with our College and hospital, much of the work which Dr. Wang used to do must of necessity be undertaken by them; and this will be increasingly so, as medical students come to the hospital for practical training. In addition to this, the students in the Medical College are going through a much more thorough scientific course than Dr. Wang had, and in a few years they will be ready to act as house surgeons and physicians. He saw these things clearly, and spoke of them to me. I had failed to get a suitable man for General Chang, so I laid his offer before Dr. Wang, who after some deliberation decided to accept it. He has been given higher rank than any medical man has ever had in Manchuria, something equivalent to a Surgeon-General, and has a free hand to organize a provincial Army Medical Service, being responsible to General Chang alone. The powerful influence which can be exercised in such a position by a man of sterling Christian character like Dr. Wang can hardly be overestimated.

Some days later General Chang called on me and thanked me most warmly for giving him so excellent a man. In the course of conversation the use of the X-rays was mentioned, which greatly interested him. He wanted to have a demonstration at once, but was disappointed to hear that we could not afford to buy it.

"Get it at once," he said, "and I will pay for it." So a complete X-ray outfit is now on its way to Moukden, which will be invaluable for both hospital and College, and I have a cheque from the General for $2000 (about £170) to cover the expense.

The history of the Republic has so far been a troubled one, but only echoes of the bloody strife in the Yang-tze valley reached Manchuria. Here all remained quiet, though there is hardly a man in the city but has his own opinion as to the political situation—changed times indeed from the old days when few knew or cared what was happening. It is well for China that, in the chaotic unrest which followed the establishment of the Republic, a strong man was at the helm of the State. That he should have right political views and devise permanently wise measures was of far less importance than that he should be powerful enough to guide the nation through the storms, and save it from the anarchy which would certainly have resulted had he failed. The statesmanship and firmness of *Yuan Shih Kai* have prevailed : the realm remains one, North and South are to have the opportunity to amalgamate, a permanent Government is established and recognized by the Powers.

We still watch anxiously for unexpected troubles which may arise, but the authorities are apparently prepared to cope with any opposition. A period of rest may be anticipated which will give the Government a chance to place the administration on a firm basis. President *Yuan Shih Kai* has shown himself just the man needed for the crisis. It now remains for him and the capable Cabinet he has gathered round him, to pacify the land and to cut the ground from under the feet of revolutionary agitators by wise and just legislation and government.

No change of the past two years is more striking than the complete revolution in the public attitude towards Christianity. Under the Manchu regime it was merely tolerated. In the elections for the Provincial Assemblies, no Christian priest nor pastor was allowed to vote. While a man's opinions were never asked, the conditions of official life and service were such that no member of a Christian Church could hold any kind of office. Christians were practically shut out from any share in the public life and government of the country. In the development of enlightened opinion which led on to the Revolution, Christian books and Christian schools had a large share. The great proportion of the English-speaking young men of China have had at least part of their training from missionaries, and most of the prominent leaders in the Revolution and in the subsequent developments are young men who speak more or less English. In addition to this, most of the Chinese books on history, political economy, etc., so eagerly studied by thousands, are written from the Christian standpoint.

DR. WANG

"The influence of a man like Dr. Wang can hardly be overestimated."

Yuan Shih Kai had no sooner been made Provisional President of the Republic than he announced in unmistakable terms that the disabilities of Christians no longer existed, and that religious liberty and equal rights were to be enjoyed by all. In many places Christians have now positions of importance, and many men in office who can hardly be called Christians are in pronounced sympathy with Christian aims. Some sixty Christian members were elected to the National Assembly, the Vice-President of the Senate was a Christian, and for a time there was a Christian Minister for Foreign Affairs. When in January, 1913, the China Medical Missionary Association met in Peking, the President received the eighty members present with great cordiality, expressed his gratitude for all that Medical Missionaries had done, and his confidence in the help they would continue to give to China.

There is one missionary organization which has gained enthusiastic support in all parts of China—the Young Men's Christian Association it is called, but it resembles rather what in Britain we call the Student Christian Union, combined with a Young Men's Club. The "Society of Youth" is its ordinary Chinese title, and in every city where it exists the young men gather to it in hundreds. Since the Revolution there is not a town of any size in Manchuria which does not want a branch of this Society, but, for lack of men to work these, it has so far been possible to start but few. There is also a demand in the larger centres for similar organizations for young women.

In the spring of 1913 large gatherings of students were held in Canton, Peking, and elsewhere, addressed by the well-known Dr. J. R. Mott. Everywhere the authorities gave sympathetic help, and the meetings were large. Last of all Dr. Mott came to Moukden. A fortnight beforehand I called on the Governor and on the Commissioner of Education, explained to them the nature of the students' meetings it was proposed to hold, and asked their advice and co-operation in getting the use of a large building for the purpose. They entered heartily into the scheme.

"Just what our students need," said the Commissioner; "every one shall be present."

No building of sufficient size existed in Moukden, so in a large open space near the ancient Fox Temple the Government at its own expense put up an enormous mat-shed. Here on a Saturday afternoon in March gathered five thousand of the flower of Moukden's youth—students, ex-students, teachers, and a good many officials. The elder boys of the Middle Schools were marched to the spot with bands playing and flags flying, and the Commissioner of Education himself presided. Dr. Mott gave a powerful address, urging the young men to rise to a higher level of living and serving their country, and emphasizing that Christianity alone can purify and elevate a nation. Then the Commissioner said a few words, urging all to take heed to Dr. Mott's advice.

Admission being by ticket only, there was a great crowd of the disappointed outside, and these were addressed from the steps of the temple where the primitive worship of the fox still lingers. Thirty years before missionaries had been stoned near that spot; and just where the shed was erected some Christians were beheaded by the Boxers in 1900. A second Students' Meeting was held the following day, without any processions, and the Commissioner again presided. Fifteen hundred were present, many of whom undertook to study the Gospels and to follow sincerely whatever Light should dawn upon them.

It was arranged that Dr. Mott should call on the Governor, who promptly returned the courtesy and thanked him warmly for his visit to Moukden and his timely words to the students. Then turning to me he said impressively

"The teaching of Dr. Mott comes at a time when it is much needed, to guide young men to higher principles. I hope it may have lasting results."

A month later, the missionaries in charge in Moukden and the Chinese pastors of the churches simultaneously received telegrams from Peking, announcing that the Government were requesting the Christians to have a Day of Prayer for China. The Governor also received the following:

> "Prayer is requested for the National Assembly now in session, for the newly established Government, for the President yet to be elected, for the Constitution of the Republic, that the Chinese Government may be recognized by the Powers, that peace may reign within our country, that strong and virtuous men may be elected to office, and that the Government may be established upon a strong foundation. Upon receipt of this telegram, you are requested to notify all Christian churches in your provinces that 27th April has been set aside as a day of prayer for the nation. Let all take part!"

The churches were crowded that Sunday, special seats being reserved in our East Church for the officials. The Governor was away from home, but sent a representative, and several other high officials were present, including the Vice-President of the Provincial Assembly, besides a considerable number of others who had never before been in a Christian church. Each worshipper on entrance received a copy of the order of service, with the Lord's Prayer, which is always repeated in unison, printed in full, as well as the hymns to be sung, and a special prayer which had been written for the occasion and in which the whole congregation joined. After an exceptionally eloquent sermon from Pastor Liu, one after another of the official visitors said a few appreciative words. In all was noticeable the note of sincerity, a genuine desire that the power of the Unseen should overshadow this

New China. The hearts of those were full that day, who remembered the day of small things, when a few despised believers met quietly in a humble room and prayed for the coming of the Kingdom of God in Manchuria.

Along with openness to the religion brought by foreigners, and eagerness for foreign clothes, houses, and knowledge of all kinds, there is in the new Republic an unwillingness for foreign interference which shows itself at every point of contact—the natural sensitiveness of a young State combined with a residuum of the old anti-foreign feeling. In Manchuria the missionaries have always sought to foster the spirit of independence, so that this increased desire for it in the Church has channels ready in which it may flow.

Manchuria is fortunate in this respect, that it has three strong missions at work, instead of, as in some provinces, a large number of comparatively weak ones which cannot but produce an unfortunate impression of rivalry on the Chinese mind. In the spring of this same year, during Dr. Mott's visit to Moukden, a gathering took place of a somewhat unique kind. At his invitation, a three-days Conference was held of representative Christian workers from all over Manchuria. There came seventy-five missionaries, being about half the total number, Scottish, Irish, and Danish, and over a hundred Chinese ministers, elders, evangelists, teachers, medical assistants, men and women. The key-note of the Conference was *Union* —Chinese with foreigner, Lutheran with Presbyterian, one great Brotherhood which shall draw under its influence the whole of Manchuria. Denominationalism is at a discount. The various missions regard their special forms of church government as but the temporary scaffolding used in building the Church of Christ in Manchuria. That Church is a Chinese one, and the Chinese alone will determine its ultimate form.

In the development of God's Kingdom among men, our

hopes are high that China will play no insignificant part. The " Church of Christ in China " cannot long remain in tutelage to the Churches of the West. Already she is breaking her bands and stretching forward, and it remains for the Christian Churches of the home lands to respond with sympathetic readiness to this movement. Only so can it be ensured that West and East shall go forward hand in hand in this work which is advancing so rapidly, of leading China into line with the Purposes of God, so that she may become a world power for good.

XXX

LOOKING FORWARD

"What is to come we know not.
We may not share
In the rich quiet of the after-glow."
W. E. Henley.

WHAT is China's future to be? What will be the outcome of this unparalleled effort of three hundred millions of people to recreate the State with a word? The wisest will prophesy least.

What is now happening is without historical precedent, and China is as unique in the length of her national existence, and in the persistence of her national characteristics, as she is in her Revolution. Dynasties have come and gone, torrents of conquest have poured over the land, still the nation remains. The original convictions of the Chinese mind endure unaltered—the all-powerfulness of Heaven and its Decrees, the obligation of ancestor-worship, the sanctity of family ties, the danger of offending spirits of all kinds. Confucius lived and wrote five centuries before Christ, and his theories, his philosophy, his standpoint towards life, are essentially those of China to this day. It is not merely that the Chinese follow Confucius; it is that the Confucian writings embodied and continue to embody Chinese thought.

Is it possible, without irretrievable disaster, to break in on the unchangingness of such a land? All these ages it has held together, notwithstanding its seemingly decreasing vitality; but must it not inevitably fall to pieces if the aggressive restlessness of the West is brought in as a disturbing element, or if any attempt is made to alter the framework of the nation in accordance with modern ideas—indeed, is not Christianity itself a disintegrating force?

In spite of her age, in spite of her apparently moribund condition of a few years ago, China is proving herself strong, is shaking herself from her lethargy, and stepping forth from her trammels as a new young nation. It was the Dynasty that was moribund, not the People. In contradiction to adverse theorizings and questionings, these are showing themselves virile, full of energetic life. The element of permanence in them is untouched, and at the same time it is being proved conspicuously that they are capable of influence by world-wide movements, that they can assimilate in a remarkable way ideas hitherto strange to them. Patriotism, Freedom, Self-Government, Equal Rights for All, Progress, Universal Compulsory Education, a State Religion—such novel expressions are constantly on men's lips and in men's minds. It will take time for the new thoughts and aspirations to penetrate and permeate the hitherto inarticulate mass of the people, but the process has begun, and there is hope that those very forces of Progress which for a time did threaten to shatter the unity of China, may yet weld her into a stronger nation than ever before.

At first it may seem that China is but imitating other nations, but sooner or later she will strike out for herself on her own new Way. The influence of the West, apparently so powerful, works for the most part on the surface, but the universal truths sink in. When these are absorbed, the unique individuality of her thought and inner life, so difficult of comprehension by Westerners, will gradually reassert itself. It is too soon to know what line the development of China will take, but all who have experience of the inherent strength of the Chinese character are convinced that she has no insignificant future before her. When the new has been assimilated by the old, a power may well be evolved quite different from anything the world has yet known.

The future of the nation rests largely with the youth of China. The unenlightened, law-abiding peasantry, who form the backbone of the land, have been stirred to expect great things of the Republic. Hopes have been raised in the hearts of many millions that their country is now about to go forward, that education, enlightenment, and material prosperity are to spread into every hamlet. A passionate patriotism has been generated which longs for settled peace, established Government, a rule of equity, whereby China may develop and prosper, and fulfil her great destiny. Among the young men who have urged forward this Revolution and this new Republic are many of marked ability and intellectual power, and with them lies the responsibility for fulfilling or disappointing the hopes of the nation. They themselves cannot reorganize the Government and regenerate the State without the co-operation of other and older men of experience and weight. It is, however, quite possible for that reorganization to be hindered and that regeneration thwarted by misdirected opposition to all measures and all men out of accord with their own views. The extent to which China will reap the fruits of her Revolution must be decided by the extent to which those to whom are offered such great opportunities, are willing and able to sink all personal considerations of pride or party, gain or glory, and to unite whole-heartedly to work for the general good of all.

The complete change in the principles of government in China has naturally its great dangers as well as its obvious benefits. The benefits lie mostly in the lap of the Future, and can hardly be realized to any great extent until the whole country settles down quietly. Now that the permanent President has been elected, and rebel factions suppressed, we may look for this settling down to be accomplished speedily. The dangers are prominently present in our midst, and are seen by all thinking men. A Parliament has been created without evolution. The position which it took Western peoples centuries of struggle and thought to attain, is claimed for China at one stroke, and much is claimed with it which will be found impossible of realization.

There is an unfortunate tendency to discard anything old simply because it is old, and to adopt blindly the new, the untried, the unknown. The old system of etiquette is laughed at. The Western freedom between the sexes is imitated and exaggerated without the Christian foundation which makes such freedom safe. The Buddhist and Taoist religions, with their idol-worship, are openly mocked, forgetting that it is better to worship ignorantly than to worship not at all. Confucius is disclaimed by many because of his attitude to the monarchical system, and his morals are set aside. The Five Relationships, so important in his theories of the State and the social system, are practically reversed. He maintained the inherent and permanent obligation of loyalty and obedience in these relationships; but now that the first of them, the relation to the Sovereign, is completely overthrown, and the people have become sovereign, what need slavishly to follow the other four? Accordingly children begin to scorn and defy their parents, age is no longer respected by Youth, pupils determine what and when and how the teacher must teach, the young claim to be the law-makers and scorn the experience of the old.

In the eyes of Chinese of standing and responsibility, the most pressing danger of the day is lack of moral principle in the rising youth of New China. Many a staunch old Confucianist would even be glad to see his sons Christians, as a safeguard against this new flood of unbridled impiety which is invading the land, ignoring all old barriers and preaching liberty from all restraint. It is striking to hear the opinions of one after another who have no manner of interest in the spiritual aspect of religion.

"The lack of China's young men to-day," remarked General *Chang Tso Lin*, for instance, " is *Tao-tê* (religion, moral principle). That is what I would like in my army in order to make my soldiers strong. I have read much about the great *Na-po-lun* (Napoleon). He was a wonderful general, but he lacked that one thing. He had power, but no moral principle, and therefore he was a menace to the whole world."

It is morals and religion in general that is desired, and to many the Christian religion is as welcome as any other. In every province the openness to Western teaching is conspicuous, religious teaching being received almost as readily as scientific. Education is the key-note of the day. Could every efficient Christian college and school be duplicated, they would still be insufficient to meet the demand. In such institutions a training is given which prepares men and women to resist the evil tendencies of the time, and to do something more than live for their own advancement and pleasure.

"What we want is not a National Religion, but a religious nation," says a Chinese Professor in a Government college. In looking forward to China's future, it is a religious nation and a Christian nation that we hope for. Christianity is not proving a disintegrating force, as some have feared. In so far as it has prevailed, it has tended to reconcile opposing elements, and to develop an enlightened and unselfish patriotism. It is the link which will bind North and South. It counteracts the dangerous tendencies special to these times. It affords an altruistic corrective to the rank individualism which prevails. It is the only effective preventative of the materialism which threatens to engulf the thought of the day. We tremble at the evolution of a powerful China without Christianity; but a strong Christian China means an irresistible force making for righteousness and world-wide peace.

SUMMARY OF EVENTS

A.D.

1583. Beginning of extension of power of Manchus, under *Nurhachu*.

1621. Moukden taken by Nurhachu and made his capital.

1644. Peking taken by the Manchus and made their capital.

1838. French Roman Catholic Mission begun in Moukden.

1870. Tientsin massacre, 18 French and 2 Russians killed.

1872. Systematic Protestant missionary work begun in Manchuria.

1876. Systematic Protestant missionary work begun in Moukden.

1883. Permanent residence in Moukden of Protestant missionaries, and organization of Medical Mission work.

1883–5. War between France and China.

1885. May. Hospital opened in Moukden.

1887. Mohammedan Rebellion.

1888. August. Great floods in Manchuria.

1894–5. CHINO-JAPANESE WAR.

1894. July. Gen. Tso sent with army to Korea.

,, 10 August. Rev. J. Wylie murdered by Manchu soldiers in Liaoyang.

15 September. Battle of Ping-yang in Korea. Gen. Tso killed.

,, 25 October. Japanese cross Yalu River and enter Manchuria.

,, 3 December. Red Cross hospitals opened in Newchwang.

A.D.	
1895.	6 March. Port of Newchwang taken by Japanese.
,,	8 May. Peace signed between Japan and China.
,,	July. Return of missionaries to Moukden.
1896.	Ordination in Moukden of first Chinese pastor in Manchuria.
,,	September. Railway concession to Russia, across North Manchuria.
1897.	1 November. Two German priests murdered in Shantung.
,,	14 November. Occupation of Kiao-chou in Shantung by Germany.
1898.	March. Occupation of Port Arthur and Ta-lien-wan by Russia, and new railway concession from Harbin to Port Arthur.
,,	June. Occupation of Wei-hai-wei by Britain.
,,	1–21 September. Reform Edicts.
,,	21 September. *Coup d'état.* Return of Empress-Dowager to power.
,,	28 September. Six Reformers executed.
1899.	Boxers organized in Shantung.
1900.	25 April. Catholics attacked by 2000 Boxers near Pao-ting-fu, Chihli.
,,	26–8 May. Railway stations burned in Chihli and railways torn up.
,,	1 June. Two English missionaries murdered by Boxers in Chihli.
,,	8 June. Mission premises burned in Pao-ting-fu and Tung-chow, Chihli.
,,	8 June. Foreigners given refuge in Peking Legations.
,,	10 June. Departure of Admiral Seymour from Tientsin for Peking with 2000 men.
,,	10 June. Arrival of first Boxers in Moukden.
,,	13 June. Hundreds of Christians killed in Peking.
,,	17 June. Taku forts, at mouth of Tientsin River, taken by Allied Fleet.
,,	17–23 June. Bombardment of Tientsin settlement by Chinese.

SUMMARY OF EVENTS

A.D.
- 1900. 20 June. German Minister killed by Boxers in Peking; attack on Legations begun.
- ,, 21 June. Missionaries privately warned to leave Moukden.
- ,, 25 June. Last Protestant missionaries leave Moukden.
- ,, 30 June. Massacre of missionaries and Chinese at Pao-ting-fu, Chihli.
- ,, 30 June. Burning of mission buildings in Moukden.
- ,, 30 June–11 August. Boxer rule in Moukden.
- ,, 9 July. Massacre of missionaries by Yü Hsien, at Tai-yuen-fu, Shansi.
- ,, 11 August. Gov.-Gen. issues Proclamation against Boxers in Moukden.
- ,, 15 August. Allied Troops relieve Peking.
- ,, 1 October. Russians enter Moukden.
- 1904. 8 February. Beginning of RUSSO-JAPANESE WAR.
- ,, 24 August–3 September. Battle of Liaoyang.
- ,, October. Battle of Sha-ho.
- 1905. January. Fall of Port Arthur.
- ,, 19 February–10 March. Battle of Moukden.
- ,, May. Naval battle of Tsu-shima; destruction of Baltic Fleet.
- ,, July. Peace signed.
- 1905–6. Abolition of opium smoking and poppy cultivation in Manchuria.
- 1907. 5 March. Opening of new hospital in Moukden.
- ,, April. Centenary Missionary Conference in Shanghai.
- ,, November. Opening of new church in East Moukden.
- 1908. Spring. Revival movement in Manchuria.
- ,, July. Site provided for Medical College in Moukden.
- ,, November. Death of Empress-Dowager and Emperor Kwang Hsü.
- 1909. January. Downfall of Yuan Shih Kai.
- ,, October. Provincial Assemblies opened in Moukden and elsewhere.

A.D.
1910–11. November to April. Epidemic of Pneumonic Plague in Manchuria.
1911. 25 January. Death of Dr. Arthur Jackson from Pneumonic Plague in Moukden.
,, April. International Plague Conference in Moukden.
,, 10 October. Outbreak of Revolution at Wuchang.
,, 9–11 November. Threatened revolutionary outbreak in Moukden.
,, November. Recall of Yuan Shih Kai. Retirement of Prince Regent.
1912. 24–6 January. Entrance Examination of Moukden Medical College.
,, 25 January. Summary executions in Moukden and suppression of revolutionaries.
,, February. Abdication of Emperor. Proclamation of Republic.
,, 28 March. Opening of Moukden Medical College.
1913. March. Dr. Mott's meetings for students in large cities of China.
,, 27 April. Day of Prayer for China.
,, 10 October. Installation of Yuan Shih Kai as Formal President of Republic.

INDEX

B

Bannermen, 12, 13
Bible Society premises, 139, 140, 142
Bible women, 190, 214
Bishop, Mrs. Isabella Bird, 72, 232, 271
Blagovestchensk, 164
Boxers, 121–122, 127–150, 154–157
British and Foreign Bible Society, 75
"Buddha's Walk," Moukden, 187
Buddhist sects, 110, 112
Buddhist temples in Moukden, 206

C

Canton, students' meetings at, 283
Chang, Blind, 116–122
Chang Hsi Lan, Governor (1812), 278, 283, 284, 285
Chang Tso Lin, General, 262–269, 279–281, 292
Chao Er Sun, Governor-General (1905–1907), 196–205, 225, 229, 244; Viceroy (1911–1912), 258–270, 273, 278
Che-kiang, guild-house of provincials, 187
Chihli, province of, 127, 129, 135
China Centenary Missionary Conference, 216
China, Christianity in, 208, 286–287, 291–292; revolution, 258–269; 278–287; day of prayer for, 285; future of, 288–292; medical theory and practice in 31–41
China, Emperor of. *See* Emperor.
China, Empress-Dowager. *See* Empress-Dowager.
China Medical Missionary Association, 223–224, 283
China, Prince Regent. *See* Prince Regent.
Chinese, adaptability for medical work, 276
— alleged dishonesty, 56–57
— attitude towards missionaries, 4–7
— customs and etiquette, 21–26, 52–54
— family life, 61–62
— fatalism, 40, 58–59, 248
— friendliness towards Russians, 165
— gratitude, 54–55, 148
— hospitality, 55
— liberality, 55
— nervous temperament, 58, 135, 211
— politeness, 21, 24–26, 56
— recuperative powers, 36, 46
— religion, 62–63
— respect for reason, 60–61
— revenge, 60
— sense of sinfulness, 210
— sufferings after the war, 184, 186, 189–196
— suicide, 59–60
— superstitions, 36–38
— sympathy with Japan, 182
Chinese New Year, 251
Chinese railways. *See* Railways

Ching, Prince, 256
Cholera, 48
Christian Arts College, Moukden, 200, 214
Christian Literature Society, 259
Christianity, revolution of public attitude towards, 282–287
Christians, persecution of by Boxers, 144–146, 155–157
Christie, Dugald, C.M.G., start for Manchuria, 1–2; work commenced at Moukden, 4–11, 26–30; experiences of the flood of 1888, 48–51; journey to Haicheng (1884), 67–70; first Sunday in Moukden, 74; journal of journey in 1886, 76–78; hospital work, 78–82; experiences of the Chino-Japanese War, 83–98; treating the wounded at Newchwang, 99–108; return to Moukden, 107; stay at Newchwang during the Boxer Rising (1900), 139; return to Moukden, 159; journey to Tientsin, 167; expedition to Kaiyuen, 173; relief work in the Russo-Japanese War, 177–195; intercourse with H.E. *Chao Er Sun*, 203, 204; views on Medical Mission work, 216–222; friendship with H.E. *Hsü Shih Chang* and Mr. *Tang*, 227; scheme for medical education in Manchuria, 229–231; return on furlough (1909), 231; fighting the plague (1910–1911), 236, 246–257; experiences of the Revolution, 265–266; appointed Director of branch of Red Cross Society, 267–268; interview with General *Chang Tso Lin*, 268; represents Manchuria at Red Cross Conference, 269; organization of the Medical College by, 270–277; friendship with *Chang Hsi Lan*, 278; assistance in organizing Army Medical Service, 279–281; assistance in organizing students' meetings, 283–284
Churches, increase in number, 207
Commercial press, 259
Committee for the Preservation of Peace, 261, 262
Confucius, 128, 288, 291
Coup d'état, 126

D

Dalny, 66, 115, 124, 159, 164, 256, 265, 273
Daly, Dr., 99
Danish Lutheran Mission, 75, 115, 274, 286
Day of Prayer for China, 285
Devil possession, 38, 134–135
Diseases prevalent in Manchuria, 46–51
Dust storm, 179–180

E

Education, 125–126, 162–163, 200–201, 207, 214, 226–227, 255, 259, 292
— Christian, 130, 163, 200, 201, 214, 259, 292
— female, 130, 200, 201, 214, 227
— medical. See Medical College
Ellerbek, Dr., 274
Emperor of China, Reform Edicts, 125–126; retirement, 126; flight, 232; death, 232
Empress-Dowager, *coup d'état*, 126; encouragement to Boxers, 129, 134, flight of, 151; Red Cross train presented by, 173; Reform Edicts, 199; death of, 232, 259–260

INDEX

F

Famine in Manchuria, 51
Feng-huang-cheng, 96
Fengtien, 14
"Firebrand," British gunboat, 101
Flood at Moukden, 48–51
Formosa, 107, 164
French missionaries. *See* Roman Catholic Mission
Fukushima, General, 194
Fulford, Mr. (Consul-General), 71

G

Gao, Mr., 27
— daughter of, 53
— son of, 95, 97
German agent, 94
German Minister at Peking, murder of, 137
Germany, aggression in Shantung, 124, 127, 128
Goforth, Rev. Jonathan, 209
Governor. *See* Chang Hsi Lan
Governor-General. *See* Chao Er Sun, Tseng Chi

H

Haicheng, 68, 96, 97
Hamerton: "Intellectual Life," 158
Han, Mr., 236
Hankow, projected railway to, 125
Harbin, 165, 256; plague in, 234, 235, 248, 256, 257
Hei-lung-kiang, missionaries sent to, 208
Hobson, Dr. 217
Hospital. *See* Moukden
Hsi Liang, Viceroy (1909–1911), 214, 235, 236, 241, 242, 243, 244, 249, 251, 252, 256
Hsin-min-tun, 168, 177, 178, 183, 187, 204; railway, 167, 227
Hsü Shih Chang, Viceroy (1907–1909), 225, 227, 230, 232, 233, 244
Hun River, 15; flooded, 48–49; picnic on, 132; Russian entrenchments on, 179; crossed by Japanese, 180
Hung, Mr., 80–81, 82

Ilu, 76, 77
Imperial edict for exterminating foreigners, 137, 138–139
— — against opium, 198
— — proclaiming a Republic, 263, 266
Imperial Proclamation of Abdication, 266
Inglis, Rev. James W., 185
Irish Mission, 75, 115, 142, 286
Italy, demand for a sea-port, 127
Itinerating, 76

J

Jackson, Dr. A. F., 237, 238–245, 250, 271
Jackson, Mrs., 243, 244
James, Sir Henry, 71
Japan, war with. *See* War
Japanese, Chinese attitude to, 83, 105, 106, 109, 182, 194–195, 247
— friendliness, 172, 194
— organization, 85, 166, 182–183
— policy, 84, 109, 165, 194
— spies, 182–183

K

Kaichow, occupation by Japanese 96, 97; battle of, 99
Kiayuan, 173; Red Cross Hospital, 174
— skirmish at, 268
Kang Yü Wei, 259
Kiao-chou, seizure of by Germans, 124, 125, 128

Kirin, medical mission work at, 76
Korea, 66, 72, 83, 84, 91, 107, 164, 165, 209, 260
Koreans, contempt of Manchurians for, 83, 209
Kuei-chou, missionary murdered at, 127
Kuroki, 177
Kuropatkin, 170, 177, 179
Kwan-cheng-tze, medical mission work at, 76
— railway to, 273

L

Li, Mr., schoolmaster, 117, 118
Li Hung Chang, 106, 123, 124
Liang, M. T., 226, 231, 233
Liao River, pirates on, 107
Liaotung Peninsula, missionaries sent to, 115
Liaoyang, 76, 87, 88, 95, 149, 152, 154; battle of, 167–169, 171, 184, mission meetings in, 209
Lieutenant-General, 137, 142, 148–149, 152, 159, 160
Liu, Pastor, 140, 147–148, 154, 285; son of, 211–212
Lockhart, Dr., 217

M

MacIntyre, Rev. John, 19, 68
MacPherson, Colonel, 203
Malaria, 51
Manchuria, country and population, 12–15; climate, 43–44; conditions of life in, 44–46; diseases prevalent in, 46–48; floods in, 50–51; famine, 51; religion in, 62–63, 291–292; travelling in, 64–73; progress of Christianity in, 74–82, 109–115, 207–215; Russian rule in, 151–163; condition after the Russo-Japanese war, 193–195; reconstructions in, 196; Revival in, 209; women of, 212–214; medical education in, 229–233; made a Viceroyalty, 225; pneumonic plague in, 234–257; revolution in, 260, 261–262, 263, 267; after the revolution, 278–279, 281; missions in, 286
Manchus, 12–13, 86, 259, 260, 265, 282, 293
Mansion House Fund, 51
Medical Assistants, 80–82, 107, 148, 211, 228–229, 266. *See also Wei*, Dr., and *Wang*, Dr.
Medical College, 3, 72, 222–224, 229–233, 243, 244, 245, 270–277, 281
Medical Mission work, 74–82, 216–224, 283
—— in Moukden, 3–11, 76–82, 130–131, 163, 188–193, 228–232, 274–275
Medicine, practice of, in China, 31–41
Merchant Guild, 157
Mission policy: admission to the Church, 80, 111–114
—— avoiding offence, 22–26, 29
—— Chinese responsibility, 75, 161, 286
—— desire for unity, 75, 286–287
—— training of evangelists, 115, 214–215
Missionary Conference, 286
Missionary Society of Manchuria, 228
Mongolia, 279
Morphia, illicit traffic in, 199
Morrison, Dr., 221
Mott, Dr. J. R., 244, 283, 284, 285, 286
Moukden, city and people, 12–20; meteorological table, 42; climate, 43–44; cholera in, 48; floods in, 48–51; famine in, 51; malaria in, 51; journey to,

INDEX 301

65-66; progress of Christianity in, 74-82; explosion at, 131; Boxers in, 133-150; condition after the Boxer Rising, 152-163; panic in, 169; occupied by Japanese, 181; refugees in, 184-188; sanitary conditions, 188; reforms in, 201-202; mission meetings in, 209; political importance recognized, 225; improvements in, 226-227; plague in, 235, 237-257; mutiny in, 269; revolution in, 258-269, 273; students' meetings at, 284; Missionary Conference at, 286

Moukden, battle of, 176-183, 190

Moukden Christian Girls' School, 201

Moukden Church, 75-76, 139, 140, 141, 153, 155, 157, 207

Moukden, Governor of, 26

Moukden Hospital, temporary building opened, 7; new building opened, 11; work at, 79-80, 115; New Hospital opened (1887), 80; tablet presented to, 88-89; donations to, 108, 131, 227; burning of, 139, 140-142; rebuilding of, 163, 203-206; extensions of, 274-275; X-ray outfit, 281

— Dispensary, 78-79, 115, 275

— Women's Hospital, 78-79, 95, 115, 140, 141, 163, 180, 188

— Medical College. *See* Medical College

Moukden Merchants' Guild, 205, 206

Muir, Dr. D. D., 273

Murray, Mr., 119

N

Nanking, projected railway to, 125

Nurhachu, 12

Nurhachu, tomb of son of, 17-18

Newchwang, 64, 66, 71, 94, 95, 96, 97, 101, 105, 107, 139, 140, 143, 154, 158, 159, 185, 204; occupation by Japanese, 103-104; hospital at, 99-103

Newspapers, 201, 241, 242, 259, 260, 272

Nodzu, 177, 179

Nogi, 177, 178, 179

North Tomb Woods, 179

O

Official customs, 24-25, 58, 97

Officials, conservative, 110, 196

— progressive, 26-27, 111, 225-226, 300

— friendship with, 3, 26-28, 88-89, 105, 203, 278

— warnings from, 96, 137

Oku, General, 177, 178, 194, 203

Opium, 136, 198-199

Oyama, Marshal, 194, 204

P

Pao-ting-fu, 135

Parker, Dr., 217

Pastors, Chinese, 115, 121, 208, 214-215, 285. *See also Liu, Pastor*

Peking, 13, 84, 91, 125, 126, 127, 128, 130, 132, 135, 136, 137, 149, 151, 167, 223, 227, 235, 256, 259, 268-269, 283, 285; School for the Blind, 119; Union Medical College, 229

" People's Army, The," 267, 268

Ping-yang, 92, 93, 104, 263

Plague, pneumonic, 234-257

" Plague Bulletin," 251

Plague bureau, 236, 246, 250

Plague conference, 254-257

Plague hospital, 246

Poppy cultivation prohibited, 198-9
Port Arthur, 96, 115, 124, 125, 164, 165, 167, 173, 194, 256; siege guns, 177, 178
Potiloff Hill, 170, 177
Prince Regent, 232, 233, 235, 256, 260

R

Railway hospital, 273
Railways, Chinese, 125, 127, 167, 204, 227, 231, 236-237
— Japanese, 194, 204, 227, 237, 238, 273, 279
— Russian, 123, 124, 130, 143, 159, 164, 237, 279
Red Cross Conference, 269
Red Cross work, 99-108, 173, 182, 189, 191, 192, 265, 266, 267, 268; at Kaiyuan, 173-174; at Shanghai, 185
Reform, 123-127, 197, 257-260, 282, 289-292
Reforms in Manchuria, 196-203, 258-259
Refugees, relief work among, 184-195, 197
"Righteous Harmony Fists," Secret Society, 128
Roman Catholic Mission, 18-19, 71, 82, 112, 141, 143, 144, 155
Ross, Rev. John, 19, 77
Russian baron, story of, 189
— friendliness, 159-60, 169, 172
— Government, invitation to Plague Conference delegates, 256
— policy, 123, 161, 164-167
— railways. *See* Railways
Russians and Boxers, 142-143, 149, 151-154
— Chinese attitude to, 130, 165, 169, 182, 189, 195

S

Saboitisch, General, 153
San Yi Miao, Temple, 188, 203, 206, 255
Scenery of Manchuria, 1, 15-16, 23-24, 66-68
Scottish United Free Church Mission, 19, 75, 115, 231, 286
Sebastopol, 172
Self-support of Chinese Church, 114, 121, 130, 162, 208
Seymour, Admiral, 130, 132, 135, 137, 138, 139
Sha-ho, 169-172, 177, 186, 189
Shan-hai-kwan, 238
Shan-si, 129
Shanghai, 125, 132, 140, 216; Red Cross Society, 100, 108, 185, 269
Shantung, 124, 128, 129, 131, 134
Small River, 11, 48, 49, 140, 141, 154, 175, 181
"Society of Progress," 264
"Society of Youth," 283
Student Christian Union, 283
Students' meetings, 283, 284
Su, Prince, 244
Suicide among Chinese, 59-60
Sun Yat Sen, 259
Sze, Hon. Alfred, 256
Szechuan, Viceroyalty of, 267

V

Vaccination, 36
Valley of Peace, 116, 117, 120
Valley of Victory, 120, 121
Viceroys. *See Hsi Liang, Hsü Shih Chang, Chao Er Sun*

W

Wang, Dr., 236, 266, 280, 281
War, Russo-Japanese, 164-195 196, 201-202

INDEX

War with France, 5, 83
— — Japan, 83–115, 162
— — Russia, 127, 134, 149, 151–163
Webster, Rev. James, 76, 77, 117–119, 185, 209*n*
Wei, Dr., 81, 105, 107, 140, 141, 142, 148, 228
Wei-hai-wei, 124, 125
Westwater, Dr. A. Macdonald, 152, 153, 268
Winter Palace tragedy, 172, 173
Women of Manchuria, 13–14, 23, 24, 27, 45, 59–60, 201, 212–214
— — Christian, 121, 130, 212–214
Wu Lien Teh, Dr., 256, 257

Wuchang, standard of revolt raised in, 260
Wylie, Rev. James, murder of, 87, 88, 94

Y

Yalu, River, 68, 91, 92, 96, 167
Yang-tze, 84, 263, 281
Young, Dr. A. R., 237, 240, 241
Young, Dr. W. A., 188, 189
Young Men's Christian Association, 283
Younghusband, Sir Francis, 71
Yü Hsien, 128, 129
Yuan shih kai, 134, 225, 232, 233, 235, 260, 263, 279, 282, 283
Yungling, 76, 78